LABOR RELATIONS AND PUBLIC POLICY SERIES

NO. 14

# OLD AGE, HANDICAPPED AND VIETNAM-ERA ANTIDISCRIMINATION LEGISLATION

*by*

JAMES P. NORTHRUP

INDUSTRIAL RESEARCH UNIT
The Wharton School, Vance Hall/CS
University of Pennsylvania
Philadelphia, Pennsylvania 19104
U.S.A.

# Foreword

In 1968, the Industrial Research Unit inaugurated its Labor Relations and Public Policy monographs as a means of examining issues and stimulating discussions in the complex and controversial areas of collective bargaining and the regulation of labor-management disputes. The first four studies and the eighth, ninth, twelfth, and thirteenth in the series dealt with aspects of the National Labor Relations Board and its administration. The fifth report contained papers read at the fiftieth anniversary conference of the Industrial Research Unit at which many aspects of labor relations and public policy were discussed. The sixth monograph—*Welfare and Strikes*—was the first empirical analysis of the impact of government payments to strikers on the American collective bargaining system and on the settlement of disputes under that system. The seventh in the series, *Opening the Skilled Construction Trades to Blacks*, was the initial attempt to determine, by detailed field analysis, what actually occurs when the federal government insists that the skilled construction trades make a serious effort to increase the number and percentage of Negroes in their work force. The tenth, *The Davis-Bacon Act*, dealt with another aspect of construction in that it involved a critical analysis of the impact and administration of the little known law under which "prevailing wages" are established in the construction industry. The eleventh monograph in the series marked the Industrial Research Unit's first published work in the public employee field since 1966.

This, the fourteenth in the series, involves the first attempt to bring together materials, cases, and opinions regarding the Age Discrimination in Employment Act of 1967, the Rehabilitation Act of 1973, and the Vietnam Era Veterans' Readjustment Assistance Act of 1974, to analyze these materials and to examine their impact upon employer personnel policies. These laws represent, in a sense, a relatively undeveloped, but potentially highly significant, aspect of a continuing and expanding public policy of creating an ever increasing number of protected groups that already comprise a majority of the labor force. Even if no new laws are enacted, the tendency of the United States Department of Labor, and often the courts, to stretch these laws to their farthest frontiers is likely to continue to compel industry and labor to reexamine their policies. As the author notes, some of these changes are fair and beneficial to society. It is likely, however, also to cost large sums directly, and perhaps even greater amounts indirectly because status and quota arrangements tend to be substituted for merit as criteria in employee selection and advancement. The cost-benefit calculus is probably impossible to determine. It is clear, however, that the process is not cost free, and is undoubtedly quite expensive.

The author, James P. Northrup, received his B.A. from the College of the University of Pennsylvania, enlisted in the U.S. Army, serving three years, including eighteen months in the Far East, and then worked in the personnel department of a major corporation. In 1975, he entered the Graduate Division of The Wharton School and received his Master of Business Administration degree in December 1976. He is the thirteenth author or co-author of a published monograph who completed his study while a student since 1968 when the Industrial Research Unit began its program of "making authors out of students." He is currently equal employment opportunity coordinator for a major corporation.

Many persons assisted in the development and completion of this work. Ms. Karen M. Rose researched, briefed and checked many of the law cases and assisted in the editing. William J. Kilberg, Esq., and Lawrence Z. Lorber, Esq., respectively, former Solicitor, United States Department of Labor, and Director, Office of Federal Contract Compliance Programs, gave freely of their time to discuss issues and to provide information. Numerous busy industrial executives spent long periods giving interviews and responding to questions. Professor Clyde W. Summers, Jefferson B. Fordham Professor of Law, University of Pennsylvania Law School, and a labor law advisor to the Industrial Research Unit, read the manuscript in detail and made extremely valuable and helpful suggestions.

The manuscript was typed by Mrs. Bonnie J. Petrauskas and edited by the Industrial Research Unit's chief editor, Michael J. McGrath, who also prepared the index. Mrs. Margaret E. Doyle, Office Manager, handled the relevant administrative matters. The research was financed by unrestricted funds provided by the sixty-five companies which comprise the Industrial

Research Unit's Research Advisory Group and by grants from the General Electric Foundation in support of industrial relations research. Final expenses, including the costs of publication, were provided from the generous grants of the Pew Memorial Trust in support of the Labor Relations and Public Policy Series. The author is, of course, solely responsible for the research and for the views expressed, which in no way should be attributed to the grantors, to the author's employer, or to the University of Pennsylvania.

HERBERT R. NORTHRUP, *Director*
Industrial Research Unit
The Wharton School

Philadelphia
April 1977

# TABLE OF CONTENTS

99089

PART FOUR

AFFIRMATIVE ACTION FOR VETERANS

# LIST OF TABLES

## LIST OF FIGURES

# PART ONE

*Introduction*

CHAPTER I

# The Nature of the Study

Governmental proscriptions against discrimination in employment concentrate, both at the federal and state level, on the problems of racial minorities and women. There are, however, other groups for which protective legislation exists, again both at the federal and state levels. These include older workers, the handicapped, and Vietnam-era veterans. Separate federal legislation has been enacted for each of the last three groups, with enforcement machinery lodged in two different agencies. These agencies in turn, are separate and distinct from the Equal Employment Opportunity Commission, the organization charged, pursuant to Title VII of the Civil Rights Act of 1964, as amended, with protecting minorities and women against discrimination.

Given the scope of the various antidiscrimination laws, most Americans are found in at least one protected class. Included are women—more than one-half of the population, but only about 40 percent of the work force; racial minorities—12-15 percent of the labor force; all persons in the labor force age 40-65; persons with handicaps of various and indeterminate kinds; disabled [1] and Vietnam-era veterans. Since one person may be black, female, 50 years of age, a Vietnam-era veteran and have a handicap, and others a member of several protected groups, we cannot add the individuals covered to arrive at a total. Obviously, however, we have moved toward protecting a variety of classes in a variety of ways.

It follows, therefore, that a person aggrieved may seek alternate solutions or forums depending upon which law that he decided to involve. Additionally, such a grievant may also depart from pursuing the administrative remedies presented by the various nondiscrimination laws and choose instead to file a

---

[1] Disabled is defined as a 30 percent rating or higher as classified by the Veterans Administration.

grievance pursuant to the union-management agreement which covers his work, or file a charge with the National Labor Relations Board on the grounds that his problem stemmed from an unfair labor practice committed by a company or union.

Moreover, federal jurisdiction over alleged discriminatory acts does not preclude a role for the states, or even in some instances, municipalities. As a result, grievants first may, or in some cases must, file with the state or municipality. In other instances, the state law is given precedence if it provides greater relief. Finally, if a grievant loses in one forum, this does not necessarily disqualify him from seeking a different result in another.

Thus an extremely complicated maze of protective laws and remedial agencies has been erected which can provide relief, regulate industry, and spur litigation. Because the issue of discrimination in employment is so large and complex, this study will be limited to three highly specialized areas which are relatively new: Part Two will deal with age discrimination; Part Three with discrimination against the handicapped; and Part Four with protective legislation relative to Vietnam-era veterans. In each section, the laws and regulations pertaining to these areas are examined and analyzed with emphasis on how they have been applied in practice.

Finally, in Part Five the questions of public policy are discussed which have been found to exist in the administration of these laws, and which are probably inherent in complex legislation designed to regulate industrial relations and personnel administration.

# PART TWO

*Age Discrimination*

# CHAPTER II

# Age Discrimination—The Background and the Law

The Age Discrimination in Employment Act of 1967 [1] was the culmination of legislative efforts which began more than twenty-five years before the Act's passage. As early as 1951, bills were introduced into Congress to promote the employment of older workers. In 1964, after efforts to include age as a protected class under Title VII of the Civil Rights Act did not succeed, a compromise was approved requiring the secretary of labor to study the problem and to make a report and recommendations to Congress. This report [2] provided the background for the 1967 legislation.

## LEGISLATIVE BACKGROUND

The 1967 Act was based on several premises, including the fact that the older workers group was a growing one that was having increasing difficulty in finding and maintaining employment; that when unemployed, persons of this age group remained unemployed longer than other groups; and that these problems were attributable to company employment policies, including discrimination.

The accuracy of these premises in fact has changed over time. The older age group is indeed a significant one (see Figure II-1), but its growth varies with demographic trends (see Table II-1) and is not consistent over time. The data in Table II-2

---

[1] *Age Discrimination in Employment Act of 1967*, 81 Stat. 602 (1967), 90 USC, S. 830, December 15, 1967.

[2] *The Older American Workers—Age Discrimination In Employment*, Report of the Secretary of Labor to the Congress under Section 715 of the Civil Rights Act of 1964 (Washington, D.C.: U.S. Government Printing Office, 1965).

7

**FIGURE II-1**
*Labor Force and Population Developments*

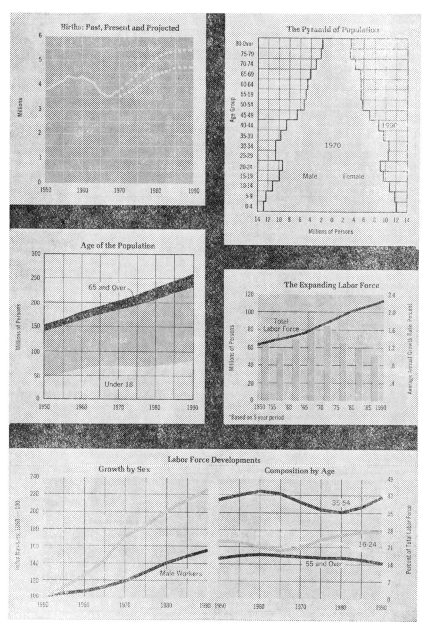

Reproduced from *A Look At Business in 1990* (Washington, D.C.: U.S. Government Printing Office, 1972), p. 51.

TABLE II-1

*Decennial Percent Increase of Population*
*by Broad Age Groups: 1950 to 2000*
*(A minus sign [—] denotes a decrease)*
*(periods extend from July 1 of initial year*
*to June 30 of terminal year)*

| Age and Projection Series | 1950 to 1960 | 1960 to 1970 | 1970 to 1980 | 1980 to 1990 | 1990 to 2000 |
|---|---|---|---|---|---|
| **SERIES B** | | | | | |
| All ages | 18.7 | 13.4 | 15.6* | 17.7* | 15.7* |
| Under 15 years | 36.8 | 3.2 | 14.0* | 33.3* | 8.6* |
| 15 to 24 years | 10.0 | 48.3 | 13.0 | —4.3* | 47.0* |
| 25 to 44 years | 3.2 | 2.7 | 28.8 | 25.9 | 3.8* |
| **SERIES E** | | | | | |
| All ages | 18.7 | 13.4 | 11.2* | 10.4* | 7.8* |
| Under 15 years | 36.8 | 3.2 | —1.5* | 10.9* | 2.3* |
| 15 to 24 years | 10.0 | 48.3 | 13.0 | —10.1* | 15.8* |
| 25 to 44 years | 3.2 | 2.7 | 28.8 | 25.9 | 0.8* |
| **ALL SERIES 45 TO 84 YEARS** | | | | | |
| 45 to 84 years | 17.4 | 15.8 | 3.8 | 3.8 | 29.4 |
| 45 to 54 years | 17.9 | 13.1 | —3.5 | 10.3 | 44.5 |
| 55 to 64 years | 16.7 | 19.3 | 13.0 | —3.1 | 11.1 |
| 65 to 84 years | 33.1 | 18.0 | 18.3 | 16.0 | 3.7 |
| 65 to 74 years | 29.9 | 13.0 | 17.8 | 14.2 | —2.5 |
| 75 to 84 years | 41.4 | 29.8 | 19.2 | 19.6 | 15.6 |
| 85 year and over | 59.3 | 51.5 [a] | (NA) [b] | (NA) | (NA) |

Source:   U.S. Department of Commerce, Social and Economic Statistics Administration Bureau of the Census, *Some Demographic Aspects of Aging in the United States* (Washington, D.C.: U.S. Government Printing Office, 1973), p. 2.

* These figures are based wholly or partly on projections of births.
a Relates to period April 1, 1960 to March 31, 1970. The 1970 census figures have been adjusted for a gross overstatement of centenarians.
b NA:   Not Available.

show that for the years 1957, 1960 and 1961—a period when the age problem was coming to the fore—older workers (those over 45 years of age) generally suffered the highest incidence of long term unemployment as a percent of the total unemployed population of any age group. Although this does not

TABLE II-2

*Long-Term Unemployed, by Age and Sex,*
*First Quarter Averages, 1957, 1960, 1961*

| Age and Sex | As Percent of Total Unemployed in Each Group | | | Percent Distribution | | | As percent of Civilian Labor Force in Each Group | | |
|---|---|---|---|---|---|---|---|---|---|
| | 1961 | 1960 | 1957 | 1961 | 1960 | 1957 | 1961 | 1960 | 1957 |
| Both sexes | 29.1 | 25.2 | 19.3 | 100.0 | 100.0 | 100.0 | 2.3 | 1.5 | 0.9 |
| Male | | | | | | | | | |
| 14 years and over | 30.9 | 26.5 | 21.0 | 72.6 | 72.1 | 73.3 | 2.5 | 1.6 | 1.0 |
| 18 to 24 years | 28.3 | 23.4 | 15.5 | 14.9 | 14.7 | 11.7 | 4.4 | 2.9 | 1.5 |
| 25 to 44 years | 28.9 | 24.2 | 18.9 | 26.4 | 24.5 | 24.0 | 2.0 | 1.2 | 0.7 |
| 45 years and over | 35.9 | 31.0 | 27.5 | 27.2 | 27.7 | 32.9 | 2.4 | 1.6 | 1.1 |
| Female | | | | | | | | | |
| 14 years and over | 25.1 | 22.2 | 15.5 | 27.4 | 27.9 | 26.7 | 1.9 | 1.3 | 0.7 |
| 18 to 24 years | 22.9 | 18.2 | 12.5 | 6.4 | 6.3 | 5.6 | 2.7 | 1.8 | 0.9 |
| 25 to 44 years | 25.5 | 20.9 | 16.7 | 11.2 | 10.1 | 11.5 | 1.9 | 1.1 | 0.7 |
| 45 years and over | 29.5 | 29.9 | 19.6 | 9.0 | 10.3 | 9.1 | 1.5 | 1.2 | 0.7 |

Source:   Jane L. Meredith, "Long-Term Unemployment in the United States,"
          *Monthly Labor Review*, Vol. 84 (June 1961), p. 605.
Note:     Because of rounding, sums of individual percentages may not add
          to 100.

mean that there were more people over 45 unemployed for the long term than any other group, it does illustrate one aspect of the employment problem faced by older people in the labor market.

During the 1950's and early 1960's, employment problems of older workers were the focus of a number of studies which almost universally concluded that older workers who were unemployed found greater difficulty than younger ones in finding new employment and tended to remain unemployed for longer periods.[3] Interestingly, most of these studies were confined to

---

[3] See, e.g., Jane L. Meredith, "Long-Term Unemployment in the United States," *Monthly Labor Review*, Vol. 84 (June 1961), pp. 601-610; Richard C. Wilcock and Walter H. Franke, *Unwanted Workers: Permanent Layoffs and Long-Term Unemployment* (New York: The Free Press of Glenco,

blue collar workers; yet, as we shall find, the main beneficiaries of the Act have been salaried lower and middle management and professional personnel. Much of the discussion in this period was related to the then current fear that automation would render the skills of older workers increasingly obsolete, particularly in relation to better educated younger workers. Although there is no basis for believing that this has occurred, there have been some significant developments which affect, both negatively and positively, employment of older workers.

## *Changing Labor Force Participation*

Since the turn of the century, the American labor market has undergone several significant changes. The improvements in plant and equipment have been the most striking. A majority of jobs today involve office or service of one type or another. There has been a steady decline in the need for manual labor and manufacturing jobs. Recent statistics on the growth of population and the growth of the labor force have revealed that between 1966 and 1976, the population grew by 19 percent, but the labor force increased by 26 percent.[4] The factor behind this surge in labor force participation is the substantial increase of women seeking and holding jobs. During this same 10 year period, the male labor force increased by 16.8 percent while the female labor force increased by 42.3 percent. Several forces have been responsible for this development: women are able to perform the majority of today's jobs; the size of the family has decreased; there has been strong government support for women who want to work; and continuing increases in the cost of living have provided a strong economic stimulus. Thus, a new and highly competitive era of labor market activity has ensued, made all the more intense by the recent recession.

It is interesting to note that much of the increase in the labor market participation rate for females has been by women in the 45-64 year age group, while, at the same time, the number of

---

1963); Louis A. Ferman and Seymour Faber, *Job Dislocation Among Older Workers: A Progress Report* (Ann Arbor: University of Michigan-Wayne State University Institute of Labor and Industrial Relations, 1958); Harold L. Sheppard, *New Perspectives on Older Workers* (Kalamazoo, Michigan: The W. E. Upjohn Institute for Employment Research, 1971); and A. H. Belitsky and Harold L. Sheppard, *The Job Hunt* (Baltimore: The Johns Hopkins University Press, 1966).

[4] John O'Riley, "The Outlook: Review of Current Trends in Business and Finance," *The Wall Street Journal*, September 20, 1976, p. 1.

men between the ages of 45-64 participating in the labor market has undergone a steady decline. This is illustrated in Table II-3 where the labor force participation rates for males in 1950 (the earliest year for which data are available) are higher for all age groups than they are projected to be by 1980. For females, just the opposite is true.

There are many factors behind the declining labor market participation by older men. They include such influences as increased retirement benefits by both public and private means; greater economic prosperity for the nation since the end of World War II; changing attitudes toward work itself coupled with increasing opportunities for leisure pursuits after retirement; and a change in the mix of jobs in the economy itself. It is not the purpose of this monograph to examine these issues in detail. Rather it is necessary only to emphasize that this decline in the labor force participation of older men is not necessarily involuntary or unwanted, and especially not necessarily an indication either of suffering or unfairness. Men in the 45-64 age group enjoy many job satisfactions. As succinctly summarized in a recent study:

> To say that men in this age category face special labor market problems is not to suggest that a majority of them are in distress. On the contrary, . . . a very large majority of them enjoy a favorable status and favorable roles in the labor market as measured by regularity of employment, occupational assignment, and degree of job satisfaction. Most of them have moved up the occupational ladder during the course of their careers and regard their current occupations the best they ever held.[5]

When such men leave the labor market, they may do so because they are retiring, or even because they are retiring early by their own choice. Nevertheless, as the above quotation notes, they do face special labor problems, and the evidence is that these problems were quite significant in the years following World War II.

*Older Worker Employment Problems*

Older persons in the labor market in the years following World War II were more vulnerable to unemployment than those in the 30-44 age bracket. One of the principal causes for

---

[5] Herbert S. Parnes et. al., *The Pre-Retirement Years*, Volume 4, U.S. Department of Labor, Manpower Administration, Manpower R & D Monograph 15 (Washington, D.C.: U.S. Government Printing Office, 1975), p. 2.

TABLE II-3
*Labor Force Participation Rates for the Population
55 Years Old and Over, by Age, Sex
For Various Years: 1950 to 1980
(Figures are annual averages)*

| Age, sex | 1950 | 1955 | 1960 | 1965 | 1970 | 1971 | 1975[a] | 1980[a] |
|---|---|---|---|---|---|---|---|---|
| Male | | | | | | | | |
| 55 to 64 | 86.9 | 87.9 | 87.5 | 84.7 | 83.0 | 82.2 | 83.9 | 83.7 |
| 55 to 59 | (NA) | (NA) | 92.3 | 90.2 | 89.5 | 88.8 | 90.5 | 90.5 |
| 60 to 64 | (NA) | (NA) | 81.8 | 78.0 | 75.0 | 74.1 | 76.3 | 75.7 |
| 65 and over | 45.8 | 39.6 | 33.2 | 27.9 | 26.8 | 25.5 | 23.4 | 21.8 |
| 65 to 69 | (NA) | (NA) | 46.8 | 43.0 | 41.6 | 39.4 | 33.8 | 31.3 |
| 70 and over | (NA) | (NA) | 24.5 | 19.1 | 17.7 | 17.0 | 17.1 | 16.0 |
| Female | | | | | | | | |
| 55 to 64 | 27.0 | 32.5 | 38.3 | 41.1 | 43.0 | 42.9 | 45.7 | 47.3 |
| 55 to 59 | (NA) | (NA) | 45.0 | 47.1 | 49.0 | 48.5 | 54.2 | 56.2 |
| 60 to 64 | (NA) | (NA) | 30.6 | 34.0 | 36.1 | 36.4 | 36.2 | 37.3 |
| 65 and over | 9.7 | 10.6 | 11.9 | 10.0 | 9.7 | 9.5 | 9.8 | 9.9 |
| 65 to 69 | (NA) | (NA) | 19.0 | 17.4 | 17.3 | 17.0 | 17.4 | 17.4 |
| 70 and over | (NA) | (NA) | 7.8 | 6.1 | 5.7 | 5.6 | 6.0 | 6.1 |

Source: U.S. Department of Commerce, Social and Economic Statistics Administration Bureau of the Census, *Some Demographic Aspects of Aging in the United States* (Washington, D.C.: U.S. Government Printing Office, 1973).
[a] Prepared before the estimates for 1970 and 1971 were available.

this difficulty could be found among institutional factors which together conspired to make re-employment for the 40-65 aged worker a serious challenge. Two factors were of special importance during this period: institutional barriers and educational attainment.

*Institutional Barriers.* For a variety of reasons, most firms have developed policies which both protect, and at the same time, unintentionally limit opportunities for the older worker. Promotion from within, hiring age limits, mandatory retirement, and other policies all have cumulative negative effects. There are, however, obvious virtues to many of these practices. For example, mandatory retirement insures that companies have promotional opportunities available for younger employees on a definite and planned basis; age limitations in hiring protect those older, more experienced employees already on the job; and promotion from within adds a high degree of security and opportunity to those older employees already in the work force. Yet, these very policies which protect the employed older worker aggravate the problems of the unemployed one and contribute to the length of his unemployment.[6]

Until recently, therefore, the likelihood of a male worker age 45-65 remaining without work once unemployed was much greater than for male workers between age 24 and 45.[7] Thus, while the probability of actually experiencing unemployment was low for the older male worker, the duration of employment was such that it pushed the rates of unemployment higher than for the younger male worker. Tables II-4 and II-5, however, while not conclusive, would appear to indicate that older workers, both male and female, have improved their relative labor market position during the latest (and most severe since the 1930's) recession. This correlates with other findings [8] which show that in the past few years, unemployment rates for males in the 45-64 age group have been similar to those 35 to 44, the cohort which typically has the lowest unemployment rate. This trend also appears to be holding for females as well. It is still true, however, as shown in Table II-6 that the duration of unemployment for older workers is higher than that of their younger counterparts.

*Educational Attainment.* Until quite recently, a substantial difference existed in the educational attainment of the 45-64 age group when compared with their younger counterparts. Before World War II this was quite pronounced, and even after the war, with the gaps in median educational levels closing, it was believed that the rapid thrust of technology would soon overtake even greater numbers of workers as they advanced with age.

---

[6] Policies such as these are frequently supported by benefit cost arguments. Yet, careful studies have demonstrated that as long as the work force is reasonably age balanced, employment of older workers need not have a negative impact on benefit costs. See Dan M. McGill, *Insurance and Pension Costs as a Barrier to the Employment of Older Workers* (Harrisburg, Pennsylvania: State Department of Labor, 1953).

[7] Parnes et al., *The Pre-Retirement Years*, p. 3.

[8] Shirley H. Rhine, "The Senior Worker-Employed and Unemployed," *The Conference Board Record*, May 1976, pp. 5-12.

## TABLE II-4

### Unemployed persons by sex and age

| Age | Males | | | | Females | | | |
|---|---|---|---|---|---|---|---|---|
| | Thousands of persons | | Unemployment rates | | Thousands of persons | | Unemployment rates | |
| | 1974 | 1975 | 1974 | 1975 | 1974 | 1975 | 1974 | 1975 |
| Total, 16 years and over | 2,668 | 4,385 | 4.8 | 7.9 | 2,408 | 3,445 | 6.7 | 9.3 |
| 16 to 19 years | 749 | 957 | 15.5 | 20.1 | 660 | 795 | 16.5 | 19.7 |
| 16 to 17 years | 391 | 440 | 18.5 | 21.6 | 301 | 390 | 18.2 | 21.2 |
| 18 to 19 years | 359 | 517 | 13.3 | 19.0 | 359 | 446 | 15.4 | 18.7 |
| 20 years and over | 1,918 | 3,428 | 3.8 | 6.7 | 1,748 | 2,649 | 5.5 | 8.0 |
| 20 to 24 years | 631 | 1,059 | 8.7 | 14.3 | 552 | 769 | 9.5 | 12.7 |
| 25 years and over | 1,288 | 2,369 | 3.0 | 5.5 | 1,196 | 1,880 | 4.6 | 7.0 |
| 25 to 34 years | 528 | 963 | 3.9 | 7.0 | 483 | 773 | 6.2 | 9.1 |
| 35 to 44 years | 263 | 502 | 2.6 | 4.9 | 294 | 445 | 4.6 | 6.9 |
| 45 to 54 years | 252 | 501 | 2.4 | 4.8 | 247 | 394 | 3.7 | 5.9 |
| 55 to 64 years | 182 | 300 | 2.6 | 4.3 | 135 | 216 | 3.3 | 5.1 |
| 55 to 59 years | 100 | 175 | 2.4 | 4.2 | 86 | 131 | 3.4 | 5.0 |
| 60 to 64 years | 81 | 124 | 2.8 | 4.4 | 49 | 85 | 3.0 | 5.2 |
| 65 years and over | 63 | 103 | 3.3 | 5.4 | 36 | 52 | 3.7 | 5.1 |
| Household heads, 16 years and over | 1,298 | 2,433 | 2.9 | 5.4 | 433 | 628 | 5.5 | 7.6 |
| 16 to 24 years | 233 | 443 | 5.5 | 10.7 | 100 | 125 | 9.8 | 11.2 |
| 25 to 54 years | 836 | 1,606 | 2.6 | 5.5 | 248 | 382 | 5.4 | 7.8 |
| 55 years and over | 229 | 384 | 2.6 | 4.4 | 85 | 121 | 3.9 | 5.5 |

Source: *Employment and Earnings*, Vol. 22 (January 1976), p. 140.

TABLE II-5

**Unemployment rates, by age and sex, seasonally adjusted**

| Age and sex | Annual average | | 1975 | | | | | | 1976 | | | | | | |
|---|---|---|---|---|---|---|---|---|---|---|---|---|---|---|---|
| | 1974 | 1975 | July | Aug. | Sept. | Oct. | Nov. | Dec. | Jan. | Feb. | Mar. | Apr. | May | June | July |
| Total, 16 years and over | 5.6 | 8.5 | 8.7 | 8.5 | 8.6 | 8.6 | 8.5 | 8.3 | 7.8 | 7.6 | 7.5 | 7.5 | 7.3 | 7.5 | 7.8 |
| 16 to 19 years | 16.0 | 19.9 | 20.5 | 20.7 | 19.4 | 19.8 | 19.0 | 19.6 | 19.9 | 19.2 | 19.1 | 19.2 | 18.5 | 18.4 | 18.1 |
| 16 and 17 years | 18.4 | 21.4 | 21.5 | 22.8 | 22.0 | 21.9 | 20.1 | 20.6 | 21.2 | 21.4 | 20.0 | 20.8 | 21.9 | 21.5 | 20.8 |
| 18 and 19 years | 14.2 | 18.9 | 19.5 | 19.4 | 18.2 | 18.2 | 18.1 | 18.9 | 19.0 | 17.5 | 18.6 | 18.2 | 16.4 | 15.6 | 15.9 |
| 20 to 24 years | 9.0 | 13.6 | 13.7 | 13.4 | 13.9 | 14.0 | 14.2 | 13.5 | 12.7 | 12.1 | 12.1 | 11.8 | 11.1 | 11.4 | 11.2 |
| 25 years and over | 3.6 | 6.0 | 6.3 | 6.0 | 6.2 | 6.3 | 6.1 | 5.9 | 5.4 | 5.3 | 5.1 | 5.1 | 5.0 | 5.5 | 5.9 |
| 25 to 54 years | 3.8 | 6.4 | 6.7 | 6.4 | 6.5 | 6.6 | 6.4 | 6.2 | 5.5 | 5.5 | 5.2 | 5.3 | 5.3 | 5.7 | 6.1 |
| 55 years and over | 2.9 | 4.7 | 4.8 | 4.7 | 4.7 | 4.9 | 5.0 | 5.0 | 4.5 | 4.8 | 4.8 | 4.6 | 4.2 | 4.7 | 4.8 |
| Male, 16 years and over | 4.8 | 7.9 | 8.3 | 8.0 | 8.2 | 8.3 | 8.1 | 7.6 | 7.1 | 6.9 | 6.8 | 6.7 | 6.8 | 7.0 | 7.2 |
| 16 to 19 years | 15.5 | 20.1 | 21.1 | 20.8 | 19.3 | 19.8 | 18.8 | 19.0 | 20.1 | 19.3 | 19.3 | 20.1 | 19.4 | 18.5 | 18.4 |
| 16 and 17 years | 18.5 | 21.6 | 22.4 | 22.9 | 22.2 | 21.6 | 19.6 | 19.3 | 21.5 | 21.0 | 20.8 | 21.5 | 23.1 | 21.3 | 21.0 |
| 18 and 19 years | 13.3 | 19.0 | 19.8 | 19.5 | 17.9 | 18.2 | 18.2 | 18.7 | 19.6 | 17.8 | 18.4 | 19.1 | 16.9 | 15.9 | 16.4 |
| 20 to 24 years | 8.7 | 14.3 | 14.9 | 14.5 | 15.3 | 15.1 | 14.6 | 13.8 | 12.8 | 11.9 | 12.0 | 11.2 | 11.3 | 11.7 | 11.9 |
| 25 years and over | 3.0 | 5.5 | 5.8 | 5.5 | 5.8 | 6.0 | 5.8 | 5.4 | 4.8 | 4.6 | 4.5 | 4.5 | 4.4 | 5.0 | 5.1 |
| 25 to 54 years | 3.1 | 5.7 | 6.1 | 5.9 | 6.1 | 6.2 | 6.0 | 5.6 | 4.8 | 4.6 | 4.3 | 4.6 | 4.5 | 5.1 | 5.4 |
| 55 years and over | 2.7 | 4.5 | 4.5 | 4.5 | 4.6 | 4.6 | 4.8 | 4.7 | 4.2 | 4.6 | 5.0 | 4.4 | 4.4 | 4.8 | 4.2 |
| Female, 16 years and over | 6.7 | 9.3 | 9.3 | 9.3 | 9.1 | 9.2 | 9.1 | 9.3 | 8.9 | 8.7 | 8.5 | 8.5 | 8.0 | 8.3 | 8.7 |
| 16 to 19 years | 16.5 | 19.7 | 19.7 | 20.5 | 19.6 | 19.9 | 19.1 | 20.3 | 19.6 | 19.1 | 18.9 | 18.1 | 17.5 | 18.2 | 17.8 |
| 16 and 17 years | 18.2 | 21.2 | 20.3 | 22.6 | 21.7 | 22.3 | 20.7 | 22.2 | 20.8 | 21.7 | 19.1 | 19.9 | 20.5 | 21.6 | 20.7 |
| 18 and 19 years | 15.4 | 18.7 | 18.8 | 19.3 | 18.5 | 18.2 | 17.9 | 19.1 | 18.4 | 17.2 | 18.8 | 17.1 | 15.9 | 15.3 | 15.3 |
| 20 to 24 years | 9.5 | 12.7 | 12.2 | 12.0 | 12.1 | 12.7 | 13.7 | 13.1 | 12.7 | 12.2 | 12.2 | 12.6 | 10.8 | 11.0 | 10.4 |
| 25 years and over | 4.6 | 7.0 | 7.1 | 6.8 | 6.8 | 6.8 | 6.7 | 6.8 | 6.4 | 6.4 | 6.2 | 6.1 | 6.0 | 6.3 | 7.1 |
| 25 to 54 years | 4.9 | 7.5 | 7.5 | 7.4 | 7.2 | 7.3 | 7.0 | 7.2 | 6.6 | 6.9 | 6.5 | 6.5 | 6.4 | 6.7 | 7.3 |
| 55 years and over | 3.3 | 5.1 | 5.2 | 5.1 | 4.7 | 5.4 | 5.3 | 5.4 | 5.1 | 5.0 | 4.5 | 4.9 | 4.0 | 4.5 | 5.8 |

Source: *Monthly Labor Review*, Vol. 99 (September 1976), p. 75.

## TABLE II-6

**Unemployed persons by duration, sex, age, color, and marital status**

| Sex, age, color, and marital status | Thousands of persons | | | | | Average (mean) duration, in weeks | Less than 5 weeks as a percent of unemployed in group | | 15 weeks and over as a percent of unemployed in group | |
|---|---|---|---|---|---|---|---|---|---|---|
| | Total | Less than 5 weeks | 5 to 14 weeks | 15 to 26 weeks | 27 weeks and over | | | | | |
| | 1975 | | | | | 1974 | 1975 | 1974 | 1975 | |
| **Total, 16 years and over** | 7,830 | 2,894 | 2,452 | 1,290 | 1,193 | 14.1 | 50.6 | 37.0 | 18.5 | 31.7 |
| 16 to 21 years | 2,581 | 1,175 | 850 | 350 | 206 | 10.3 | 57.1 | 45.5 | 13.1 | 21.5 |
| 16 to 19 years | 1,752 | 846 | 588 | 209 | 110 | 9.2 | 57.9 | 48.3 | 12.2 | 18.2 |
| 20 to 24 years | 1,828 | 690 | 575 | 319 | 244 | 13.1 | 52.3 | 37.8 | 16.1 | 30.8 |
| 25 to 34 years | 1,736 | 587 | 541 | 308 | 299 | 14.8 | 49.6 | 33.8 | 19.1 | 35.0 |
| 35 to 44 years | 948 | 307 | 292 | 178 | 171 | 15.9 | 47.7 | 32.4 | 20.6 | 36.8 |
| 45 to 54 years | 894 | 270 | 272 | 160 | 191 | 17.8 | 42.7 | 30.2 | 26.0 | 39.3 |
| 55 to 64 years | 516 | 153 | 147 | 87 | 129 | 19.3 | 37.8 | 29.7 | 32.0 | 41.9 |
| 65 years and over | 155 | 39 | 37 | 29 | 50 | 24.5 | 32.4 | 25.2 | 34.8 | 51.0 |
| **Males, 16 years and over** | 4,385 | 1,459 | 1,399 | 776 | 750 | 15.3 | 46.9 | 33.3 | 21.2 | 34.8 |
| 16 to 21 years | 1,424 | 605 | 472 | 216 | 131 | 11.1 | 54.6 | 42.5 | 14.5 | 24.4 |
| 16 to 19 years | 957 | 444 | 321 | 125 | 66 | 9.8 | 55.7 | 46.4 | 13.8 | 20.0 |
| 20 to 24 years | 1,059 | 350 | 338 | 206 | 165 | 14.5 | 48.5 | 33.0 | 18.0 | 35.0 |
| 25 to 34 years | 963 | 281 | 314 | 178 | 189 | 16.2 | 43.9 | 29.2 | 23.0 | 38.2 |
| 35 to 44 years | 502 | 139 | 158 | 101 | 104 | 17.4 | 42.7 | 27.6 | 25.0 | 40.9 |
| 45 to 54 years | 501 | 138 | 154 | 93 | 116 | 18.9 | 39.9 | 27.6 | 29.2 | 41.6 |
| 55 to 64 years | 300 | 79 | 90 | 52 | 78 | 20.1 | 35.7 | 26.4 | 35.2 | 43.5 |
| 65 years and over | 103 | 27 | 23 | 20 | 32 | 24.2 | 27.1 | 26.5 | 37.7 | 51.3 |
| **Females, 16 years and over** | 3,445 | 1,435 | 1,053 | 513 | 443 | 12.6 | 54.7 | 41.7 | 15.4 | 27.8 |
| 16 to 21 years | 1,157 | 571 | 378 | 134 | 75 | 9.2 | 60.0 | 49.3 | 11.5 | 18.0 |
| 16 to 19 years | 795 | 402 | 266 | 83 | 79 | 8.6 | 60.5 | 50.5 | 10.5 | 16.0 |
| 20 to 24 years | 769 | 341 | 237 | 113 | 79 | 11.2 | 56.6 | 44.3 | 13.9 | 24.9 |
| 25 to 34 years | 773 | 306 | 227 | 130 | 110 | 13.0 | 55.9 | 39.6 | 14.8 | 31.0 |
| 35 to 44 years | 445 | 168 | 134 | 76 | 66 | 14.1 | 52.2 | 37.8 | 16.8 | 32.1 |
| 45 to 54 years | 394 | 132 | 118 | 68 | 76 | 16.4 | 45.5 | 33.6 | 22.7 | 36.4 |
| 55 to 64 years | 216 | 74 | 57 | 35 | 51 | 18.1 | 40.6 | 34.2 | 27.7 | 39.6 |
| 65 years and over | 52 | 12 | 14 | 8 | 18 | 25.1 | 41.6 | 22.8 | 29.7 | 50.3 |
| **White** | 6,371 | 2,371 | 2,005 | 1,038 | 958 | 14.0 | 51.7 | 37.2 | 17.9 | 31.3 |
| Males | 3,597 | 1,213 | 1,150 | 632 | 602 | 15.1 | 47.9 | 33.7 | 20.5 | 34.3 |
| Females | 2,774 | 1,158 | 855 | 406 | 356 | 12.5 | 56.0 | 41.7 | 15.0 | 27.5 |
| **Negro and other races** | 1,459 | 523 | 448 | 252 | 236 | 14.8 | 46.1 | 35.9 | 20.7 | 33.4 |
| Males | 787 | 246 | 249 | 144 | 148 | 16.3 | 42.4 | 31.2 | 24.2 | 37.2 |
| Females | 671 | 277 | 199 | 107 | 83 | 13.1 | 50.0 | 41.3 | 17.0 | 29.1 |
| **Males:** | | | | | | | | | | |
| Married, spouse present | 2,044 | 603 | 649 | 399 | 393 | 16.4 | 43.2 | 29.5 | 24.5 | 38.7 |
| Widowed, divorced, or separated | 401 | 103 | 125 | 79 | 95 | 18.8 | 40.7 | 25.6 | 27.8 | 43.4 |
| Single (never married) | 1,939 | 753 | 626 | 299 | 261 | 13.4 | 50.6 | 38.8 | 17.6 | 28.9 |
| **Females:** | | | | | | | | | | |
| Married, spouse present | 1,680 | 669 | 494 | 266 | 250 | 13.6 | 55.6 | 39.8 | 14.7 | 30.7 |
| Widowed, divorced, or separated | 601 | 229 | 185 | 95 | 91 | 14.2 | 48.5 | 38.1 | 20.0 | 31.0 |
| Single (never married) | 1,164 | 537 | 373 | 152 | 102 | 10.5 | 56.6 | 46.1 | 14.2 | 21.8 |

Source: *Employment and Earnings*, Vol. 22 (January 1976), p. 144.

In fact, this was one of the main arguments brought forth by proponents of age discrimination legislation,[9] and, at that time, the conclusion was not without merit.

More recent statistical data and analysis, however, show greater gains made by the older members of the labor force than were previously thought possible. Between 1959 and 1974, the median years of schooling completed by the 25 to 44 year old group increased by one one-half a year, while for the 45 to 54 year old group the gain was more than one and one-half years. Best of all, however, were the two oldest age groups, the 55 to 64 year old cohort and the 65 year and older cohort. They each rose by more than three years.[10] Table II-7 shows the ed-

---

[9] See, for example, *The Older American Worker-Age Discrimination in Employment, loc. cit.*

[10] Rhine, "The Senior Worker," p. 9.

## TABLE II-7
### *Educational Attainment of Persons in the Labor Force by Age and Sex, March 1974*

| Years of school completed and sex | All persons | | | | | | |
| --- | --- | --- | --- | --- | --- | --- | --- |
| | Total | 16 to 19 years | 20 to 24 years | 25 to 34 years | 35 to 44 years | 45 to 54 years | 55 years and over |
| **BOTH SEXES** | | | | | | | |
| Total:    Number (thousands) | 89,633 | 8,052 | 12,654 | 20,927 | 16,600 | 17,150 | 14,249 |
| Percent | 100.0 | 100.0 | 100.0 | 100.0 | 100.0 | 100.0 | 100.0 |
| Less than 4 years of high school | 30.8 | 59.0 | 14.5 | 18.1 | 27.9 | 33.9 | 47.4 |
| Elementary:    8 years or less | 12.7 | 5.0 | 3.6 | 6.2 | 12.0 | 17.3 | 30.1 |
| High school:    1 to 3 years | 18.1 | 54.1 | 10.9 | 11.9 | 15.9 | 16.6 | 17.4 |
| 4 years of high school or more | 69.2 | 40.9 | 85.5 | 81.9 | 72.1 | 66.1 | 52.6 |
| High school:    4 years | 39.2 | 34.5 | 44.3 | 40.9 | 41.4 | 40.3 | 30.9 |
| College:    1 to 3 years | 15.1 | 6.4 | 29.1 | 18.0 | 12.7 | 11.5 | 10.1 |
| 4 years or more | 15.0 | (¹) | 12.1 | 22.9 | 18.0 | 14.4 | 11.5 |
| Median school years completed | 12.5 | 11.5 | 12.8 | 12.8 | 12.5 | 12.4 | 12.1 |
| **Men** | | | | | | | |
| Total:    Number (thousands) | 54,312 | 4,382 | 6,969 | 13,170 | 10,324 | 10,480 | 8,987 |
| Percent | 100.0 | 100.0 | 100.0 | 100.0 | 100.0 | 100.0 | 100.0 |
| Less than 4 years of high school | 32.7 | 63.8 | 17.5 | 18.9 | 29.0 | 36.0 | 49.9 |
| Elementary:    8 years or less | 14.7 | 6.9 | 4.2 | 7.3 | 14.0 | 19.4 | 32.6 |
| High school:    1 to 3 years | 18.0 | 56.9 | 13.3 | 11.6 | 15.0 | 16.6 | 17.3 |
| 4 years of high school or more | 67.3 | 36.2 | 82.5 | 81.1 | 71.0 | 64.0 | 50.1 |
| High school:    4 years | 36.0 | 30.8 | 43.2 | 38.8 | 37.1 | 35.4 | 28.0 |
| College:    1 to 3 years | 14.9 | 5.3 | 29.0 | 18.4 | 13.0 | 11.7 | 9.6 |
| 4 years or more | 16.4 | .1 | 10.3 | 23.9 | 20.9 | 16.9 | 12.5 |
| Median school years completed | 12.5 | 11.3 | 12.8 | 12.8 | 12.6 | 12.4 | 12.0 |
| **Women** | | | | | | | |
| Total:    Number (thousands) | 35,321 | 3,670 | 5,685 | 7,757 | 6,276 | 6,670 | 5,262 |
| Percent | 100.0 | 100.0 | 100.0 | 100.0 | 100.0 | 100.0 | 100.0 |
| Less than 4 years of high school | 27.8 | 53.4 | 10.8 | 16.8 | 26.1 | 30.5 | 43.2 |
| Elementary:    8 years or less | 9.7 | 2.6 | 2.9 | 4.5 | 8.7 | 13.9 | 25.7 |
| High school:    1 to 3 years | 18.1 | 50.8 | 7.9 | 12.3 | 17.5 | 16.6 | 17.5 |
| 4 years of high school or more | 72.2 | 46.6 | 89.2 | 83.2 | 73.9 | 69.5 | 56.8 |
| High school:    4 years | 44.2 | 38.9 | 45.7 | 44.5 | 48.3 | 48.0 | 36.0 |
| College:    1 to 3 years | 15.2 | 7.7 | 29.2 | 17.4 | 12.3 | 11.1 | 11.0 |
| 4 years or more | 12.8 | (¹) | 14.2 | 21.4 | 13.3 | 10.4 | 9.8 |
| Median school years completed | 12.5 | 11.8 | 12.9 | 12.7 | 12.5 | 12.4 | 12.2 |

¹ Less than 0.05 percent.

Source:    Beverly J. McEddy, "Educational Attainment of Workers, March 1974," *Monthly Labor Review*, Vol. 98 (February 1975), p. 66.

ucational attainment of persons in the labor force by age and sex in the first quarter of 1974. It can be seen that the median years of school completed for both sexes totals 12.5 and that the two older cohorts do not vary as much as they once did years ago. An interesting highlight in the table is revealed by the comparatively high educational attainment for women, something that may herald an important development in the near future.

The projected educational attainment of the civilian labor force by age and sex from data available in 1970 is shown in Table II-8. It appears to offer further encouragement to the expectation that as our century progresses into its final decades, the median level of education possessed by the different working age cohorts will approach that of the highest group. The data are especially encouraging because these 1970 projections are conservative when compared with the data available for 1974, for example in Table II-7. The median educational levels in Table II-7 for all working age categories either exceeded or equaled the projected 1970 figures.

Another interesting feature of educational achievement that is often not cited, especially for the over 35 age group, is the return of school for further job skill improvement.

> Adults go back to school for many reasons. Some workers may feel that they are handicapped by obsolete skills or may recognize that they are at a disadvantage when competing with those with more education. Others may wish to brush up in new developments in their fields. Housewives, planning to rejoin the labor force when their children no longer require constant attention, may return to school to complete education which was halted many years earlier when they married.[11]

Finally, educational attainment based upon number of years of schooling completed is at best a rough measure. Certainly, the recent reports of a steady decline in achievement tests among secondary school and college-bound students raises serious questions about any superior educational attainments of younger workers.[12]

## Occupational Distribution and Income

Despite recent gains in unemployment incidence and educational attainment, older workers may be generally "underrepresented" in rapidly expanding occupational classifications. Part

---

[11] Anne McDougall Young, "Going Back To School at 35 and Over," *Monthly Labor Review*, Vol. 98 (December 1975), p. 47.

[12] See B. Bruce-Briggs, "The Great Classroom Debacle," *The Wall Street Journal*, July 20, 1976, p. 16.

*Antidiscrimination Legislation*

## TABLE II-8

Projected educational attainment of the civilian labor force 25 years old and over, by age and sex, 1975, 1980, and 1985
[Percent distribution]

| Age and years of school completed | 1975 | | | 1980 | | | 1985 | | |
|---|---|---|---|---|---|---|---|---|---|
| | Both sexes | Male | Female | Both sexes | Male | Female | Both sexes | Male | Female |
| **25 YEARS AND OVER** | | | | | | | | | |
| Total: Number (in thousands) | 69,803 | 44,713 | 25,090 | 76,327 | 48,665 | 27,662 | 83,644 | 53,282 | 30,362 |
| Percent | 100.0 | 100.0 | 100.0 | 100.0 | 100.0 | 100.0 | 100.0 | 100.0 | 100.0 |
| Less than 4 years of high school [1] | 33.7 | 34.9 | 31.5 | 28.7 | 29.6 | 27.0 | 24.1 | 24.6 | 22.9 |
| 4 years of high school or more | 66.3 | 65.0 | 68.4 | 71.3 | 70.4 | 73.2 | 75.9 | 75.4 | 77.1 |
| Elementary: Less than 5 years [1] | 2.4 | 2.9 | 1.5 | 1.8 | 2.1 | 1.1 | 1.3 | 1.6 | .7 |
| 5 to 7 years | 5.3 | 5.7 | 4.7 | 4.0 | 4.3 | 3.4 | 2.9 | 3.1 | 2.4 |
| 8 years | 8.2 | 8.7 | 7.2 | 6.1 | 6.6 | 5.4 | 4.5 | 4.8 | 4.0 |
| High school: 1 to 3 years | 17.8 | 17.6 | 18.1 | 16.8 | 16.6 | 17.1 | 15.4 | 15.1 | 15.8 |
| 4 years | 39.9 | 36.9 | 45.2 | 42.4 | 39.7 | 47.2 | 44.4 | 42.3 | 48.2 |
| College: 1 to 3 years | 11.2 | 11.3 | 11.0 | 12.0 | 12.0 | 12.0 | 12.7 | 12.6 | 12.9 |
| 4 years or more | 15.2 | 16.8 | 12.2 | 16.9 | 18.6 | 14.0 | 18.8 | 20.5 | 16.0 |
| Median years of school completed | 12.4 | 12.4 | 12.4 | 12.5 | 12.5 | 12.5 | 12.6 | 12.6 | 12.6 |
| **25 TO 34 YEARS** | | | | | | | | | |
| Total: Number (in thousands) | 21,301 | 14,339 | 6,962 | 25,474 | 17,054 | 8,420 | 28,264 | 18,840 | 9,424 |
| Percent | 100.0 | 100.0 | 100.0 | 100.0 | 100.0 | 100.0 | 100.0 | 100.0 | 100.0 |
| Less than 4 years of high school [1] | 21.2 | 21.9 | 20.1 | 17.8 | 18.2 | 17.1 | 14.9 | 15.0 | 14.6 |
| 4 years of high school or more | 78.7 | 78.1 | 79.9 | 82.2 | 81.9 | 82.9 | 85.1 | 85.0 | 85.4 |
| Elementary: Less than 5 years [1] | 0.9 | 1.1 | 0.5 | .7 | .9 | .4 | .5 | .6 | .3 |
| 5 to 7 years | 2.0 | 2.3 | 1.6 | 1.3 | 1.5 | 1.0 | .9 | 1.0 | .7 |
| 8 years | 3.1 | 3.4 | 2.6 | 2.2 | 2.4 | 1.8 | 1.5 | 1.6 | 1.3 |
| High school: 1 to 3 years | 15.2 | 15.1 | 15.4 | 13.6 | 13.4 | 13.9 | 12.0 | 11.8 | 12.3 |
| 4 years | 46.2 | 44.8 | 49.0 | 47.3 | 46.6 | 48.8 | 48.1 | 48.1 | 48.1 |
| College: 1 to 3 years | 13.5 | 13.5 | 13.5 | 14.2 | 14.0 | 14.5 | 14.6 | 14.2 | 15.3 |
| 4 years or more | 19.0 | 19.8 | 17.4 | 20.7 | 21.3 | 19.6 | 22.4 | 22.7 | 22.0 |
| Median years of school completed | 12.6 | 12.6 | 12.6 | 12.7 | 12.7 | 12.7 | 12.7 | 12.7 | 12.7 |
| **35 TO 44 YEARS** | | | | | | | | | |
| Total: Number (in thousands) | 16,044 | 10,246 | 5,798 | 18,386 | 11,682 | 6,704 | 23,009 | 14,616 | 8,393 |
| Percent | 100.0 | 100.0 | 100.0 | 100.0 | 100.0 | 100.0 | 100.0 | 100.0 | 100.0 |
| Less than 4 years of high school [1] | 30.6 | 30.9 | 29.9 | 25.6 | 26.2 | 24.8 | 21.2 | 21.2 | 20.9 |
| 4 years of high school or more | 69.5 | 69.1 | 70.1 | 74.3 | 73.8 | 75.2 | 78.8 | 78.7 | 79.0 |
| Elementary: Less than 5 years [1] | 2.0 | 2.4 | 1.2 | 1.4 | 1.7 | .9 | 1.0 | 1.2 | .6 |
| 5 to 7 years | 4.5 | 5.0 | 3.6 | 3.1 | 3.5 | 2.4 | 2.0 | 2.2 | 1.6 |
| 8 years | 6.0 | 6.3 | 5.4 | 4.3 | 4.6 | 3.9 | 3.1 | 3.2 | 2.8 |
| High school: 1 to 3 years | 18.1 | 17.2 | 19.7 | 16.8 | 16.4 | 17.6 | 15.1 | 14.6 | 15.9 |
| 4 years | 42.3 | 38.8 | 48.4 | 44.7 | 41.7 | 49.9 | 46.5 | 44.3 | 50.1 |
| College: 1 to 3 years | 11.2 | 11.6 | 10.6 | 12.1 | 12.2 | 11.9 | 12.9 | 12.8 | 13.7 |
| 4 years or more | 16.0 | 18.7 | 11.1 | 17.5 | 19.9 | 13.4 | 19.4 | 21.6 | 15.7 |
| Median years of school completed | 12.5 | 12.5 | 12.4 | 12.5 | 12.6 | 12.5 | 12.6 | 12.6 | 12.6 |
| **45 TO 54 YEARS** | | | | | | | | | |
| Total: Number (in thousands) | 17,145 | 10,579 | 6,566 | 16,252 | 9,995 | 6,257 | 15,987 | 9,834 | 6,153 |
| Percent | 100.0 | 100.0 | 100.0 | 100.0 | 100.0 | 100.0 | 100.0 | 100.0 | 100.0 |
| Less than 4 years of high school [1] | 38.3 | 40.8 | 34.3 | 35.2 | 37.4 | 32.0 | 29.5 | 30.6 | 27.5 |
| 4 years of high school or more | 61.7 | 59.2 | 65.7 | 64.7 | 62.6 | 68.0 | 70.6 | 69.4 | 72.5 |
| Elementary: Less than 5 years [1] | 2.9 | 3.6 | 1.8 | 2.4 | 3.1 | 1.4 | 1.9 | 2.4 | 1.1 |
| 5 to 7 years | 6.4 | 7.1 | 5.2 | 5.5 | 6.3 | 4.3 | 4.1 | 4.6 | 3.2 |
| 8 years | 9.4 | 10.5 | 7.6 | 7.9 | 8.9 | 6.3 | 5.8 | 6.3 | 4.9 |
| High school: 1 to 3 years | 19.6 | 19.6 | 19.7 | 19.4 | 19.1 | 20.0 | 17.7 | 17.3 | 18.3 |
| 4 years | 38.3 | 33.2 | 46.5 | 39.4 | 34.4 | 47.4 | 43.3 | 39.2 | 49.7 |
| College: 1 to 3 years | 10.1 | 10.1 | 10.0 | 10.6 | 10.8 | 10.3 | 11.3 | 11.6 | 10.9 |
| 4 years or more | 13.3 | 15.9 | 9.2 | 14.7 | 17.4 | 10.3 | 16.0 | 18.6 | 11.9 |
| Median years of school completed | 12.3 | 12.3 | 12.3 | 12.4 | 12.4 | 12.4 | 12.5 | 12.5 | 12.5 |
| **55 TO 64 YEARS** | | | | | | | | | |
| Total: Number (in thousands) | 12,184 | 7,507 | 4,677 | 12,947 | 7,844 | 5,103 | 12,981 | 7,847 | 5,134 |
| Percent | 100.0 | 100.0 | 100.0 | 100.0 | 100.0 | 100.0 | 100.0 | 100.0 | 100.0 |
| Less than 4 years of high school [1] | 46.7 | 49.7 | 41.7 | 39.5 | 42.4 | 35.1 | 36.2 | 39.1 | 31.7 |
| 4 years of high school or more | 53.4 | 50.3 | 58.4 | 60.5 | 57.6 | 64.8 | 63.8 | 60.9 | 68.3 |
| Elementary: Less than 5 years [1] | 3.6 | 4.6 | 2.0 | 2.8 | 3.6 | 1.5 | 2.3 | 3.0 | 1.2 |
| 5 to 7 years | 8.7 | 9.1 | 8.0 | 6.7 | 7.2 | 5.8 | 5.7 | 6.4 | 4.5 |
| 8 years | 14.7 | 15.6 | 13.2 | 10.8 | 11.7 | 9.5 | 8.7 | 9.7 | 7.2 |
| High school: 1 to 3 years | 19.7 | 20.4 | 18.5 | 19.2 | 19.9 | 18.3 | 19.5 | 20.0 | 18.8 |
| 4 years | 33.2 | 29.7 | 38.8 | 37.8 | 33.3 | 44.7 | 38.3 | 33.0 | 46.5 |
| College: 1 to 3 years | 9.4 | 9.5 | 9.2 | 10.1 | 10.3 | 9.8 | 10.6 | 10.8 | 10.4 |
| 4 years or more | 10.8 | 11.1 | 10.4 | 12.6 | 14.0 | 10.3 | 14.9 | 17.1 | 11.4 |
| Median years of school completed | 12.1 | 12.0 | 12.2 | 12.3 | 12.2 | 12.3 | 12.4 | 12.3 | 12.4 |
| **65 YEARS AND OVER** | | | | | | | | | |
| Total: Number (in thousands) | 3,129 | 2,042 | 1,087 | 3,268 | 2,090 | 1,178 | 3,403 | 2,145 | 1,258 |
| Percent | 100.0 | 100.0 | 100.0 | 100.0 | 100.0 | 100.0 | 100.0 | 100.0 | 100.0 |
| Less than 4 years of high school [1] | 58.9 | 62.2 | 52.6 | 53.1 | 56.6 | 47.0 | 47.0 | 50.7 | 40.8 |
| 4 years of high school or more | 41.0 | 37.7 | 47.4 | 46.8 | 43.5 | 52.9 | 53.0 | 49.4 | 59.2 |
| Elementary: Less than 5 years [1] | 6.7 | 7.6 | 5.1 | 4.4 | 5.2 | 3.0 | 2.7 | 3.5 | 1.4 |
| 5 to 7 years | 13.2 | 13.3 | 12.9 | 11.0 | 11.2 | 10.7 | 8.8 | 9.2 | 8.3 |
| 8 years | 22.3 | 23.9 | 19.2 | 19.3 | 20.8 | 16.7 | 16.3 | 17.8 | 13.7 |
| High school: 1 to 3 years | 16.7 | 17.4 | 15.4 | 18.4 | 19.4 | 16.6 | 19.2 | 20.2 | 17.4 |
| 4 years | 20.2 | 18.1 | 24.1 | 24.4 | 22.1 | 28.7 | 29.3 | 26.0 | 34.8 |
| College: 1 to 3 years | 9.1 | 7.7 | 11.8 | 9.9 | 8.7 | 12.1 | 10.5 | 9.6 | 12.2 |
| 4 years or more | 11.7 | 11.9 | 11.5 | 12.5 | 12.7 | 12.1 | 13.2 | 13.8 | 12.2 |
| Median years of school completed | 10.4 | 9.9 | 11.8 | 11.5 | 11.0 | 12.1 | 12.1 | 11.9 | 12.3 |

[1] Includes persons reporting no formal education.

Source: Denis F. Johnston, "Education of Adult Workers: projections to 1985," *Monthly Labor Review*, Vol. 93 (August 1970), p. 46.

of the reason for this is that a number of these technical or professional occupations simply did not exist several decades ago or, if they did, the demand was such that most people with abilities in these areas channeled them into other careers. Moreover, in older and declining industries, older male workers also tend to be overrepresented since little hiring is done. The railroads would be a good example of this phenomenon.

Median earnings by age and occupation are shown in Table II-9. For males, the pattern is clear. For jobs requiring a higher median level of education, the peak earning years are between 45 and 54 while for jobs which require specific work skills more limited in application, the 35-44 year age group is the leader.

Females, on the other hand, have experienced a different result for a number of reasons. Female labor force participation has been characterized by a more flexible entry and exit pattern of participation because of the responsibilities encountered in child rearing. Also, until very recently, women have played a less assertive role in the labor market, a factor which is now undergoing rapid change. Thus, for females, peak earning years are more typically near the older age levels in both the 45-54 and 55-64 age cohorts. It has been at this point in a woman's life where family responsibilities have diminished so that greater concentration can be placed upon career goals, and for many, it marks the years of greatest job seniority, although it would not be as high as the male levels. The differences among women wage earners may also be less pronounced, because for those women today, opportunities were often not available which are now open to those women currently entering the labor market.

## Labor Market Problems—Final Comments

Institutional, education, and policy barriers to the employment of older workers have indeed existed. The extent and severity of the problems of older workers have varied over time and will undoubtedly fluctuate in the future. Business cycle changes, secular variations in the birthrate and consequent changes in the labor force, labor force participation rates, technological and educational developments, social patterns, and federal and state legislation will all affect older worker opportunity. The Age Discrimination in Employment Act, summarized in the balance of this chapter, was designed to affect just employment and personnel policies of employers, primarily, but also those of unions and employment agencies. As we have seen, the study upon

## TABLE II-9
*Median Earnings in 1969 by Occupational Group, Age and Sex*

| Occupation | Males | | | | | Females | | | | |
|---|---|---|---|---|---|---|---|---|---|---|
| | 18-24 Years | 25-34 Years | 35-44 Years | 45-54 Years | 55-64 Years | 18-24 Years | 25-34 Years | 35-44 Years | 45-54 Years | 55-64 Years |
| Experienced Civilian Labor Force | $5,467 | $8,601 | $9,640 | $9,310 | $8,225 | $4,340 | $5,069 | $4,832 | $4,881 | $4,698 |
| Professional, technical and kindred workers | 6,469 | 10,344 | 13,064 | 13,529 | 12,476 | 5,865 | 7,039 | 6,998 | 7,279 | 7,313 |
| Managers and administrators, except farm | 6,505 | 10,103 | 12,484 | 12,725 | 11,492 | 5,132 | 6,355 | 6,254 | 6,264 | 6,110 |
| Sales workers | 5,256 | 9,359 | 10,999 | 10,629 | 9,331 | 2,843 | 3,790 | 3,565 | 3,650 | 3,617 |
| Clerical and kindred workers | 5,236 | 7,904 | 8,805 | 8,808 | 8,338 | 4,509 | 5,275 | 5,265 | 5,456 | 5,522 |
| Craftsmen and kindred workers | 6,063 | 8,655 | 9,437 | 9,272 | 8,614 | 4,498 | 5,278 | 5,367 | 5,442 | 5,346 |
| Operatives, except transport | 5,561 | 7,599 | 8,000 | 7,937 | 7,510 | 3,826 | 4,326 | 4,453 | 4,491 | 4,347 |
| Transport equipment operatives | 5,432 | 7,755 | 8,250 | 7,975 | 7,262 | 4,514 | 4,962 | 4,895 | 4,686 | 5,063 |
| Laborers, except farm | 4,258 | 6,652 | 6,946 | 6,726 | 6,194 | 3,497 | 4,189 | 4,181 | 3,995 | 3,975 |
| Farmers and farm managers | 3,633 | 5,808 | 6,243 | 5,668 | 4,791 | 2,071 | 3,073 | 2,972 | 2,970 | 2,459 |

Source: U.S. Department of Commerce Bureau of the Census, *1970 Census of Population, Detailed Characteristics, United States Summary* PC (1)-D1, June 1973.

which the Act was based did not accurately portray the progress of older workers nor understandably foresee such labor force developments as the decline in labor force participation of older men, the sharp rise in female labor force participation, and the decline in the birthrate.

## THE AGE DISCRIMINATION ACT

The Age Discrimination in Employment Act of 1967 (ADEA) was enacted as an amendment to the Fair Labor Standards Act (FLSA) with the recordkeeping investigation and enforcement features of the ADEA being closely patterned after the FLSA. It is for this reason that the Department of Labor's Wage and Hour Division is charged with enforcement of the ADEA. Despite this, the ADEA bears a close relationship to Title VII of the Civil Rights Act of 1964. The interpretation and administration of the ADEA are therefore a mixture of the Title VII and FLSA procedures.

The purpose of ADEA is the outlawing of discrimination based upon age although this is confined to those over 40 and under 65 years of age.[13] The Act thus covers a large portion of the labor force (which will vary over time). It applies to all employers employing 20 or more persons, in addition to employment agencies and labor unions. There have been many interesting developments in the interpretation of the ADEA because its regulatory mechanism is essentially the litigation process. But before the developing age discrimination law can be discussed, the basic provision of the Act itself will be reviewed.

### Prohibition of Age Discrimination

Section 4 of the ADEA contains the language which provides for the express prohibition of discrimination in employment because of age. As shown in Figure II-2, it is unlawful for an employer to take any personnel action involving an individual in the protected age group because of that individual's age. This includes all aspects of personnel policy such as hiring, retirement, promotions, pay, demotions, etc.

Section 4 also requires employment agencies to strike all age criteria from their activities pertaining to employment. This includes listing job vacancies with age qualifications, failing to refer applicants to prospective employers because of their age,

---

[13] *Age Discrimination in Employment Act of 1967*, Section 12.

FIGURE II-2

*Excerpts from Age Discrimination in Employment Act*

Pub. Law 90-202                                              December 15, 1967
81 STAT. 603

## PROHIBITION OF AGE DISCRIMINATION

SEC. 4. (a) It shall be unlawful for an employer—

(1) to fail or refuse to hire or to discharge any individual or otherwise discriminate against any individual with respect to his compensation, terms, conditions, or privileges of employment, because of such individual's age;

(2) to limit, segregate, or classify his employees in any way which would deprive or tend to deprive any individual of employment opportunities or otherwise adversely affect his status as an employee, because of such individual's age; or

(3) to reduce the wage rate of any employee in order to comply with this Act.

(b) It shall be unlawful for an employment agency to fail or refuse to refer for employment, or otherwise to discriminate against, any individual because of such individual's age, or to classify or refer for employment any individual on the basis of such individual's age.

(c) It shall be unlawful for a labor organization—

(1) to exclude or to expel from its membership, or otherwise to discriminate against, any individual because of his age;

(2) to limit, segregate, or classify its membership, or to classify or fail or refuse to refer for employment any individual, in any way which would deprive or tend to deprive any individual of employment opportunities, or would limit such employment opportunities or otherwise adversely affect his status as an employee or as an applicant for employment, because of such individual's age;

(3) to cause or attempt to cause an employer to discriminate against an individual in violation of this section.

(d) It shall be unlawful for an employer to discriminate against any of his employees or applicants for employment, for an employment agency to discriminate against any individual, or for a labor organization to discriminate against any member thereof or applicant for membership, because such individual, member or applicant for membership has opposed any practice made unlawful by this section, or because such individual, member or applicant for membership has made a charge, testified, assisted, or participated in any manner in an investigation, proceeding, or litigation under this Act.

(e) It shall be unlawful for an employer, labor organization, or employment agency to print or publish, or cause to be printed or published, any notice or advertisement relating to employment by such an employer or membership in or any classification or referral for employment by such a labor organization, or relating to any classification or referral for employment by such an employment agency, indicating any preference, limitation, specification, or discrimination, based on age.

(f) It shall not be unlawful for an employer, employment agency, or labor organization—

(1) to take any action otherwise prohibited under subsections (a), (b), (c), or (e) of this section where age is a bona fide occupational qualification reasonably necessary to the normal operation of the par-

FIGURE II-2 (Continued)

ticular business, or where the differentiation is based on reasonable factors other than age;

(2) to observe the terms of a bona fide seniority system or any bona fide employee benefit plan such as a retirement, pension, or insurance plan, which is not a subterfuge to evade the purposes of this Act, except that no such employee benefit plan shall excuse the failure to hire any individual; or

(3) to discharge or otherwise discipline an individual for good cause.

See Appendix A for the full text of the law.

advertising for young applicants, and other practices of a similar nature.

Section 4 includes labor unions as well, requiring them to provide equal representation to persons in the protected age class in all aspects of their operations including hiring hall, membership, disciplinary action, and other activities under a labor organization's control.

*Exceptions to the Age Discrimination Prohibitions*

Certain exceptions to the prohibitions against age discrimination are also found in Section 4 of the Act. These are based upon the legal theory of a "bona fide occupation qualification" (BFOQ). To the layman, this appears to provide, that for an employer to be able successfully to engage in business and to survive in the market place, the law's application may, under special circumstances, be waived. In civil rights law, the BFOQ has been interpreted in a rather narrow way. The ADEA's BFOQ has application to two basic areas of employment activity, employment and terminations. Section 4 provides that "it shall not be unlawful for employers, employment agencies, or labor organizations . . . to take any action otherwise prohibited under . . . this section where age is a bona fide occupational qualification reasonably necessary to the normal operation of a particular business, or where the differentiation is based on reasonable factors other than age." [14] In addition, the section specifically excludes mandatory retirement under the provisions of a "bona fide" retirement plan of any type "which is not a subterfuge to evade the purposes of this Act . . ." and it specifically excludes discharging or disciplining an individual in the protected class "for good cause."

---

[14] *Ibid.*, Sec. 4.

## Recordkeeping, Investigation, and Enforcement

Section 7 of the ADEA specifies how Congress intended the Act to be applied. As mentioned in the introduction, the ADEA derives its basic recordkeeping, investigative, and enforcement procedures from the Fair Labor Standards Act. This indicates that employment records kept for compliance under the ADEA should be maintained for three years because the FLSA applies a two year statute of limitations to the recovery of back wages, except in the case of willful violations for which the statute is three years.[15]

The Wage and Hour Division compliance officers are responsible for initial ADEA enforcement similar to FLSA enforcement, except for one important provision. Section 7(b) states that "before instituting any action . . . the Secretary shall attempt to eliminate the discriminatory practice or practices alleged, and to effect voluntary compliance with the requirements of this Act through informal methods of conciliation, conference, and persuasion." [16] Whether this actually always occurs is not clear.[17] The Wage and Hour Division does, however, have an operating procedure which is generally well known. It strives for "flexible" enforcement of the Act. In practice, this means that conciliation of cases involving complainants occurs as do fully organized investigations of places of business.

Because the ADEA is largely complaint-oriented, conciliation is often the first step of the enforcement process. Depending upon the outcome of the conciliation, the employer may find the case dropped, a limited investigation made of his place of business, or a full-fledged investigation conducted of all of his employment practices and policies during the preceding two year period. The deciding factor, at least initially, of determining if a more thorough investigation is necessary will be the compliance officer. If the officer is "convinced" that a pattern or practice of age discrimination exists at the place of employment, the probability of a full investigation is high. The process may also

---

[15] U.S. Department of Labor, Employment Standards Administration, Wage and Hour Division, *Handy Reference Guide to the Fair Labor Standards Act,* WH Publication 1282 (Washington, D.C.: U.S. Government Printing Office, 1975), p. 16.

[16] *Age Discrimination in Employment Act,* Section 7(b).

[17] See, for example, *Brennan* v. *Ace Hardware Corporation,* 495 F.2d 368 (8th Cir., 1974), in which failure to conciliate caused dismissal of complaint.

begin with a full investigation if the Department of Labor is so disposed. There need not be an apparent reason as such for the investigation, but if the facts warrant in the opinion of the officer or the Department, the investigation will be limited in scope (See Figure II-3 for sequence of procedures under the Act.)

In using this type of enforcement approach, the Department of Labor is, in a sense, seeking litigation because it reasons that it is only through the litigation process that the interpretative issues in the application of the ADEA are resolved. Although the Act in Section 7(c) provides for aggrieved individuals to bring a "civil action in any court . . . for such legal or equitable relief as will effectuate the purposes of this Act . . . ," many of the most important cases were either instituted or aided by the Department of Labor. This policy has been enunciated by the former Solicitor of Labor who stated that it is incumbent upon the Department to push the ADEA to its virtual judicial limits.[18]

Section 7(d) contains the notification requirements of persons desiring either to bring civil action or to enlist the aid of the Department of Labor. These requirements provide that if an aggrieved individual is to proceed under civil action, he or she must give the Department of Labor "not less than sixty days' notice of an intent to file such action;" and, furthermore, that the notice shall be filed either within 180 days after the alleged discriminatory practice occurred or, if the aggrieved individual decides to proceed under a state age discrimination law as noted below, then the requirement of notice of intent to sue to the Department of Labor shall be within 300 days after the occurrence of the alleged discriminatory practice. If the state involved terminates its proceedings in the case and notifies the aggrieved individual that it has done so, the individual then has only 30 days to notify the Department of Labor of his or her intent to proceed with the case. But in any case involving state action, the applicable notice requirement period is always the one which is the earliest of the two described above.

---

[18] "Statement of Labor Solicitor Kilberg on Age Discrimination Submitted to Subcommittee on House Select Committee on Aging," *Daily Labor Report*, No. 33, February 18, 1976, p. E-1. This assertive view of its role is interestingly not a feature of the Department's view in the case of the Landrum-Griffin Act in which unions are the focal recipients of complaints.

## Figure II-3

### Procedures for Filing Complaints under the Age Discrimination in Employment Act

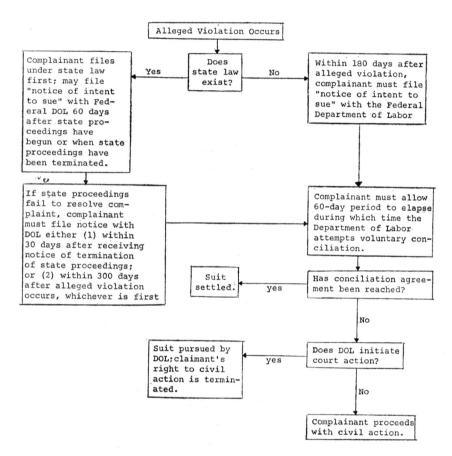

*Concurrent Jurisdiction*

As in the case with the FLSA, the ADEA allows states to enforce their own age discrimination laws even if they differ from the federal statute. Section 14 of the ADEA provides that federal action against an employer, employment agency, or labor union shall supersede any state action once the federal action has begun. In every other respect, however, state activity is separate and independent from federal activity. This is an important issue because in fourteen jurisdictions the state law protects persons generally, irrespective of age; in ten others, the protection starts at the earliest employment age; in eight, varying age limits exist; and only thirteen have the same 40-65 year age limits as the federal statute. Thus, thirty-two states have coverage which differs from the provisions of the ADEA, creating new affected classes and extra potential liabilities.[19] It should be noted that Title VII of the Civil Rights Act also provides for concurrent jurisdiction of state legislation.

## Coverage

The ADEA was amended in 1974. The amendments extended coverage to federal, state, and local government employees; broadened the application of the Act to include private employers with twenty or more employees instead of twenty-five as under the prior law; and increased the authorized funding level from $3 million to $5 million dollars for enforcement activities. Since that date, the U.S. Supreme Court has ruled that Congress cannot constitutionally extend its wage setting powers to state and municipal employees.[20] The question of whether this also voids the coverage of antidiscrimination laws to such employees is not settled and will be discussed with other matters of litigation in Chapter III.

---

[19] See Appendix B for a summary of state laws pertaining to old age discrimination.

[20] *National League of Cities v. Usery,* 96 S. Ct. 2465 (1976).

# Enforcement and Litigation of ADEA

The Age Discrimination in Employment Act has been enforced on a case by case basis. Although the Department of Labor has issued an interpretative bulletin [1] explaining the Department's position on the issues created by the Act, this bulletin has often been contradicted by the results of litigation. Therefore, the importance of knowing both the position which the Department of Labor takes in enforcing the various provisions of the ADEA and the decisions of the federal courts which have ruled on the application of the law is readily apparent.

## ENFORCEMENT—AN OVERVIEW

From 1968, the year that the Wage and Hour Divison began enforcing the ADEA, through 1976, there has been a rapid increase in all areas of enforcement activity. Table III-1 shows the progression of dollar awards made to employees who have sought and won relief pursuant to ADEA. The Department has received a steady and ever-increasing rise in the number of complaints involving age discrimination. This has been attributable partly to the increased efforts of the Wage and Hour Division, to more budgeted dollars for age discrimination enforcement, and to the impact of uncertain economic conditions since 1974. The data in Table III-2 demonstrate that people are becoming increasingly more aware of their rights in this area. Articles about older workers challenging their employers on such issues as compulsory early retirement, dismissals, failure to employ and other age related personnel decisions have given further evidence to the increased labor force awareness of the ADEA as well as to the more active role of the Department of Labor during the

---

[1] U.S. Department of Labor, Wage and Hour Division, *Age Discrimination in Employment Act of 1967*, Interpretive Bulletin, Title 29, Part 860 of The Code of Federal Regulations, WH Publication 1296 (Washington, D.C.: U.S. Government Printing Office, 1972).

## TABLE III-1
### *Affected Employees, Money and Jobs Awarded, ADEA, 1969-1976*

| Fiscal year | Individuals | | | Income restored | | Individuals aided | Job opportunities made available |
| | Discriminated against | Due damages | Amount found due | Individuals | Amount | | |
|---|---|---|---|---|---|---|---|
| 1969 | a | 48 | $39,875 | a | a | a | a |
| 1970 | a | 131 | 129,514 | a | a | a | a |
| 1971 | a | 655 | 738,074 | a | a | a | a |
| 1972 | a | 964 | 1,650,039 | a | a | a | a |
| 1973 | 14,386 | 1,031 | 1,866,226 | 304 | $662,324 | 8,849 | 39,667 |
| 1974 | 3,800 | 1,648 | 6,315,484 | 637 | 2,507,448 | 2,744 | 84,207 |
| 1975 | 5,540 | 2,350 | 6,574,409 | 728 | 1,676,171 | 3,376 | 27,217 |
| 1976 | 12,951 | 1,908 | 8,631,432 | 742 | 3,491,658 | 2,351 | 31,964 |
| 1976 b | 421 | 284 | 1,066,210 | 141 | 385,402 | 204 | 2,443 |

Source: U.S. Department of Labor Employment Standards Administration, *Age Discrimination In Employment Act of 1967—The 1976 Report*, (Washington, D.C.: U.S. Government Printing Office, 1977), p. 7.

a Not available or not comparable.
b Transition quarter, June 21, 1976-September 20, 1976.

## TABLE III-2
### *Complaints Received, ADEA, 1969-1976*

| Fiscal year | Complaints received | Percent increase |
|---|---|---|
| 1969 | 1,031 | — |
| 1970 | 1,344 | 30 |
| 1971 | 1,658 | 23 |
| 1972 a | 1,862 | 12 |
| 1973 | 2,208 | 19 |
| 1974 | 3,040 | 38 |
| 1975 b | 4,717 | 55 |
| 1976 b | 5,121 | 9 |
| 1976 (transition quarter) | 1,105 | — |

Source: U.S. Department of Labor Employment Standards Administration, *Age Discrimination In Employment Act of 1967* (Washington, D.C.: U.S. Government Printing Office, 1977), p. 8.

a Excludes one area office for which data were not available because of a flood.
b In fiscal year 1975, complaints were also counted on an individual basis for the first time. In that year, 5,424 complaints were recorded, 5,826 in 1976, and 1,226 in the transition quarter.

past several years.[2] Underscoring this increasingly active role, the Department of Labor had instituted a total of approximately 260 law suits by the end of 1976. Although this represented only a small percentage of the total number of allied age discrimination charges handled by the Department, litigation data are significant because the majority of cases is concluded at the administrative level. Furthermore, these figures do not include the large number of cases settled by the Department before court litigation was inaugurated.

## *The Case by Case Approach and the SOCAL Case*

The indications are that age discrimination complaints to the Department of Labor will continue to rise unabated into the foreseeable future. The case-by-case method of enforcement appears almost certain to encourage litigation and to produce new liabilities for employers. In the absence of detailed policy and rules, neither employers nor complainants can be certain as to the nature or complete extent of their liability or rights under the ADEA. The results of litigation can be unfair because past practices which originated before the adoption of present case law can be found vulnerable to attack. Employers have discovered that their total liability for age discrimination charges extended backwards in time even though they were unaware of violating the law; conversely, actions which have been found violative of the Act by one court, have been termed legal by another.

The Standard Oil of California (SOCAL) consent decree made ADEA well-known.[3] SOCAL had decided to reorganize its marketing operations because of the changing nature of the petroleum business. In 1973, the Arab Oil Boycott permanently altered the marketing thrust of most major oil companies. No longer was aggressive expansion of all gasoline and oil markets

---

[2] See, for example, Walter Mossberg, "Older U.S. Workers Challenging Employers on Forced Retirement," *The Wall Street Journal*, October 13, 1975, p. 1; Ralph E. Winter, "More Office Workers Battle Being Fired by Suing Their Bosses," *The Wall Street Journal*, June 18, 1975, p. 1; Lesley Oelsner, "High Court to Rule in Test Suit Against Retirement at Age 50," *The New York Times*, May 16, 1976, p. 26; Jane Gregory, "Spotlight—He's 72 and Set to Fight (in court) For a Job," *The Sunday Bulletin* (Philadelphia), September 4, 1976, p. 10.

[3] "Consent Decree Providing For Reinstatement and Back Pay For Standard Oil Employees For Age Discrimination," *Daily Labor Report*, No. 96, May 16, 1974, pp. G-1, 2.

possible or, since the boycott, even socially desirable. As a result, the company found itself, as did others, with a surplus of marketing personnel.

One way to handle this situation would have been to eliminate from employment all people under age 40 or wherever seniority provided for a cut-off age. This policy would have been in compliance with the ADEA, but it also would have created a considerable hardship among those employees who had young families, severe immediate financial obligations, and considerable long term company potential.

Another possible approach which the company could have employed would have been to terminate personnel on the basis of "merit." This policy has much to recommend, but it also creates hardship for those laid off. Often, in a sizeable reduction-in-force, good performing people will be terminated because the numbers involved are too large for careful merit analysis, or even for absorbing all meritorious employees.

A third approach, and the one taken by SOCAL, was to retire involuntarily those employees who had vested retirement benefits. To alleviate hardship in a difficult situation, and to cushion the blow of separation as much as practicable, SOCAL added separation allowances. Although in many respects this approach might seem to provide for the greatest equity for the greatest number, it ran afoul of the ADEA as interpreted by the Department of Labor. Although SOCAL agreed to the consent decree with the Department of Labor, it still maintained that it was not in violation of the Act, but that the consent decree would produce a better solution than litigation for everyone involved.

The SOCAL backpay awards totalling approximately $2,000,000 are, to date, the largest to result from any age discrimination case, but that figure does not tell the complete story. One hundred-twenty former employees were offered reinstatement. If a great injustice had been committed in retiring these employees involuntarily, one would think that the overwhelming majority would react with strong approval at the prospect of receiving backpay *and* returning to active employment until their "normal" retirement dates. Yet, over 60 percent of the affected class chose to remain retired.

For most of that 60 percent, the additional benefits were not so overwhelming as to suggest that they were "bought off" by the settlement. It would seem to indicate, therefore, that the original company decision was not, for the majority of the employees affected, either negative or inconsiderate.

Whether SOCAL made the "right" decision in agreeing to the consent decree is a moot point. It is now history, and it was more responsible than any single action up to 1974 for putting age discrimination enforcement into the forefront. The huge dollar award and the attendant publicity apparently sparked the Department of Labor into augmenting its ADEA compliance activities. ". . . [P]lans to step up enforcement of the anti-age discrimination law (had) been under consideration for some time, and the Labor Department's success in the SOCAL case settled the issue. [Solicitor of Labor] Kilberg ordered a review of all age discrimination complaints pending in regional offices. . . ." [4]

In every report which the Department releases concerning its activities in age discrimination enforcement, and before every congressional committee to which testimony is given regarding the Department's record in enforcing the ADEA, the SOCAL consent decree is always prominently mentioned, especially its large dollar award. This figure, more than any other criterion, appears to be the most important measurement of success for the Department of Labor's staff. Emphasis on this aspect of enforcement ignores the fact that there are two parties to every age discrimination suit, that the public through the market price system pays the cost of these awards, and that the strong emphasis on backpay as the measurement of success in litigation gives employers very little incentive to do anything less than maintain a strong adversary position. This, in turn, fosters mistrust on the part of employers toward the efforts of conciliation and the development of reasonable compromise solutions to problems which are usually neither precise nor highlighted by clear boundaries of equity.

The Department's emphasis on litigation and backpay also places in jeopardy the language of Section 7(b) of the Act which requires the Department of Labor "to effect voluntary compliance with the requirements of this Act. . . ." Many employers wonder how cooperation and voluntary compliance can be effectuated when the threat of backpay looms so large. What voluntary compliance seems to mean, if the employers interviewed for this study are correct, is that the employer will voluntarily

---

[4] "Age discrimination moves into the limelight," *Business Week*, June 15, 1974, p. 104.

make the backpay award himself without requiring the Department to litigate. This was the situation in the SOCAL consent decree and this is what should generally be expected as the Department's position when an employer faces a charge of age discrimination.

## PROCEDURAL ISSUES

The procedural requirements of the ADEA have been the subject of much of the litigation involving the Act. Cases involving these issues have both interpreted the law and caused dismissal of more than two-thirds of the suits brought by individuals. This has led the Department of Labor to seek a conflict with the "unfavorable" court rulings so that it can "become a vehicle for bringing these procedural issues to the Supreme Court." [5] The procedural issues include notice and other prerequisites to suits, state agency relationships, conditions for class action suits, conciliation requirements, what constitutes willful violations, right to jury trials, and constitutionality of coverage of state and municipal employees.

### *Notice Requirements*

Section 7(d) of the Act states:

> No civil action may be commenced by any individual . . . until the individual has given the Secretary (Department of Labor) not less than sixty days notice of an intent to file such action. Such notice shall be filed—
>
> (1) within one hundred and eighty days after the alleged unlawful practice occurred, . . .

The reason for the 60-day notice is simple. It allows the Department of Labor to seek the elimination of the alleged discriminatory practice by informal methods of conciliation, and to attempt *voluntary* compliance as stipulated by Section 7(b) of the Act so that, in the words of the *Powell* case,

> potential defendants would become aware of their status and the possibility of litigation reasonably soon. . . . In turn, this would promote the good faith negotiation of employers during the 60 day conciliation period and provide an opportunity for preserva-

---

[5] "Statement of Solicitor Kilberg On Age Discrimination Submitted to Subcommittee On House Select Committee On Aging," *Daily Labor Report*, No. 33, February 18, 1976, p. E-1.

tion of evidence and records for use at a trial necessitated by failure of negotiation.[6]

A problem of interpretation has arisen concerning the legal nature of the notice. Most courts have ruled that the notice requirement is "jurisdictional"[7]; that is, failure to comply with the letter of the law is an absolute bar to bringing an action in court against the employer. Other courts[8] have ruled that the notice requirement is "directional" in nature, that is, the time limitations are somewhat analogous to statutes of limitation and are subject to equitable modifications. On February 21, 1977, the U.S. Supreme Court granted certiorari in the *Dartt v. Shell Oil Case* and will presumably settle the issue.

The two positions of the appellate are illustrated by the *Powell* and *Moses* cases. In the former, an employee filed a complaint alleging age discrimination hiring by the Southwestern Bell Telephone Company. Because the facts would not support her case, the Department of Labor notified Powell that it would not pursue the matter. Powell waited beyond the 180 day period to give notice to the Department of Labor that she intended to bring private action against the phone company. The court stated:

> . . . our sympathy is an insufficient basis upon which to justify an extension of the tolling theory to meet her predicament. She was expressly alerted to the time limitations for possible action, both private and agency assisted. To consider informal action by the Secretary (Department of Labor) in her behalf as tolling the 180 day requirement would be to read the notice section out of the statute, an action we are not prepared to take.[9]

In the *Moses v. Falstaff Brewing Case,* the issue was when does the notice period commence. Moses was terminated from employment after 23 years of service at age 48. She was notified of her termination on November 12, 1973, but continued to work out the week, her last day of work being November 16, 1973. In addition, she received pay through November 30 to

---

[6] *Powell v. Southwestern Bell Telephone Company,* 494 F.2d 485 (5th Cir. 1974).

[7] *Ibid.,* and *Hiscott v. General Electric Company,* 521 F.2d 632 (6th Cir. 1975).

[8] *Dartt v. Shell Oil Company,* 539 F.2d 1256 (10th Cir. 1976), *cert. granted,* U.S. Supreme Court, February 21, 1977; also *Moses v. Falstaff Brewing Corporation,* 525 F.2d 92 (8th Cir. 1975).

[9] *Powell, supra,* note 6.

cover vacation time due her, part of which was the Thanksgiving holiday that the company added to her pay period. Moses filed with the Department of Labor on May 24, 1974, advising the Secretary of Labor that she intended to file a private suit.

The appeals court, on appeal, overturned the district court's ruling barring the suit for lack of timeliness by saying,

> A procedural requirement of the Act, of doubtful meaning in a given case, should not be interpreted to deny an employee a claim for relief unless to do so would clearly further some substantial goal of the Act.[10]

The court, therefore, used the date that the employee was administratively terminated from the company. This interpreted the Act in favor of the employee, and in the court's opinion, served to achieve the Act's purpose of protecting the employee from discrimination.

The courts also do not require any special form for the notice to file.[11] It may even be given orally.[12] Moreover, if the employer fails to post a notice in a conspicuous place explaining the features of ADEA, the plaintiff may be excused from the notice requirement.[13]

Since the ADEA has by now received much publicity, and since Congress did indeed legislate time limits, it does seem that the courts should adhere to these limits, and most have. There will always be "late filers" no matter what limits are established. To enhance employer liability and costs to accommodate tardiness with the Act's provisions seems at best questionable equity.[14]

## State Relationships

When the state in which the alleged unlawful practice has a law against age discrimination and an agency to enforce that

---

[10] *Moses v. Falstaff Brewing, supra,* note 8.

[11] *Burgett v. Cudahy Company,* 361 F. Supp. 617 (D.C. Kansas 1973).

[12] *Woodford v. Kinney Shoe Corporation,* 369 F. Supp. 911 (N.D. Ga. 1973).

[13] *Gebhard v. GAF Corporation,* 59 FRD 504 (D.D.C. 1973); *Bishop v. Jelleff Associates,* 398 F. Supp. 579 (D.D.C. 1974). FRD stands for Federal Rules Decisions and is published by West Publishing Company.

[14] For a different view, see Thomas P. Donahoe, "Procedural Aspects of the Age Discrimination in Employment Act of 1967," *University of Pittsburgh Law Review,* Vol. 36 (Summer 1975), pp. 914-932. This article has been helpful in writing this section.

law, no suit can be brought under the ADEA until sixty days after proceedings have begun under state law, or unless state proceedings have been terminated. When the state has an applicable law, individuals have 300 days, instead of 180, to file notice of intent to sue with the Secretary, or thirty days after they receive notice of the termination of state proceedings, whichever occurs first.

Because of this deference to the state law, state agencies must be given the first opportunity to act, although after the initial 60 day conciliation period an individual may eschew state or federal remedies and initiate his own suit. That does not mean that state remedies must be exhausted, but that the state must be given a reasonable opportunity to attempt to settle the matter.[15] An exception to this rule has been made in cases in which the plaintiff relied upon official advice in neglecting a state remedy, or lacked a definitive ruling on the legal question involved.[16]

The Department of Labor has followed a policy of attempting to begin the 60 day conciliation period immediately after a "notice to file suit" has been given by a plaintiff, regardless of the standing of the case in a state agency. In such an instance the Department will not interfere with state proceedings. The Department will, however, proceed on its own with conciliation. It is, therefore, at least theoretically possible for an employer to be dealing simultaneously with federal and state agencies, in addition to having to prepare for the private litigation that can commence as soon as the 60 day conciliation period ends.

This approach would seem to conflict with the view of the Court of Appeals, Third Circuit which, after noting that "no suit may be brought until after 60 days have elapsed from the time of commencing proceedings under state law," declared: "Ordinarily plaintiff's failure . . . to avail himself of the state administrative remedy would be fatal to his course of action." [17] Thus, it would appear that the Department may not rescue a case by deferring to a state *after* a suit has been filed in court.

---

[15] *Goger v. H. K. Porter Company, Inc.*, 492 F.2d 13 (3rd Cir. 1974).

[16] *Vaughn v. Chrysler Corporation*, 382 F. Supp. 143 (E.D. Mich. 1974); and *Rogers et al. v. Exxon Research and Engineering Company*, —— F.2d —— (3rd Cir., January 20, 1977).

[17] *Rogers et al. . . . , supra*, note 16.

## Private v. Federal Suit

If an action is begun by the Secretary of Labor, the right to bring a private suit is terminated.[18] Thus, two suits on one alleged violation do not appear possible under the Act.

## Class Action Suits

Because the Fair Labor Standards Act limits class action suits to those that give their consent in writing to become a party and file such consent in court, some courts have limited ADEA class action litigants to this procedure.[19] Other courts drawing an analogy from Title VII of the Civil Rights Act of 1964, have applied Rule 23 of the Federal Rules of Civil Procedure, which is less stringent in limiting the litigant class.[20]

## Conciliation Requirement

The ADEA explicity requires that the Secretary of Labor must, through the Department's staff, seek to settle ADEA-based complaints by voluntary compliance. If he fails to do so, even though the employer may have violated the Act, judgment may be found for the employer. The lead case involved a situation where the Department of Labor made two visits and one telephone call, and then four months later, filed suit. The Department's compliance officer failed to follow its field operations handbook to request that the employee be made whole; to advise the employer that his file was referred for review and possible litigation; or to give the employer an opportunity to discuss the situation from his point of view. The court reminded the Department that the employer had a right for the government to be concerned about his plight, as well as that of the complainant, and declared that,

> . . . government officials must approach their service with a spirit and an attitude of helpfulness and concern for all persons with whom they deal and not with ambiguity, nonchalance, and heavy handedness of an all-pervasive federal bureaucracy. . . . Persuasion cannot be accomplished if the desired goal is unknown. The Secretary by not informing the employer that back wages are recoverable under the Act and by later instituting a law suit for

---

[18] *Ibid.*

[19] *Hull v. Continental Oil Company,* 58 FRD 636, (S.D. Texas 1973).

[20] *Bishop v. Jelleff Associates, supra,* note 13.

such damages, is defeating the very purpose of attempting to persuade the employer to comply with the Act.[21]

District courts apparently have discretion to stay proceedings to permit the Department of Labor to attempt conciliation. This would probably meet the requirements of the Act and has been advocated by one commentator.[22] The district court in the case just described declined to do this after the Department of Labor requested it to do so. Whether conciliation at this stage would serve a purpose would depend on the extent to which the Department of Labor, seemingly already committed to litigation, as well as the defendant employer, would be capable of flexibility.

## Willful Violations

Suits to enforce the ADEA must be brought within two years after the alleged violation unless a willful violation in which a three year statute of limitations is effective. The courts have disagreed on what is "willful." One ruling required that the violations be committed in bad faith and with a definite knowledge that the Act was being violated,[23] another, that it be intentional, knowingly and voluntary rather than careless, unknowing and unintentional.[24] The later decision applied a three year statute of limitations. Liquidated damages may also be recovered where violations are willful. Attorney's fees may be granted whether or not the violations are willful.

## Right to Jury Trial

The courts of appeal are split on the right of an employee to a jury trial in an action for lost wages brought under the Act. The Fourth Circuit has stated that, if requested, a jury trial must be granted; the Third Circuit seems to agree. The Sixth Circuit, however, disagrees.[25] Thus, the issue must await resolution by the U.S. Supreme Court.

---

[21] *Brennan v. Ace Hardware Company*, 495 F.2d 368 (8th Cir. 1974).

[22] Donahoe, "Procedural Aspects."

[23] *Bishop v. Jelleff Associates, supra*, note 13.

[24] *Hodgson v. Ideal Corrugated Box Company*, 8 EPD 9805, (D.C. W.Va. 1974). EPD stands for Employment Practice Decisions published by Commerce Clearing House, Inc.

[25] *Morelock et al. v. The NCR Corporation*, —— F.2d —— (6th Cir. 1976); *Rogers, supra*, note 16; and *Pons v. Lorillard*, —— F.2d —— (4th Cir. 1977).

## Damages for "Pain and Suffering"

The weight of judicial opinion is that the ADEA does not authorize damages for "pain and suffering." The most important case regarding this issue is *Rogers v. Exxon Research Engineering Company.*[26] In *Rogers,* the plaintiff alleged that Exxon was responsible for lost earnings, physical and emotional ailments, and fewer retirement benefits due to his involuntary early retirement at age 60. Specifically, the plaintiff claimed that the emotional and physical problems he suffered entitled him to a jury trial and a recovery of damages for "pain and suffering." The district court agreed, and an award of $550,000 was made.

The appeals court vacated the award on the grounds that the ADEA does not permit "monetary damages for 'pain and suffering' in the nature of emotional distress." The court based its ruling on the following points:

—there is no specific provision in the Act which authorizes a recovery for emotional or psychic distress.

—the damages provided for in the ADEA relate directly to the FLSA and are money damages in amounts measured by "unpaid minimum wages . . . and liquidated damages."

—there is no evidence in the congressional history of the ADEA that such awards were meant to be granted.

—Congress explictly restricted the penalty provisions of the Act to doubling the amount of lost earnings for willful violations.

—and perhaps most importantly, the granting of pain and suffering would dramatically alter the impact of available administrative remedies.

The thrust of ADEA's enforcement provisions is that private lawsuits are secondary to administrative remedies and suits brought by the Secretary of Labor. . . . The introduction of a claim for psychic and emotional distress would present serious administrative problems . . . it would induce an element of uncertainty *which would impair the conciliation process.*[27]

---

[26] *Rogers, supra,* note 16.

[27] Emphasis supplied. A strong statement against awarding pain and suffering damages was earlier contained in *Sant v. Mack Trucks, Inc.,* 13 FEP Cases 854 (N.D. Cal. 1976). The opposite opinion was reached in *Combes v. Griffin Television, Inc.,* 13 FEP Cases 1455 (W.D. Okla. 1976).

## Coverage of State and Municipal Employees

In the *National League of Cities Case*,[28] the United States Supreme Court ruled that the 1974 Fair Labor Standards Act amendments were invalid in so far as they attempted to extend the Act's minimum wage and overtime regulations to state and municipal employees.

According to one respected law professor, this means that ". . . [p]resumably, the federal law prohibiting discrimination because of age, extended to public employees by the 1974 amendments, will also be held not applicable to state and local government workers."[29] On the other hand, the former solicitor of the Department of Labor has argued the opposite on the grounds that the ADEA does not interfere with legitimate state interests and represents justifiable exercises of federal power to combat discrimination pursuant to the Fourteenth Amendment.[30]

As of January 1977, two district courts had decided that the former solicitor was correct and unheld the constitutionality of the application of the ADEA to state employees.[31] It may, however, be a considerable period before this issue is definitively determined.

## BURDEN OF PROOF

The question of where the burden of proof lodges is basic to all age discrimination cases. In general, the precedents established in cases involving Title VII of the Civil Rights Act of 1964, as amended, are followed.[32] Thus the complainant must demonstrate that age was a factor in the action which secured. He need es-

---

[28] 96 S. Ct. 2465 (1976).

[29] From a speech by Professor Benjamin Aaron, quoted in "Significant Decisions in Labor cases," *Monthly Labor Review*, Vol. 99 (December 1976), p. 50.

[30] "Statement of Solicitor William Kilberg," *Daily Labor Report*, No. 33, Feb. 18, 1976, p. E-1.

[31] *Usery v. Board of Education of Salt Lake City*, 421 F. Supp. 718, (D.C. Utah, September 1, 1976); and *Usery v. Bettendorf Community School District*, 423 F.Supp. 637 (S.D. Iowa, 1976). There have also been few federal district court cases upholding the constitutionality of extending the Equal Pay Act to state and municipal employees. (See Aaron, "Significant Decisions." pp. 50-51). The Equal Pay Act is also an amendment to the FLSA.

[32] See for example: *Muziz v. Beto*, 434 F.2d 697 (5th Cir. 1970), *Weeks v. Southern Bell Telephone and Telegraph Company*, 408 F.2d 228 (5th Cir. 1969); and *McDonnell Douglas Corporation v. Green*, 411 U.S. 792 (1973).

tablish only a "prima facie case of unlawful discrimination at which point the burden of proof shifts to the defendant to justify the existence of any disparities. Once the plaintiff has made out his prima facie case, we look to the defendant for an explanation since he is in a position to know whether he failed to hire a person for reasons which would exonerate him." [33]

The burden of proof will be switched to the defendant whenever the evidence shows that the action taken by the employer was "tainted with the impermissible criterion of age." [34] Therefore, if a prima facie case of discrimination has been established, the charge of age discrimination can be sustained even if there is an affirmative showing that there were other factors which might have justified the employer's action.[35]

Examples by which a prima facie case of discrimination may be shown are numerous. For example, there can be evidence of overt discrimination, such as a notation on the application form that the applicant is "too old to do the job"; or that an applicant was not employed because of his age even though he seemed to possess all the requisite qualifications for the job; or that the person discharged had good performance reviews and that age was apparently a factor in his termination. There may also be evidence gleaned from the employment statistics at a place of work indicating a "disparate" impact on the protected age group which cannot be explained by random selection. In fact, the Department of Labor relies upon the development of elementary statistical analysis to show prima facie cases of discrimination. The former Solicitor of Labor has stated:

> The development of meaningful statistics is essential to the successful prosecution of the large pattern and practice cases and thus is the kind of case that we intend to develop more of. This does not mean that we will continue to bring cases involving a single employer. We will. At the same time we must concentrate our efforts on those cases which will have the greatest impact on the community and which will establish precedent for more important legal issues. . . .[36]

---

[33] *Hodgson v. First Federal Savings and Loan Association of Broward County, Florida,* 455 F.2d 818 (5th Cir. 1972).

[34] *Wilson v. Sealtest Food Division of Kraft Company Corporation,* 501 F.2d 84 (5th Cir. 1974).

[35] *Laugesen v. Anaconda Company,* 510 F.2d 307 (6th Cir. 1975).

[36] "Statement of Labor Solicitor Kilberg," *Daily Labor Report,* No. 33, February 18, 1976, p. E-2.

Because of this stress on statistics it behooves companies to develop supporting data, to make decisions on the basis of as objective evidence as possible, and to maintain clear and unequivocal records. When this approach has been followed, charges of age discrimination may be overcome.[37] As one court noted:

> Thus, while the principal thrust of the Age Act is to protect the older worker from intimidation by arbitrary classification on account of age, we do not believe that Congress intended automatic presumptions to apply whenever a worker is replaced by another of a different age.[38]

Discrimination must therefore be proved by a preponderance of evidence. A prima facie case transfers the burdens of proof to the defendant, but it does not establish that the defendant is guilty.[39] The defendant must then establish his proof which in turn must go beyond just rebuilding the prima facie case. Where the defendant company, union or employment agency is able:

> to articulate some legitimate, nondiscriminatory reason for the employee's rejection . . . [this] suffices to meet the prima facie case, but the inquiry must not end there. . . . [Plaintiff] must . . . be afforded a fair opportunity to show that . . . [the] stated reason . . . was in fact pretext.[40]

Thus, although an employee may be discharged for unsatisfactory work, he may not be discharged if equally unsatisfactory younger workers are retained, and if the reason for his selection for discharge is age.

## ADVERTISING AND JOB APPLICATIONS

The first efforts of the Department of Labor in ADEA enforcement were designed to alter advertising of job vacancies and job applications. Compliance has been achieved with little litigation.

### Advertising

The Department of Labor's efforts to bring advertising into compliance have been quite successful. Almost 3,903 complaints

---

[37] *Mastel et al. v. Great Lakes Steel Corporation*, Case No. 3801 (Ed. Mich. December 20, 1976).

[38] *Laugesen v. Anaconda Company, supra*, note 35.

[39] *Mastel et al. v. Great Lake Steel Corporation, supra*, note 37.

[40] *McDonnell Douglas Corporation v. Green, supra*, note 32.

in this category were processed during 1974, 1975, and 1976, with the number declining each year.[41] Section 4(e) of the Act prohibits "an employer . . . from using any notice or advertisement relating to employment . . . indicating any preference, limitation, specification, or discrimination based on age." The Department has interpreted this to mean that most forms of job advertising which specify age as a requirement for applying for a job are illegal. There are several exceptions. For example, "help wanted notices or advertisements which include a term or phrase such as college graduate or other educational requirement, that specify a minimum age less than 40, such as not under 18, or not under 21, are not prohibited by the statute." [42]

There has been only one important appellate court decision [43] regarding job advertising and here the Department of Labor's position was held. The case involved an employment agency which advertised in its capacity as an employer for "college students," "girls," "boys," and "June graduates" to work for the agency itself. The Department's position was that such advertisements were violative of the ADEA and that the court should grant an injunction to prohibit this type of advertising. The agency argued that because it employed fewer than 25 personnel (the Act was amended in 1974, after the case was initiated, to include employers of 20 or more persons) and since it had acted in its capacity as an employer, the ADEA did not apply to the advertising. The district court agreed on the grounds that the agency had failed to meet the statutory definition of "employer." On appeal, however, the Department's position was sustained because a "pragmatic" test was applied—would the advertisement keep qualified jobseekers in the protected age group from applying? The court's answer to that question was affirmative, thereby placing strong restrictions on all job advertising. Only jobs which meet the requirement of a bona fide occupational qual-

[41] U.S. Department of Labor Employment Standards Administration, *Age Discrimination In Employment Act of 1967—A Report Covering Activities Under The Act During 1975* (Washington, D.C.: U.S. Government Printing Office, 1976), p. 9; also see *Age Discrimination In Employment Act of 1967—A Report Covering Activities Under the Act During 1976* (Washington, D.C.: U.S. Government Printing Office, 1977), p. 12.

[42] *Age Discrimination in Employment Act of 1967, Interpretive Bulletin,* CFR Title 29, Sec. 860.92, p. 3.

[43] *Hodgson v. Approved Personnel Services, Inc.,* 529 F.2d 760 (4th Cir. 1975).

ification may be generally exempt from this provision of the Act.

As job advertising has been considered a "non-monetary" violation, it is both easy and painless for employers to correct. The success of the Department of Labor in eliminating age-related advertisements may be measured by a casual reading of any newspaper "want-ad" section. This will provide testimony to the overall level of awareness of the requirements of Section 4 (e).

## *Job Applications*

Job applications may provide for age information from applicants as long as they are not used in any way to restrict or deter the inquiries for employment or function by persons in the protected age group.[44] Although there have been no major court cases devoted to the actual construction of job applications, the use of age questions on applicants or comments written on them by employment personnel have often been the starting point for age discrimination suits. This is the type of "overt" age discrimination which compliance officers attempt to uncover. A notation on the application itself that the applicant is "too old," or words to that effect, can be discriminatory. Although this is not a frequent occurrence, it has led to several major actions by the Department of Labor.[45]

## BONA FIDE OCCUPATIONAL QUALIFICATIONS

A key question associated both with the decision to employ and with mandatory retirement is what constitutes a "bona fide occupational classification" (BFOQ). The BFOQ has two related, but somewhat distinct aspects. First, the employer may in some circumstances specify age as a qualification and it may be allowed as a BFOQ. Second, the employer may impose some other qualification, such as a physical examination which has a disparate impact on older employees. This may be permitted in spite of the disparate impact if the particular qualification is one which is essentially job related. Among the cases discussed

---

[44] *ADEA Interpretive Bulletin*, CFR Title 29, Sec. 860.95, p. 3.

[45] For example, a multimillion dollar suit against the Goodyear Tire and Rubber Company has been launched, in part, because a personnel officer noted age qualifications on all applicant's forms at one of the firm's plants. As the Department considers this a form of overt discrimination, its willingness to conciliate is correspondingly diminished.

below, the *Greyhound* one involves the first problem, the *Spurlock* one the second. Here we will first examine the relation of the BFOQ to employment criteria; later we look at it in relation to early retirement.

## Definition and Interpretations

A bona fide occupational qualification (BFOQ) relates to those jobs, positions, or duties in a place of business that require special skills, attainment levels of performance, safety needs, physical condition, or any number of unique combinations that restrict applicability to performance in a given line or work. Obvious examples exist such as movie or stage roles, wet nurses, or professional athletes. Between the obvious and the ordinary, however, there exists a host of occupations which to some degree require highly specialized skills, attributes, or physical qualities that most people over age 40 generally cannot be expected to possess. Are those over 40 people entitled to identify this job as a BFOQ within the meaning of the ADEA?

The Department of Labor's interpretations of a BFOQ state that:

> [w]hether occupational qualifications will be deemed bona fide and reasonably necessary to the normal occupation of the particular business, will be determined on the basis of all the pertinent facts surrounding each particular situation. It is anticipated that this concept of a bona fide occupational qualification will have limited scope and application. Further, as this is an exception it must be construed narrowly, and the burden of proof in establishing that it applies is the responsibility of the employer. . . .[46]

To augment further the application of a BFOQ, the Act and therefore the regulations, also address the issue of "differentiations based on reasonable factors other than age."[47] The Department of Labor again states that to define with precision such a phrase as "differentiations" would be futile. Instead, such decisions will be "made on a case by case basis of all the particular facts and circumstances surrounding each individual situation."[48] In determining the merit of a "differentiation," the

---

[46] *ADEA, Interpretive Bulletin,* CFR Title 29, Sec. 860.102, p. 4.

[47] *Age Discrimination In Employment Act of 1967,* 81 Stat. 603, 90 U.S.C., 1967, Section 4(f)(1).

[48] *ADEA, Interpretive Bulletin,* CFR Title 29, Sec. 860.103, p. 4.

Department's position is that the applicability of an exception to the law will be construed in the narrowest possible fashion. The courts, however, have not always agreed with the Department's interpretation of a BFOQ. An examination of the key cases will further illustrate the complexity of the issue and the difficulty of establishing a BFOQ exception with age as the employment criterion.

## Precedent Cases Based Upon Title VII Civil Rights Decisions

As in burden of proof issues under the ADEA, the BFOQ also follows precedent from Title VII cases. The most important precedents in this regard are to be found in *Weeks v. Southern Bell Telegraph Company*,[49] *Diaz v. Pan American World Airways, Inc.*,[50] and *Spurlock v. United Airlines, Inc.*[51]

In *Weeks*, the telephone company was faced with a charge of sex discrimination for refusing to consider women for the position of "switchman." The company claimed that because most women would be physically unable to perform the duties of the job which required the "strenuous activity" of lifting weights in excess of thirty pounds, the job should be declared a BFOQ, thereby relieving the company's obligation to hire women for the position. In discussing the burden of proof required to be met by the company, the court stated:

> We hold that in order to rely on the bona fide occupational qualification exception an employer has the burden of proving that he had reasonable cause to believe, that is, a factual basis for believing that all or substantially all women would be unable to perform the duties of the job involved.

The court found that the company had failed to meet its burden of proving the BFOQ exemption was valid because it would not accept the contention that on the basis of a "stereotyped characterization" few or no women could safely lift thirty pounds while all men would be treated as if they could.

The only other alternative for the employer in the *Weeks* test would be for him to demonstrate "that it is impossible or highly impractical to deal with women on an individualized basis." If

---

[49] 408 F.2d 235 (5th Cir. 1969).

[50] 442 F.2d 385 (5th Cir. 1971).

[51] 475 F.2d 216 (10th Cir. 1972).

this situation exists, then the employer may apply a "reasonable general rule."

In *Diaz*, the court analyzed the question of business necessity and how it relates to hiring practices and, more specifically, to the BFOQ exception. Here, the company had refused to hire men for the job of flight cabin attendant. The court's analysis of a "BFOQ reasonably *necessary* to the normal operation of that . . . particular business," was seen as a "business necessity test, not a business *convenience* test." The court stated that, "the primary function of an airline is to transport passenger safety . . ." and that the sex of flight cabin attendants had no measurable impact upon that function. Therefore, the essence of the business serves as a benchmark in determining whether a company can claim a BFOQ exception for a particular job.

In *Spurlock*, United Airlines was charged with racial discrimination in the hiring of aircraft pilots. The plaintiff alleged that the rigorous preemployment testing and other job qualifications discriminated against blacks because, as a group, they tended to do poorer on the total qualification ratings than did white applicants. The court found this argument unpersuasive. It stated that:

> . . . when the job clearly requires a high degree of skill and the economic and human risks involved in hiring an unqualified applicant are great, the employer bears a correspondingly lighter burden [of proof] to show that his employment criteria are job related . . . [and meet the requirements of a BFOQ].

Therefore, it was not necessary for United to show that a disproportionate impact upon blacks would not result from its hiring policy, but rather that the job requirements themselves were directly related to the essence of the company's business.

These cases have been directly relied upon in several of the most crucial decisions regarding the ADEA to date, a discussion of which follows.

## The Greyhound Decision [52]

Greyhound Bus Lines, Inc. has had a long established policy of not hiring persons over the age of thirty-five for the job of intercity bus driver. Without the concept of a BFOQ, the company would be undeniably discriminating against persons in the

---

[52] *Hodgson v. Greyhound Lines, Inc.*, 354 F. Supp. 230 (N.D. Ill. 1973), *reversed* 499 F.2d 859 (7th Cir. 1974), *cert. denied*, 419 U.S. 1122 (1975).

protected age class. But the BFOQ is not an automatic excuse for a company to restrict its hiring policies. There must be compelling reasons related to the very survival of the business for the BFOQ exemption to be acceptable to the Department of Labor and the challenge of judicial review. Greyhound's policy of not hiring persons in the protected age class was based upon company data which showed that the safest driver was one who had sixteen to twenty years of driving experience and was between fifty and fifty-five years of age—an optimum blend of age and experience which could never be attained in employing an applicant forty years of age or over. Furthermore, the most difficult driving assignments, the "extra board duty," [53] were given to the drivers with the least seniority. This, coupled with other statistical evidence of safety performance by drivers of different ages, and the fact that the degenerative changes caused by aging impact adversely on driving skills and are not readily detectible by physical examination, were Greyhound's reasons for having a hiring policy based in part upon age.

Greyhound did not, however, rely exclusively upon its own corporate data in establishing the 35 years hiring age limit. Safety requirements are established by the Bureau of Motor Carriers Safety of the Department of Transportation. These regulations state that a carrier is free to establish more stringent rules relating to safety.[54]

The Department of Labor's *Interpretive Bulletin,* also recognizes the issue of safety. It states that:

> age limitations . . . without reference to the individual's actual physical condition [would be considered a possible bona fide occupational qualification] when such conditions are clearly imposed for the safety and convenience of the public.[55]

---

[53] "Extra board duty" requires a driver to perform long distance driving subject to brief notice. The term refers to that part of the bus operations which are not part of the regularly scheduled operations. Drivers are assigned "extra board" work on a first-in, first-out basis so that as a driver completes an assignment, he is then placed at the bottom of the "extra board" list. The driver has little freedom or choice in the matter and must take whatever assignments come up. Since extra board drivers are on call twenty-four hours per day, seven days per week and must be prepared to go anywhere in the continental United States on short notice, the work is both demanding and physically exhausting.

[54] U.S. Department of Transportation, Bureau of Motor Carrier Safety, Title 49, Parts 390-396 of *The Code of Federal Regulations.*

[55] *ADEA, Interpretive Bulletin,* CFR, Title 29, Sec. 860.102(d), p. 4.

Because the Department of Labor is, in part, concerned about establishing the farthest limits of the ADEA's applicability, suit was brought against Greyhound to enjoin the company's practice of not hiring persons in the protected ages of 40 to 65. The Department's main position in the case was that Greyhound could not maintain the job of intercity bus driver as a BFOQ because the age limit would eliminate all persons in the protected age group even though there would be some individuals who could qualify physically for the job. The Department of Labor was, therefore, advocating that Greyhound establish hiring practices on the basis of individual functional age rather than its current practice of excluding persons over 35 on the basis of their chronological age.

Before the court could determine which mode of hiring was proper for Greyhound, the question of what constituted a BFOQ had to be answered. In order to achieve its objective, Greyhound was required to carry its burden of proof that the qualification of age was, under the circumstances, a BFOQ. This was a complicated problem because proof of the BFOQ essentially required evidence concerning many aspects of the business. The appeals court in *Greyhound* found that the district court had erred. The district court had relied on *Weeks v. Southern Bell Telephone,* which held that:

> In order to rely on the bona fide occupational qualification exception, an employer has the burden of proving that he had reasonable cause to believe, that is, a factual basis for believing that all or substantially all (applicants) would be unable to perform safely and efficiently the duties of the job involved.[56]

For the bus driving job that Greyhound held to be a BFOQ, however, the appeals court noted that, in addition to the welfare of the applicant, the company's concern by definition had to extend to the well-being and safety of bus passengers and other highway motorists. Therefore, a different burden of proof test was required for Greyhound because of the added dimension of safety. In order to arrive correctly at a satisfactory burden of proof, Greyhound's business had to be defined in terms of necessity; that is, what ingredient above all others, over which all applicants had a direct influence, was the sustaining factor in the company's success? The answer is that "the essence of Greyhound's business is the safe transportation of its passengers."

---

[56] *Weeks v. Southern Bell Telephone and Telegraph Company, supra,* note 49.

The next step was to answer these questions. Does the job require a high degree of skill? What are the consequences of hiring an unqualified applicant? Are the preemployment standards commensurate with the degree of risk the company faces when hiring an applicant? Precedent involving airline pilots [57] indicated that the higher degree of skill required and the greater the economic and human risk involved, the lighter the burden of proof was for the employer in demonstrating that his employment criteria were job-related.

Therefore, because the essence of Greyhound's business was deeply enmeshed with safety, and because the risk to Greyhound and to the public in having qualified applicants employed for that job was great, the company must demonstrate only that it had a "rational basis in fact to believe that elimination of its hiring age would increase the likelihood of risk or harm to its passengers."

Greyhound did present such evidence. Furthermore, the company pointed out that the only way to prove with a very high degree of certainty that the hiring of persons over the age of forty was, in fact, safe would be to experiment with the lives of the public. In addition, the medical testimony and evidence clearly indicated that there is no way to detect functional age with certainty. Medical science does not have the capability adequately to screen out degenerative disabilities occasioned by age in the 40-65 age bracket and to assure the fitness of people on a regular basis. Accordingly, the court found that Greyhound had successfully proved the need for age as a BFOQ.

## The Tamiami Trail Tours Case [58]

The only other case which centered on a company's failure to hire members of the protected age class because of a BFOQ involved a bus company similar to Greyhound which also has a hiring age limit for its bus drivers. Although the hiring age limit at Tamiami was age 40 (at Greyhound it is age 35), the issue of the BFOQ exception was identical. The Department of Labor, attempting to overcome the *Greyhound* decision, challenged the company's BFOQ on the grounds that it was not made on a

---

[57] *Spurlock v. United Air Lines, Inc., supra,* note 51.

[58] *Usery v. Tamiami Trail Tours, Inc.,* 531 F.2d 224 (5th Cir. 1976).

factual basis and that functional rather than chronological age should be used as a basis for determining the physical job requirements of applicants.

The appeals court in this case used a two-step approach in determining whether the company successfully met the requirements of its burden of proof. Although the *Greyhound* decision required only that the essence of the company's business would be endangered by hiring drivers over 40, the *Tamiami* case incorporated an additional standard. This required the company to prove that all, or substantially all, members of the affected class would be unable to perform safely and efficiently the duties of the job involved. This is a difficult task and Tamiami had no way actually of proving this except by heuristic methodology. The court, realizing the uncertainty and risks involved, allowed this test to be met by having the employer "establish that some members of the discriminated against class possess a trait precluding safe and efficient job performance that cannot be ascertained by means other than knowledge of the applicants' membership in the class." Thus, the issue of functional verses chronological age is of equal importance to safety in this decision, whereas in *Greyhound*, safety was the overriding concern. The court in the *Tamiami* case stated that the employer must not only prove that the essence of the business is endangered by dropping the BFOQ, but in addition, that there is no practical way for the company rationally to determine the qualified from the unqualified among the affected class other than by a blanket policy, which is the BFOQ.

## Hiring and the BFOQ—A Summary

It is clear from the limited case law available that a BFOQ in hiring must meet a difficult burden of proof. At the very least, the BFOQ must be reasonably necessary to the essence of the employer's business, and the essence of the business defined must relate directly to the likelihood of harm to the applicant, to the applicant's fellow workers, to the public, or to a combination of all three. In addition, the employer will be required to show that he had a factual basis for his BFOQ, or he must demonstrate in a very convincing fashion that there is no possible or practical way to deal with persons in the affected class on an individual basis.

## MANDATORY RETIREMENT BEFORE AGE 65— NON-BFOQ ISSUES

The Age Discrimination in Employment Act authorizes employees to be retired pursuant to the terms of a bona fide employee retirement or pension plan as long as it is not a subterfuge to evade the purposes of the Act. Therefore, when the issue of a BFOQ is not involved, the involuntary retirement of employees before age 65 must not be for the purposes of evading the ADEA, that is, discriminating against those employees in the protected ages of 40-65.

To the layman, it would appear that mandatory retirement under a bona fide pension plan at various ages would be permissible. When considering the Act, Congress rejected attempts led by the AFL-CIO to outlaw mandatory retirement at any age, and in the words of the Third Circuit, "Congress continued to regard retirement plans favorable and chose, therefore, to legislate only with respect to discharge." [59]

The *Interpretative Bulletin* issued by the Department of Labor soon after the enactment of the statute clearly supports this view. It stated in part:

> Thus the Act authorizes involuntary retirement *irrespective of age*, provided that such retirement is pursuant to the terms of a retirement or pension plan meeting the requirements of section 4(f)(2). The fact that an employer may decide to permit certain employees to continue working beyond the age stipulated in the formal retirement program does not, in and of itself, render an otherwise bona fide plan invalid insofar as the exception provided in section 4(f)(2) is concerned. [60]

In its report on the ADEA for 1975, however, the Department of Labor drastically altered its views, stating:

> [R]etirements [before 65] are unlawful unless the mandatory retirement provision: (1) is contained in a bona fide pension or retirement plan, (2) is required by the terms of the plan and is not optional, and (3) is essential to the plan's economic survival or to some other legitimate purpose—i.e., is not in the plan for

---

[59] *Zinger v. Blanchette et al.,* —— F.2d ——, (3rd Cir. 1977). The opinion in this case contains an excellent review of the ADEA's legislative history with regard to retirement.

[60] *Idem* citing *ADEA, Interpretive Bulletin,* CFR Title 29 Sec. 860.110. (Emphasis supplied.)

the sole purpose of moving out older workers, which purpose has now been made unlawful by the ADEA.[61]

It is the latter view which the Department of Labor has been urging in court, and which was litigated in three appellate cases.

## *The Taft Broadcasting Case* [62]

The company's profit sharing retirement plan was installed in 1963 and employees were then solicited to participate. A formal copy of the plan was never communicated to the employees although a summary of the plan was posted at the place of work. The plaintiff was not told about the normal retirement age of 60 under the plan until two years before the date of his scheduled retirement.

The Department of Labor challenged the mandatory retirement by holding that the "Profit Sharing Retirement Plan" did not qualify as a bona fide employee benefit plan as defined by Section 4(f)(2) and that even if it could qualify, the compulsory retirement feature was not communicated to the participants and, therefore, was not bona fide; and that the company discriminated against the plaintiff/retiree by not rehiring him after his forced retirement.

The appeals court found that the "Profit Sharing Retirement Plan" was bona fide and qualified for the Section 4(f)(2) exception for several reasons. First, it was not a subterfuge to evade the purposes of the Act because it was "effectuated far in advance of the ADEA and because it was a benefit plan within the meaning of the Statute." The plan paid benefits, did not discriminate against employees in terms of benefits paid because of age, and the plan fit into the clear meaning of the Act. The court believed that in this instance, the "use of legislative history to override the unambiguous language of the statute" would be wrong. The court also said the same would apply to the use of the "Congressional purpose" argument. Finally, as to the contention that the retired employee should be rehired, the court stated:

> The Secretary [of Labor]'s construction would render meaningless the statutory language allowing employers to 'observe the

---

[61] *Idem* citing Department of Labor's January 1975 report pertaining to activities in connection with the *Age Discrimination in Employment Act of 1967* (1975), p. 17.

[62] *Brennan v. Taft Broadcasting Company*, 500 F.2d 212 (5th Cir. 1974).

terms of bona fide employee benefit plans such as retirement . . .
plans.' If retired employees must be rehired immediately, the
right to insist on compliance with the plan is an illusion. Congress could not have possibly intended or directed, such a contradictory, irreconcilable result.

## *The United Airlines Case* [63]

The opinion in the *Taft Broadcasting* case has been disputed
by at least one district court case [64] and one circuit court case,
*United Airlines.* In the former, the Department of Labor's
revised interpretation was given great weight and the court
also found the benefits inadequate—judgment based on nothing
that would appear subject to judicial determination.

The *United Airlines* case is not finalized but it does appear
that the Fourth Circuit disagrees with *Taft Broadcasting.* Here
an employee was classified in the "technical-specialist aircraft
systems" job classification at United, and he began his participation in the pension plan in 1964. As the plan was operating before the passage of the ADEA and as the employee elected
to participate in the plan (which was bona fide within the meaning of the Act), United requested a summary judgment of the
charges based upon the precedent set in the *Taft* decision.

The court, however, felt that the language of the statute was
not entirely unambiguous and that legislative history and intent
were crucial to define the true meaning of the Act, which is the
prevention of age discrimination for all individuals in the protected class. Therefore, if a company involuntarily retires an
employee at age 60 simply because the employee is 60 years old,
it must constitute a prima facie case for age discrimination.

> Stated otherwise, there must be some reason other than age for
> a plan, or a provision of a plan, which discriminates between em-
> ployees of different ages. At this state of the proceeding, United
> has offered no nonarbitrary justification for the age 60 retirement
> provision of its plan.

When contacted about the case, a spokeswoman for United's
employee benefits office stated that the reason for the plaintiff's
retirement at age 60 was his grouping in the pilot's pension plan
program. This was done because all employees who are pilot

---

[63] *McMann v. United Airlines,* 542 F.2d 217 (4th Cir. 1976), *cert. granted,*
U.S. Supreme Court, February 21, 1977.

[64] *Dunlop v. Hawaiian Telephone Company,* 415 F. Supp. 330 (D.C. Hawaii,
1976).

qualified—and the company stated that the plaintiff was pilot qualified—are placed in the pilot's pension plan. Pilots must retire at age 60 because of the Federal Aviation Administration's regulations and these regulations have been uniformly upheld by the courts.[65] What appears to have happened is that the Fourth Circuit simply could not agree with the *Taft* ruling, and therefore, would require United to prove on retrial that the plaintiff's job is a BFOQ, as discussed below. Instead of a retrial, however, United appealed to the U.S. Supreme Court which granted certiorari on February 21, 1977. Thus, the issue will probably be definitively determined.

## *The Zinger Case* [66]

A ruling strongly supporting mandatory retirement was issued by the Third Circuit in January 1977. The plaintiff, Zinger, was retired one year before age 65 pursuant to a bona fide pension plan of the Penn Central railroad. The court affirmed the legality of such retirement after reviewing the legislative history of the Act and Congressional intent as summarized above, and examining the conflicting Department of Labor regulations. It accepted the original rules with this caustic comment about their later revision:

> In adopting this stance, the Secretary ignored the obvious and important distinction implicit in his previous bulletin between discharge without pay and retirement on a pension. Moreover, the Secretary's latter position is not only contrary to that taken by his predecessor contemporaneously with the consideration and passage of the Act, but also to the views of Congressional Committees which declined that proposal when it was forthrightly presented to them.
>
> Thus, rather than proposing an amendment to Congress, as Congress had instructed, the Secretary seeks to change the Act by court decision or administrative fiat.

## *The Murgia Case*

In June 1976, the U.S. Supreme Court upheld the right of the Commonwealth of Massachusetts to retire state policemen at age

---

[65] See, for example, *Airline Pilots Association, International v. Quesada*, 286 F.2d 319, (2d Cir. 1961); and *O'Donnell v. Shaffer*, 491 F.2d 59 (D.C. Cir. 1974).

[66] See *supra*, note 59.

fifty.[67] The case was not brought under the ADEA, but on the constitutional ground of a right to state employment. The extent to which the Supreme Court will follow this case in mandatory retirement matters relating to ADEA must await its ruling in the *United Airlines* case. The *Murgia* case was cited by the Third Circuit in the *Zinger* case, particularly noting the Supreme Court's comment therein that "the drawing of lines that create distinctions is peculiarly a legislative task and an unavoidable one." This augurs well for the belief that the Third Circuit's interpretation in *Zinger* will prevail.

## The BFOQ and Mandatory Retirement Before Age 65

If the Department of Labor's current interpretation of the right to retire employees prior to age 65 prevails (which does not appear likely), or if the Act is amended, the bona fide occupational qualification exception could be the only legal rationale to permit such retirement. The leading case on this subject is *McDonnell Douglas,*[68] which also illustrates the right to use age as a criterion for job performance in highly critical circumstances.

McDonnell Douglas removed an employee at age 50 from the job of test pilot, but simultaneously offered him other employment in the company. The plaintiff, however, refused to accept a number of jobs with pay comparable to the test pilot job, insisting instead that he be either kept on as a test pilot or made an executive vice-president of the company. The company went ahead and assigned the plaintiff to a job supervising an aspect of the testing program, but he did not perform well largely because of his discontent, and was terminated.

The issue in the case can therefore be seen as twofold: is the age requirement for test pilots for military fighter aircraft at McDonnell Douglas a BFOQ such that upon attaining age 50 an individual may no longer qualify on the basis of age alone? Once this question was answered, then the question of the plaintiff's termination from the company for poor performance in his newly assigned job could be considered.

Because there is no uniform burden of proof test to be applied other than those set forth in the *Greyhound* [69] and *Tamiami* [70]

---

[67] *Massachusetts Board of Retirement et al. v. Murgia,* 96 S. Ct. 2562 (1976).

[68] *Houghton v. McDonnell Douglas Corporation,* 413 F. Supp. 1230 (E.D. Mo. 1976); *reversed and remanded,* U.S. Court of Appeals, Eighth Circuit, April 1977.

[69] *Supra,* note 52.

[70] *Supra,* note 58.

cases, which conflict to some degree, the district court in this case felt compelled to consider the unique facts presented in the evidence before choosing which test to use. After finding that "functional age, as distinguished from chronological age, cannot be determined with sufficient reliability to meet the special safety obligations which are imposed upon . . . McDonnell Douglas," the court concluded that there is no alternative to establishing an arbitrary age limit.

The burden of proof test applied by the court was the one enunciated in the *Tamiami* case. This involved a two step process. First, the defendant must overcome the "threshold" burden of proof, the *Diaz* [71] test in which the BFOQ must be analyzed in terms of business necessity. Business necessity here refers to the very essence of the business; that is, is the BFOQ necessary to preserve the essence of the business rather than simply making the BFOQ something convenient for business operations. After this "threshold" burden of proof has been overcome, the defendant must then satisfy the second level burden of proof, the *Weeks* [72] test, in which the company must successfully demonstrate that all, or substantially all, of the affected class cannot perform the job or else demonstrate that the task of assembling such data is either impossible or impracticable. The court found that Mc-Donnell Douglas passed this test as well. It concluded, in part that:

> [i]t does not require a quantum leap in logic to infer that a test pilot operating an aircraft within the far reaches of the flight design envelope is under far more strain than a bus driver proceeding from point to point, or an airline pilot on a normally scheduled and established flight.

As if this were not enough, the court reminded the Department of Labor that in its own age discrimination regulations,[73] the BFOQ exception was illustrated by the example of mandatory retirement at age 60 of "airline pilots within the jurisdiction of the Federal Aviation Agency."

After the question of the BFOQ was resolved, the court arrived at its conclusion of the case. "The evidence clearly shows that the termination of plaintiff's employment was not due to his age

---

[71] *Supra,* note 50.

[72] *Supra,* note 49.

[73] *ADEA, Interpretive Bulletin,* CFR Title 29, Section 860.102(d).

but was due to his negative attitude upon removal from flying status."

On appeal, the decision was reversed. The appeals court felt that the district court had not considered all the evidence, and ordered the plaintiff installed as a test pilot. McDonnell Douglas is appealing the extraordinary decision.

### *Mandatory Retirement Before Age 65—Final Comment*

The legality of mandatory retirement prior to age 65 is now before the Supreme Court. Although the decisions are more favorable than not, there is also considerable support to end mandatory retirement of any kind by amending the ADEA. Until the matter is definitively settled, it would appear that employers must handle this issue with the utmost of care, especially if economic or reorganizational necessities require that a large number of employees in the protected age group will be affected.

## CONCURRENT STATE JURISDICTION

A problem, particularly for multistate employers, is the applicability of the various state laws in relation to the ADEA. As discussed in the previous chapter, a large number of jurisdictions have age discrimination laws which differ significantly in coverage from the federal statute.[74] These laws have concurrent jurisdiction with the ADEA, and have precedence where the state provision is more stringent. This becomes especially important where the state law does not provide for a 65 year age cutoff of protection, or includes provisions not found in the ADEA.

### *The Providence Washington Insurance Case*

The most important case on this subject to date, and the only federal level case specifically directed at this issue is *Simpson v. Alaska State Commission for Human Rights.*[75] The case involved a former employee of the Providence Washington Insurance Group who had been discharged after he reached the normal

---

[74] The various state laws and their major provisions are found in Appendix B.

[75] 423 F. Supp. 552 (D.C. Alaska 1976).

retirement age of 65. Because Alaska is one of seven states with no upper age limit, Simpson filed the required notices and brought suit in state court alleging discrimination because of age. The qualifications for Simpson's job could not be easily defended by the company as a BFOQ. Therefore, the company elected to challenge the conflicting requirements of the state and federal statutes. The company's main argument was that the state law had an implied upper age limit of 65 in order to make it consistent with public policy and, alternatively, that the federal government had preempted the field of age discrimination with the enactment of the ADEA. Finally, the company contended that the lack of an upper age limit in the state law was unenforceably vague and overbroad.

The court refused to accept any of these arguments, finding that the ADEA would be preempted only when compliance with both federal and state regulations was "physically impossible," and that public policy which generally accepts age 65 as the normal retirement age should not be controlling.

> While it is true that many retirement programs require retirement at 65, such an age is hardly recognized as a universal constant. Without belaboring the innumerable exceptions to this alleged universally accepted age of retirement, the court notes that the retirement age for civil service employees is 70.

The conflict with the federal statute was disposed of in a similar fashion. The court stated that the burden of accepting this conflict was "the price that an interstate business pays for operating in our system of government."

The practical problem of a no upper age limit of protection has been encountered in other states. In New Mexico, for example, a man applied by telephone for a job and after some discussion, revealed his age as 70. The employment interviewer thoughtlessly replied that "the company would never employ a person that old." Under New Mexico's law, this was a violation for which the company paid a penalty.[76] Such an experience could occur in any of the seven states with similar provisions.

## COMPANY EXPERIENCES

During 1976, the author interviewed approximately fifty companies, all large "Fortune 500" concerns, in order to gain in-

---

[76] Interview with company personnel department, New York City, March 1975.

formation about experiences with ADEA problems. A number of companies surveyed had interesting age discrimination charges brought against them. Although this is by no means a representative sample, it is instructive in that the cases disclose, in a very real sense, how age discrimination charges materialize and how an employer will often respond to those charges.

1. One manufacturer had four cases filed against it. In one case, a former vice-president of the company applied for a supervisory job after his retirement. A company employment manager wrote the retired officer that the firm desired a younger man to fill the position. Because of this indiscretion, the company was held liable for discriminating because of age and was forced to grant backpay, even though the company was under no statutory obligation to employ the man.

In the second case, a welder who had recently retired from an area steel company was not hired. He contacted the Wage and Hour Division claiming discrimination because of his age. When the company offered to employ him and grant thirty days backpay, the retired welder refused the job. The company has reason to believe that he was trying to "set them up" because his demands included an earlier starting date with retroactive seniority or approximately twice as much as the company offered.

The third case involved an older salesman who became an extremely poor performer. Because he was close to retirement, the company gave him a less demanding work assignment rather than retire him early with a somewhat lower pay rating. In addition, he was given an extension at his request so that his retirement benefits would meet the next higher benefits level. When he commenced his retirement, he filed an age discrimination charge with the Department of Labor. The case was dismissed as without merit.

The fourth case involved an employee who, during layoffs in 1974, was given the option of early retirement or accepting another job within the company, although the firm could not tell him at that time where the job would be. The employee chose early retirement instead of the transfer. Six months later, the company learned that he has filed age discrimination charges to obtain full retirement benefits. The charges were dismissed by the Department of Labor.

2. Another company has experienced "several" age discrimination cases. The charges all stemmed from a Wage and Hour Division investigation regarding an employee who claimed he

was not properly rated in the company's performance pay plan and would, therefore, receive a lower merit increase than he believed he deserved. The Wage and Hour investigator examined all promotional and performance ratings for all employees at that location as well as conducting interviews with a substantial number of employees. The company was concerned that if the case were lost at this location, it would result in a company-wide investigation for similar "deficiencies."

3. An age case at this particular firm involved a confusing combination of the Wage and Hour Division, the Office of Federal Contract Compliance Programs (OFCCP), both U.S. Department of Labor agencies, and the Pennsylvania State Department of Labor. It began with a compliance review pursuant to Executive Order No. 11246 by the OFCCP regarding an apprenticeship program at one of the company's operating locations. The OFCCP judged the program inadequate in its utilization of minorities. Accordingly, the company sought to hold several places in the program for minorities. It notified the union that this action would be taken and that the current seniority and job-bidding systems in the collective-bargaining agreement would be bypassed until the required "utilization" had been reached.

No sooner had this been accomplished then the company was hit with an age discrimination charge because of the thirty-nine year age limit for entry into the program. Although this limit had been determined pursuant to the collective bargaining agreement with the union, it was nonetheless the object of legal action instituted by four unionized employees, one of whom was a local official in that union. It appeared that this was the union's way of harassing the company for bypassing the membership in favor of minority ascension into the apprenticeship program.

In addition, the company had promised to rewrite the apprenticeship program so that it would satisfy both Wage and Hour and OFCCP objections. The program was rewritten, and although state approval was forthcoming, neither Wage and Hour nor OFCCP have approved the program or communicated their objections to the company at the time of the interview. The company has seriously considered the elimination of its in-house apprenticeship training altogether to avoid future harassment and possible litigation. This would, of course, result in fewer opportunities for minorities and women because the supply of qualified minority crafts workers is severely limited at that location.

4. There have been a number of minor age discrimination cases against this company most of which resulted from closing an entire division, but there has also been a major investigation for failure to hire by the state of California. The state investigator began his inquiry by looking for a pattern and practice of age discrimination in hiring and probably any other type of age discrimination that could be discerned. He left only to return several weeks later to demand that the company develop and initiate a complete affirmative action program for employing people in the 40 to 65 age group. The state had "monitored" applicant flow and claimed a disparate effect upon this group in hiring. This was despite the fact that employment applications did not ask for age and that there was a good age mix in the plant itself. Nothing has come of this investigation as yet.

The other age discrimination cases have all been attributable to reductions in force. The company took all individuals affected and performance-ranked their records. The firm believes it was very careful during this period, and did not include age as one of the factors to be considered. Because the company was trying to do the same amount of work with fewer people, it was imperative that the best people be kept. It believes that age discrimination charges were filed by individuals looking for backpay.

One case involved a statistical response to a charge of age discrimination by an employee who was dismissed for performance reasons. Both the New York State Human Relations Division and the Wage and Hour Division of the Department of Labor were involved in the investigation. After three years of investigation, the case was dropped in favor of the company.

The other two cases were handled by Wage and Hour exclusively and involved the failure to employ. The individuals involved were seeking professional positions at the company's headquarters and were turned down in favor of more qualified applicants. The company's defense rested on basic statistics—there was no discernible pattern or practice of age discrimination in hiring. The cases were still pending at the time of the interview.

## CONCLUDING REMARKS

The Age Discrimination in Employment Act has granted significant protection to the 40-65 age group in industry. Moreover, the U.S. Department of Labor, through litigation, is strenuously endeavoring to stretch that protection to undetermined limits. Mandatory retirement, early retirement, and policies which question the ability of this age group to perform are all under attack and are on the defensive as a result.

Interestingly, an examination of the cases indicates that middle management, professional and supervisory employees are the principal beneficiaries of ADEA. Hourly workers are protected by seniority in union contracts which require layoffs of junior workers; moreover, hourly workers are less mobile than salaried ones. Thus, although the Act seems to have been based on problems of hourly workers, it has become largely a device to challenge management decision making concerning salaried workers.

It seems undeniable that discrimination against older workers —partly unintentional, partly as a matter of policy—was widespread prior to passage of the ADEA. Undoubtedly, such discrimination has been considerably lessened by the Act. One can applaud this result as a benefit.

On the other hand, little concern has been expressed about the costs involved. To what extent, for example, will the ADEA make it more difficult for younger persons to be employed and to progress? Will ADEA deny industry and government sufficient fresh views of younger persons in key jobs so that innovation, progress and employment suffer? How much litigation costs are the results of the expansive interpretation of ADEA pushed by the Department of Labor and often rebuffed by the courts?

We have no answer to these questions, but they certainly should be asked. Industry has great resiliency to assume costs, but such capacity is not unlimited. For every benefit, there is a cost, and social benefits are no exception. The benefits of ADEA are undoubtedly great. The costs have not been defined, but they, too, can be large.

# PART THREE

*Discrimination Against the Handicapped*

CHAPTER IV

# The Rehabilitation Act of 1973

The Rehabilitation Act of 1973 [1] has its origins in the state-federal programs of vocational rehabilitation. These were instituted because of a growing awareness of our industrial society's need for institutionalizing what was formerly considered to be a family problem. The original Vocational Rehabilitation Act [2] provided programs of rehabilitation services for handicapped people which included medical care and job training. In addition, another law, the Wagner-Peyser Act of 1933, required every local office of the state employment service system to allocate resources for the handicapped in the form of training and job search assistance. The programs of this law, as amended, remain in effect. [3]

Other programs for the handicapped population are administered by the Social Security Administration, the Social Services Administration, the Veterans Administration, and the system of sheltered workshops. The economic viability of the last is

---

[1] *Rehabilitation Act of 1973*, 87 Stat. 355, H.R. 8070, 93rd USC, September 26, 1973. The key sections of the Act are found in Appendix C.

[2] *Vocational Rehabilitation Act*, 68 Stat. 652, 29 USC, pp. 31-42.

[3] The programs initiated under this act are still operative, and they seek to provide the handicapped with:

(a) equal opportunity for employment and equal pay in competition with other applicants;

(b) employment at the highest skill permitted by their physical abilities and other occupational qualifications;

(c) satisfactory adjustment to their chosen occupations and work situations; and

(d) employment that will not endanger others or aggravate their own disabilities.

(From the U.S. Department of Labor Program Highlights, Consumer Information Leaflet No. USDL-7 (ETA-3), "Program for the Handicapped," November 1975.)

in part maintained through an amendment to the Fair Labor Standards Act.[4]

As comprehensive and as far-reaching as many of these programs have been, there remained no mechanism, other than private initiative, to encourage the employment of handicapped persons within the mainstream of American enterprise. The passage of the Rehabilitation Act of 1973 altered the traditional approach toward employing the handicapped. Charity was discarded in favor of affirmative action. The Act required employers affirmatively to hire the handicapped. Enforcement procedures of the Act linked compliance to the federal government's procurement process.

The ramifications of this law may be far-reaching, depending upon the results of litigation which is still in the formative stage. As in other areas of civil rights law, the enforcement agency must proceed cautiously until the case law develops to a point where reasonable certainty exists concerning the duties and responsibilities of employers and the rights of the protected groups. The Rehabilitation Act has yet to reach this stage of development, thereby generating far more questions to be answered. An analysis of these questions follows, and through this process, it is hoped that some of the sought after answers will begin to emerge. The potential for vast corporate liability will also clearly emerge from this discussion.

## HOW MANY HANDICAPPED?

The handicapped population of the United States will vary in size depending upon the definition of handicapped that is being used. There has been little attempt until recent years actually to discover what the real numbers are. The Bureau of the Census first sampled for the number of adult handicapped persons in the country during the 1970 census. For a definition of a handicap, the census relied upon the individuals sampled to decide if they were in fact handicapped subject to parameters such as these:

> Does this person have a health, mental or physical condition which limits the kind or amount of work he can do at a job? Does his health, mental or physical condition keep him from holding

---

[4] The Fair Labor Standards Act was amended in 1966 to allow sheltered workshops to certify the employment of handicapped individuals at less than, but at least 50 percent of, the prevailing minimum wage.

any job at all? If yes to either, how long has he been limited in his ability to work?

Did this person work at any time last week? How many hours did he work last week (at all jobs)? Where did he work last week?

The results of this survey can be seen in Tables IV-1 and IV-2. Table IV-1 shows the percent of the adult population by schooling, income, poverty status, and labor force status as compared with the handicapped population. It can be seen that in all factors which are important ingredients to successful employment, the handicapped lag behind the general adult population. This is especially pronounced as the qualitative increases occur, for example, level of education.

In Table IV-2, the same factors are listed for the handicapped population by age and sex. It is readily apparent again, that the handicapped population surveyed has less education, less income, and greater poverty than the general population. It also has much greater unemployment *if* those not in the labor force are counted among the unemployed. If only those who are counted as unemployed, as defined by the Department of Labor, are included in the analysis, then in 1969, the unemployment rates for the handicapped were about the same as the unemployment rates for the nation's labor force.

The reason for speculating on the appropriateness of the unemployment rates for the handicapped population is that a far greater proportion of the handicapped population is not considered in the labor force than is the case with the general population. There are a number of reasons for using this approach to measure the employment problems of the handicapped. For example, in 1974, handicapped persons not in the labor force but among those "wanting a job now" constituted 15 percent of the handicapped population. On the other hand, the handicapped constituted only 8 percent of the general population not in the labor force listed as "not wanting a job now." [5]

Table IV-3 gives the percent of the disabled population, as defined by the Bureau of the Census, by age compared to the total adult population. This shows that the disabled population is considerably older than the general adult population. This has implications for employers because it points to the fact that much of the handicapped population are also affected by the same problems which have traditionally been associated with

---

[5] U.S. Department of Labor, Bureau of Labor Statistics, *Employment and Earnings*, Vol. 22, No. 7 (January 1976), p. 156.

## TABLE IV-1

### CHARACTERISTICS OF THE NONINSTITUTIONAL POPULATION: 1970

| | Percent of Total Population 14 to 64* | | | Percent of Population 16 to 64 Years Old With Work Disability of Six Months or More | | |
|---|---|---|---|---|---|---|
| Total | Total 129,296,315 | Male 63,044,274 | Female 66,252,041 | Total 11,264,830 | Male 5,962,160 | Female 5,302,670 |
| **YEARS OF SCHOOL COMPLETED** | | | | | | |
| Elementary:   Less than 8 years | 11 | 12 | 10 | 22 | 23 | 22 |
|   8 years | 11 | 11 | 10 | 14 | 14 | 14 |
| High school:   1 to 3 years | 25 | 24 | 25 | 24 | 22 | 26 |
|   4 years | 32 | 28 | 35 | 25 | 24 | 26 |
| College:   1 to 3 years | 12 | 13 | 12 | 9 | 11 | 8 |
|   4 years or more | 9 | 11 | 7 | 5 | 7 | 4 |
| **INCOME IN 1969** | | | | | | |
| None | 26 | 11 | 40 | 23 | 8 | 40 |
| $1 to $999 | 12 | 9 | 15 | 15 | 11 | 20 |
| $1,000 to $1,999 | 8 | 7 | 9 | 14 | 13 | 15 |
| $2,000 to $2,999 | 6 | 5 | 7 | 8 | 9 | 8 |
| $3,000 to $4,999 | 12 | 10 | 14 | 12 | 15 | 10 |
| $5,000 to $6,999 | 11 | 13 | 9 | 9 | 14 | 4 |
| $7,000 or more | 25 | 45 | 7 | 18 | 31 | 3 |
| **POVERTY STATUS** | | | | | | |
| Family or unrelated individual income | (178,926,999) | (157,140,210) | (21,786,789) | | | |
|   Under .75 of poverty level | 8 | 5 | 29 | 15 | 13 | 17 |
|   Under 1.00 of poverty level | 12 | 9 | 38 | 21 | 19 | 24 |
|   Under 1.25 of poverty level | 17 | 13 | 46 | 27 | 25 | 30 |
| **LABOR FORCE STATUS (EMPLOYABLE)** | | | | | | |
| Employed or in Armed Forces | 59 | 76 | 42 | 42 | 58 | 24 |
| Unemployed | 3 | 3 | 2 | 2 | 3 | 2 |
| Not in labor force | 38 | 21 | 55 | 15 | 8 | 23 |

*Data for the age groups 16-64 was not available for this study.

Source:   President's Committee on Employment of the Handicapped, *One in Eleven; A Survey Based on 1970 U.S. Census Data* (Washington, D.C.: U.S. Government Printing Office, 1975), p. 8.

## TABLE IV-2

## Characteristics of the Noninstitutional Population 16 to 64 Years Old With Work Disability of Six Months or More: 1970

| UNITED STATES SUMMARY | Males Total | Percent Distribution of Males by Age | | | | | Females Total | Percent Distribution of Females by Age | | | | |
|---|---|---|---|---|---|---|---|---|---|---|---|---|
| | | 16 to 24 years | 25 to 34 years | 35 to 44 years | 45 to 54 years | 55 to 64 years | | 16 to 24 years | 25 to 34 years | 35 to 44 years | 45 to 54 years | 55 to 64 years |
| Total | 5,962,160 | 15 | 12 | 15 | 25 | 33 | 5,302,670 | 9 | 10 | 16 | 27 | 37 |
| **YEARS OF SCHOOL COMPLETED** | | | | | | | | | | | | |
| Elementary: Less than 8 years | 1,362,963 | 6 | 8 | 14 | 26 | 46 | 1,176,865 | 5 | 7 | 13 | 26 | 48 |
| 8 years | 817,622 | 6 | 7 | 13 | 27 | 48 | 768,151 | 4 | 6 | 12 | 27 | 51 |
| High school: 1 to 3 years | 1,338,087 | 20 | 10 | 16 | 25 | 29 | 1,364,457 | 13 | 11 | 18 | 27 | 32 |
| 4 years | 1,412,436 | 19 | 16 | 17 | 26 | 22 | 1,380,508 | 11 | 14 | 19 | 29 | 27 |
| College: 1 to 3 years | 631,952 | 29 | 15 | 14 | 21 | 20 | 408,710 | 15 | 13 | 16 | 25 | 31 |
| 4 years or more | 399,100 | 11 | 20 | 20 | 25 | 24 | 203,979 | 6 | 17 | 18 | 25 | 34 |
| **INCOME IN 1969** | | | | | | | | | | | | |
| None | 476,999 | 35 | 11 | 12 | 17 | 25 | 2,140,736 | 9 | 10 | 17 | 30 | 35 |
| $1 to $999 | 632,556 | 32 | 9 | 11 | 17 | 30 | 1,040,445 | 13 | 10 | 13 | 23 | 42 |
| $1,000 to $1,999 | 774,970 | 18 | 7 | 10 | 20 | 44 | 783,663 | 8 | 8 | 14 | 25 | 46 |
| $2,000 to $2,999 | 539,535 | 18 | 8 | 11 | 23 | 40 | 414,657 | 9 | 11 | 18 | 27 | 35 |
| $3,000 to $4,999 | 896,288 | 15 | 12 | 14 | 24 | 36 | 510,515 | 9 | 14 | 20 | 27 | 30 |
| $5,000 to $6,999 | 821,735 | 11 | 15 | 17 | 26 | 31 | 231,469 | 8 | 14 | 19 | 30 | 30 |
| $7,000 to $9,999 ($7,000 or more for females) | 940,259 | 6 | 16 | 20 | 31 | 28 | 181,185 | 4 | 12 | 18 | 31 | 35 |
| $10,000 to $14,999 (males only) | 586,382 | 2 | 14 | 23 | 35 | 26 | | | | | | |
| $15,000 or more (males only) | 293,436 | 1 | 8 | 21 | 38 | 32 | | | | | | |
| **POVERTY STATUS** | | | | | | | | | | | | |
| Family or unrelated individual income | | | | | | | | | | | | |
| Under .75 of poverty level | 788,540 | 12 | 10 | 15 | 23 | 40 | 919,920 | 8 | 10 | 15 | 24 | 42 |
| Under 1.00 of poverty level | 1,125,371 | 12 | 10 | 15 | 23 | 40 | 1,276,976 | 8 | 10 | 16 | 24 | 42 |
| Under 1.25 of poverty level | 1,467,396 | 12 | 10 | 16 | 23 | 38 | 1,608,479 | 8 | 11 | 16 | 24 | 42 |
| **LABOR FORCE STATUS (EMPLOYABLE)** | | | | | | | | | | | | |
| Employed or in Armed Forces | 3,426,887 | 15 | 14 | 18 | 28 | 26 | 1,254,302 | 12 | 13 | 20 | 29 | 26 |
| Unemployed | 165,328 | 27 | 14 | 16 | 22 | 21 | 92,133 | 21 | 16 | 20 | 26 | 18 |
| Not in labor force | 488,419 | 36 | 8 | 8 | 15 | 33 | 1,230,963 | 12 | 13 | 18 | 26 | 31 |

Source: President's Committee on Employment of the Handicapped, *One in Eleven; A Survey Based on 1970 U.S. Census Data* (Washington, D.C.: U.S. Government Printing Office, 1975), p. 17.

## TABLE IV-3

### AGE OF NONINSTITUTIONAL POPULATION 16 TO 64: 1970

| UNITED STATES SUMMARY | Percent of Total Population | | | Percent of Disabled Population With a Work Disability Of Six Months or More | | |
|---|---|---|---|---|---|---|
| | Total | Male | Female | Total | Male | Female |
| TOTAL .......... | 120,985,414 | 58,797,898 | 62,187,516 | 11,264,830 | 5,962,160 | 5,302,670 |
| **AGE** | | | | | | |
| 16-24 ................ | 26 | 26 | 25 | 12 | 15> | 9 |
| 25-34 ................ | 21 | 21 | 20' | 11 | 12> | 10 |
| 35-44 ................ | 19 | 19 | 19 | 16 | 15 | 16 |
| 45-54 ................ | 19 | 19 | 19 | 26 | 25 | <27 |
| 55-64 ................ | 15 | 15 | 16 | 35 | 33 | <37 |

Source: President's Committee on Employment of the Handicapped, *One In Eleven; A Survey Based on 1970 U.S. Census Data* (Washington, D.C.: U.S. Government Printing Office, 1975), p. 10.

the older working population in the country: lower educational attainment, obsolete job skills, stronger geographical attachments, etc. It also shows that a majority of our handicapped citizens are also covered by the Age Discrimination in Employment Act of 1967—more than 61 percent were so covered in 1970—and therefore have the added protection of this law.

The Department of Labor's Employment Standards Administration has also developed data on the handicapped population as defined by the Rehabilitation Act.[6] The number of persons in the adult U.S. population with a handicap is estimated by this agency at 7.2 million, and "this probably does not include people with cancer, heart disease, diabetes, and many other diseases which are barriers to employment."

## Defining the Meaning of "Handicapped"

It should now be clear that the data available on the number of handicapped people vary among agencies counting them. This variation is the result of a lack of a precise, or at least a consensus, definition of what constitutes a handicap. Nevertheless, the definition of who is a handicapped individual is crucial to the interpretation of the employment requirements of the

[6] U.S. Department of Labor Employment Standards Administration, *Fact Sheet: Who are the Handicapped?* Data from 1970 census. See discussions below in regard to the changed definition of handicapped. The figure of 7.2 million was developed prior to the definition change in 1974.

Rehabilitation Act. The Act originally defined a handicapped individual as "any individual who (A) has a physical or mental disability which for such individual constitutes or results in a substantial handicap to employment and (B) can reasonably be expected to benefit in terms of employability from vocational rehabilitation services pursuant [to] this Act." [7] Other definitions have, however, been used in prior government programs which were more direct in their attempt to pinpoint exactly who was, in fact, handicapped.

For example, the Bureau of Employment Security used this definition:

> A handicapped applicant is one who:
>
> (a) Has a physical or mental disability or disease, as listed in the Employment Security Manual (upper or lower extremities; trunk, spine, and abdominal defects; vision, hearing, and speech; cardiovascular; respiratory except asthma; neuromuscular; neuropsychiatric; retardation; skin, cosmetic, and allergy conditions; generalized or systematic diseases; gastrointestinal; and genitourinary).
>
> (b) Has a physical, mental, or emotional impairment or characteristic (other than listed above) which meets one or more of five criteria: 1) requires applicant to modify or change occupation; 2) makes it difficult to get employer acceptance for suitable work; 3) requires special consideration to prevent undertaking work likely to aggravate the disability, or jeopardizing health and safety of others; 4) restricts entry level opportunities; 5) employability is improvable through use of adjustment services of another agency.
>
> (c) Has a service-connected disability rated 10 percent or more by the Veterans Administration, or which resulted in retirement from the armed forces.[8]

Another example is found in a Social Security survey of disabled adults. Here, the handicapped were categorized by a ranking of disability related to their work limitation:

> (a) *Severely Disabled:* unable to work at all or unable to work regularly.
>
> (b) *Occupationally Disabled:* able to work regularly, but unable to do the same work as before onset of disability or unable to work full time.

---

[7] *Rehabilitation Act of 1973*, Section 7(6).

[8] U.S. Department of Labor, Bureau of Employment Security, *Employment Security Manual*, Sections 8225, 8227, 8228 (Revised May 17, 1965).

(c) *Secondary Work Limitations:* able to work regularly, full time, and at the same occupation, but with limitations in the amount or kind of work they can perform in their jobs.[9]

A most important work on this subject by the American Medical Association and one which was used by the Office of Federal Contract Compliance Programs in developing regulatory standards, carefully describes the differences between impairment and disability and defines why the differences exist:

(1) *Permanent Impairment*—This is a purely medical condition. Permanent impairment is an anatomic or functional abnormality or loss after maximal medical rehabilitation has been achieved, which abnormality or loss the physician considers stable or non-progressive at the time evaluation is made. It is always a basic consideration in the evaluation of permanent disability.

(2) *Permanent Disability*—This is not a purely medical condition. A patient is "permanently disabled" or "under a permanent disability" when his actual or presumed ability to engage in gainful activity is reduced or absent because of "impairment" which, in turn, may or may not be combined with other factors. A permanent condition is found to exist if no fundamental or marked change can be expected in the future.

(3) *Evaluation (Rating) of Permanent Impairment*—This is a function that physicians alone are competent to perform. Evaluation of permanent impairment defines the scope of medical responsibility and therefore represents the physician's role in the evaluation of permanent disability. Evaluation of permanent impairment is an appraisal of the nature and extent of the patient's illness or injury as it affects his personal efficiency in one or more of the activities of daily living. These activities are self-care, communication, normal living postures, ambulation, elevation, traveling, and nonspecialized hand activities.

(4) *Evaluation (Rating) of Permanent Disability*—In the last analysis, this is an administrative and not solely a medical responsibility and function. Evaluation of permanent disability is an appraisal of the patient's present and future ability to engage in gainful activity as it is affected by such diverse factors as age, sex, education, economic and social environment, in addition to the definite medical factor—permanent impairment. The first group of factors has proved extremely difficult to measure. For this reason, permanent impairment is in fact the sole or real criterion of permanent disability far more often than is readily acknowledged. However, in actual practice the final determination of permanent

---

[9] Lawrence D. Haber, "Identifying the Disabled: Concepts and Methods in the Measurement of Disability," *Social Security Bulletin*, Vol. 30, (December 1967), p. 17.

disability is an administrative decision as to the patient's entitlement.[10]

*Congress Changes the Definition*

The Department of Labor's original guidelines prescribed that a qualified handicapped individual must have benefited from the types of services offered pursuant to Titles I and II of the Act or their equivalent. Congress, however, did not agree with, or could not accept, these limitations to coverage and therefore in December 1974 passed Public Law 93-516 which amended the Rehabilitation Act's definition of handicap to read:

> . . . any person who (1) has a physical or mental impairment which substantially limits one or more of such person's major life activities; (2) has a record of such impairment; or (3) is regarded as having such an impairment.

It is therefore obvious that Congress has removed the evaluation rating of permanent disability as far as possible from the medical definition and placed it within the scope of administrative regulation. The scope of this regulation, moreover, is such that the political imperatives of determining who is qualified versus who is not qualified to be covered under the Act in all probability overrule strictly medical qualifications. This is certainly one reason why there is deep concern about the direction of the Act and the potential cost implications flowing from its currently open-ended definition of handicap.

## THE REHABILITATION ACT OF 1973

The Rehabilitation Act of 1973, as amended, represents a complete overhaul of the Vocational Rehabilitation Act, as amended. Four sections of the Act concern employment of the handicapped, and one of these, Section 503, is the really significant one in so far as private industry is concerned. Section 502 of the Act addresses the problem of architectural accommodation and establishes a government committee to study the problem.

Section 504 of the Act provides for nondiscrimination under the program of federal grants. This brings under the Act's protection handicapped individuals who may be involved with programs, institutions, or other organizations which receive federal funds. This section is very brief and states:

---

[10] American Medical Association Committee on Rating of Mental and Physical Impairment, *Guides to the Evaluation of Permanent Impairment* (Chicago: American Medical Association, 1971), p. iii.

No otherwise qualified handicapped individual in the United States . . . shall, solely by reason of his handicap, be excluded from participation in, be denied the benefits of, or be subjected to discrimination under any program or activity receiving federal financial assistance.

Section 504 would thus have application to hospitals, universities, among other institutions, and to states and municipalities which receive federal grant funds, and places them under the necessity of adhering to the provisions of the Act.

Section 501(b) requires each "department, agency, and instrumentality" of the federal government to submit to the Civil Service Commission and to the Interagency Committee on Handicapped Employees, which Section 502(a) established "an affirmative action plan for the hiring, placement, and advancement of handicapped individuals. . . ." The Civil Service Commission is required by Section 501(c) to develop such programs and encourage state agencies to adopt them.

## Section 503

Section 503 is a strong statement of the responsibilities of "covered contractors." It reads as follows:

### EMPLOYMENT UNDER FEDERAL CONTRACTS

SEC. 503. (a) Any contract in excess of $2,500 entered into by any Federal department or agency for the procurement of personal property and nonpersonal services (including construction) for the United States shall contain a provision requiring that, in employing persons to carry out such contract the party contracting with the United States shall take affirmative action to employ and advance in employment qualified handicapped individuals as defined in section 7(6). The provisions of this section shall apply to any subcontract in excess of $2,500 entered into by a prime contractor in carrying out any contract for the procurement of personal property and nonpersonal services (including construction) for the United States. The President shall implement the provisions of this section by promulgating regulations within ninety days after the date of enactment of this section.

(b) If any handicapped individual believes any contractor has failed or refuses to comply with the provisions of his contract with the United States, relating to employment of handicapped individuals, such individual may file a complaint with the Department of Labor. The Department shall promptly investigate such complaint and shall take such action thereon as the facts and circumstances warrant, consistent with the terms of such contract and the laws and regulations applicable thereto.

(c) **The** requirements of this section may be waived, in whole or in part, by the President with respect to a particular contract or subcontract, in accordance with guidelines set forth in regulations which he shall prescribe, when he determines that special circumstances in the national interest so require and states in writing his reasons for such determination.[11]

The three paragraphs of Section 503 thus call for "affirmative action" on the part of employers to hire the handicapped and vest interpretative, investigative, and enforcement powers with the Department of Labor. Section 503 is applied to all covered government contractors, which is also the basis of such other affirmative action programs as the one applying to Vietnam-era veterans, and to those pertaining to minorities pursuant to Executive Order No. 11246.

## REGULATIONS PURSUANT TO SECTION 503 OF THE ACT

Through the Office of Federal Contract Compliance Programs (OFCCP) the Department of Labor has the responsibility of enforcing Section 503. On April 16, 1976, the OFCCP issued a revised set of regulations [12] which delineated the affirmative action obligations of all covered employers under the Act. Although the handicapped program is administered by the OFCCP along with other "contract compliance" programs, the enforcement mechanism differs from that found under Executive Order No. 11246, which pertains to race and sex discrimination and affirmative action of contractors in those regards. Under the handicapped (and Vietnam-era) programs, the OFCCP retains the sole power to answer complaints from aggrieved individuals while the various government department and agency contracting branches assume a supportive role only to the extent of insuring that individual contractors actually have a handicapped policy and affirmative action program in place. They do not take on the investigative role assigned to their offices by General Order No. 14 pursuant to Executive Order No. 11246. This implies, that for the present, compliance reviews will not be conducted as part of the enforcement mechanism of Section 503. A checklist, however, has been developed by the OFCCP and

---

[11] *Rehabilitation Act of 1973*, Section 503.

[12] U.S. Department of Labor, Employment Standards Administration, Office of Federal Contract Compliance Programs, "Affirmative Action Obligations of Contractors and Subcontractors for Handicapped Workers," *Federal Register*, Vol. 41, No. 75, Part 60-741, April 16, 1976, pp. 16147-16155.

disseminated to all government department and agency compliance officers to serve as a guideline for their activity. It is in Appendix D.

## Coverage and Recordkeeping

The new regulations obligate all covered contractors and subcontractors holding contracts of $50,000 or more and fifty or more employees to prepare and to maintain a written affirmative action program (AAP) for employment of the handicapped. The previous regulation stipulated that the OFCCP be sent a copy of the AAP plus an annual progress update contract if the contract called for performance in ninety days or more and for an amount greater than $500,000. If the dollar amount was greater than $2,500 but less than $500,000, the contractor did not have to send his AAP to Washington. Both groups were, however, obligated to disseminate their complete AAPs to all employees, a burdensome task. This is no longer required, although the AAP must now be kept on file for employees to inspect if they so desire. The $50,000 and 50 employee criteria were chosen because they are also the criteria under Executive Order No. 11246.

Job applicants or employees filing complaints under the law are no longer required to be certified as handicapped, a rule that was particularly resented by those whom the Act was designed to protect. In addition, the recordkeeping requirements were reduced from three years to one in an effort to help ease the paperwork burden placed on employers.

## Definitions and Their Applications

The revised regulations changed the original definition of "handicapped individual" from that of the Rehabilitation Act before its amendment of 1974 to that of the definition found in the amended Act. To repeat, that definition states that "a handicap is any impairment which substantially limits one or more of a person's major life activities." The earlier definition did not use the word "impairment." The definition also includes any person who "has a record of such impairment and is regarded as having such an impairment." [13] The key to understanding the definition is the concept of employability. If for any reason a past, present or future impairment were to affect

---
[13] *Ibid.*, p. 16149.

the employability of that person in any way, then he or she would be covered by Section 503 of the Act. Appendix A (see Figure IV-1) was added to the revised guidelines in order to provide additional clarification to the definition of handicapped individual.

The OFCCP gives further refinement to the amended definition of a handicap by stating what is meant by a "qualified handicapped individual." This means an individual who is capable of performing a particular job, with *reasonable accommodation* (emphasis added) to his or her handicap." [14] What is not stated, although it may be implied, is where the handicap, accommodation, and productivity meet. Does the handicapped individual have to meet only minimum productivity standards? Does he have to meet a level of productivity that will offset the cost of the accommodation made by the employer?

The test to be used, according to the regulations, will be that of "business necessity and financial cost and expenses." [15] This is a very general concept applied by the courts in other areas of civil rights litigation where it is frequently associated with determining whether a defendant employer has met the burden of proof regarding the personnel decision that brought about the alleged discrimination. It is a difficult test for employers. Thus, there is no suggestion that the accommodation be a reasonable one from the employer's viewpoint, only from the viewpoint of the handicapped applicant.

## Medical Examinations and Job Qualifications

Another significant aspect of the revised regulations concerns information obtained from medical examinations and preemployment physicals for job applicants with a handicap. The regulations specify that every physical and mental qualification must be justified by the particular job standards for which the handicapped person is being considered. That is, the contractor must attempt to "screen in" qualified handicapped applicants rather than screen them out through the preemployment physical. It should be noted that, as in other civil rights employment practices, employers cannot rely upon traditional methods of determining fitness for a job. The job placement decision must have as much uncertainty removed as possible. The excuse of

---

[14] *Ibid.*

[15] *Ibid.*, p. 16150.

## FIGURE IV-1

### Appendix A.  Guidelines on the Application of the Definition "Handicapped Individual"

The Rehabilitation Act of 1973, as amended, defines a handicapped individual for the purposes of the program as any person who has a physical or mental impairment which substantially limits one or more of such person's major life activities, has a record of such impairment, or is regarded as having such an impairment.

*"Life activities"* may be considered to include communications, ambulation, selfcare, socialization, education, vocational training, employment, transportation, adapting to housing, etc. For the purpose of section 503 of the Act, primary attention is given to those life activities that affect employability.

The phrase *"substantially limits"* means the degree that the impairment affects employability. A handicapped individual who is likely to experience difficulty in securing, retaining or advancing in employment would be considered substantially limited.

*"has a record of such an impairment"* means that an individual may be completely recovered from a previous physical or mental impairment. It is included because the attitude of employers, supervisors, and coworkers toward that previous impairment may result in an individual experiencing difficulty in securing, retaining, or advancing in employment. The mentally restored, those who have had heart attacks or cancer often experience such difficulty. Also, this part of the definition would include individuals who may have been erroneously classified and may experience discrimination based on this misclassification. This group may include persons such as those who have been misclassified as mentally retarded or mentally restored.

*"is regarded as having such an impairment"* refers to those individuals who are perceived as having a handicap, whether an impairment exists or not, but who, because of attitudes or for any other reason, are regarded as handicapped by employers, or supervisors who have an effect on the individual securing, retaining or advancing in employment.

Source:   Office of Federal Contract Compliance Programs.

"we know someone with a handicap cannot perform this job," without medical and, for example, industrial engineering production evidence, will probably not survive a challenge by the OFCCP or the courts.

Accommodation raises a problem that will eventually reach all covered employers. When is accommodation sufficient so that the liability for failing to hire an otherwise qualified handicapped individual may be waived? In other words, does a contractor's laudatory past performance in hiring the handicapped and in accommodating their needs at any point in time become satisfactory so that no further accommodation is necessary? The regulation's only answer appears to be business necessity and financial cost and expenses, to be determined by the OFCCP, or finally through litigation.

In April 1977, a Department of Labor attorney who was responsible for drafting the regulations, stated that the objective of "reasonable accommodation" is to enable the handicapped person to qualify for a particular job. According to this person, what the Department will deem "reasonable" will vary depending upon the nature of the handicap involved, the size of the contractor and the size and frequency of his government contracts.[16] Obviously, this leaves a lot of discretion to the Department of Labor compliance personnel.

This same spokesman gave these examples of accommodation:

>Modify building architecture to include wheelchair ramps, wider bathroom stalls, and raised door numbers for the blind;
>Install alternative warning devices for the deaf and blind;
>Eliminate heat-activated elevators and replace them with elevators that persons with artificial limbs can operate;
>Initiate an outside interviewing and application process to make the contractor more accessible to the handicapped;
>Initiate alternative testing methods for handicapped individuals who can't take traditional tests, i.e., oral tests for the blind;
>Restructure job duties where possible;
>Create opportunities for job-sharing, part-time work, and work at home where possible; and
>Purchase special aids for the handicapped to help them do the job, such as special telephones for the blind.[17]

Some of these suggested accommodations are reasonably easy to accomplish; others can be quite expensive; and still others often impractical (work at home, job sharing, etc.). They all indicate that there are serious problems ahead for industry in conforming with the law.

### Sheltered Workshops

Sheltered workshops may be considered a part of the contractor's affirmative action program only if the sheltered workshop trains employees for the contractor and the contractor is then obligated to employ those trainees. By not allowing any credit for the use of sheltered workshops except as mentioned, the regulations give no credit to employers who have contracted for goods and services from sheltered workshops in the past. To the extent that employers used sheltered workshops out of the concept of self-help may limit the amount of funds available for such goods and services in the future, especially if accommodation proves to be expensive.

---

[16] *Daily Labor Report*, No. 64, April 1, 1977, p. A-4.

[17] *Ibid.* Regulations embodying similar requirements have been issued by the Department of Health, Education, and Welfare covering hospitals, universities, and other institutions receiving federal aid or grants. The cost has been estimated in the billions of dollars for these already financially poor institutions.

## Collective Bargaining Agreements

The revised regulations still provide for the disruption of collective bargaining agreements if there were a conflict with the purposes of the Act. An example of a situation where this problem could easily arise would be when a qualified handicapped applicant applied for work at a firm where entry level jobs could not be accommodated to the individual's handicap, but a third level job could easily be accommodated. In this case, the regulations would call for the abridgement of seniority or job progression provisions in the collective bargaining agreement so that the handicapped applicant would be allowed entry into the third level vacancy rather than be rejected for the unaccommodative first level vacancy. The regulations' mechanism for achieving this goal would be through the director of the OFCCP who "shall use his or her best efforts to cause any labor union . . . to assist in the implementation of the purposes of the Act." [18] This is somewhat ambiguous as to whether a labor union can in fact be required to revise a collective bargaining agreement. It appears as though they can be revised, but at the same time there is no provision for real enforcement other than asking the union for help or enforcing action against the contractor. Thus, there exists the possibility of a conflict between the employer's obligation under the labor agreement—which he cannot alter unilaterally without violating the National Labor Relations (Taft-Hartley) Act, as amended—and the employer's obligations under Section 503. Since unions are usually not contractors, they cannot be reached directly pursuant to Section 503. This type of employer jeopardy for union noncooperation is present in all procurement-enforced civil rights activities.

## Enforcement

The enforcement procedures require that a complaint of discrimination be "filed within 180 days from the date of the alleged violation unless the time for filing is extended by the director for good cause shown." [19] There may be difficulty with this provision because the grounds for a determination of "good cause" are not defined. Although the regulations require that covered employers maintain records of handicapped applicants

---

[18] U.S. Department of Labor, *supra*, note 12, p. 16155.

[19] *Ibid.*, p. 16156.

for one year, there exists the real possibility of an alleged violation going unreported for a period greater than 360 days. If the employer has eliminated these records from his files, a situation may result which is unfair to either the employer or the applicant or both, unless the 180 day limitation is not extended.

## The Concept of Accommodation and Other Regulating Issues

The accommodation factor is a new concept replacing goals and timetables. It is to be considered in the areas of physical access to the work site, job or work restructuring, or the adaptation or design of tools and equipment to the handicap. These positive programs must be related to recruitment, hiring, job placement, assignment, promotion, training, transfers, layoffs, termination, working conditions, and benefits—that is, to all conditions of employment. The reason accommodation exists, instead of goals and timetables, is simply that the handicapped cannot be thought of as a minority in the traditional application of the term. Each disabled person is unique and, more so than any other minority would be within his own classification. Therefore, the affirmative action program required of contractors must reflect this uniqueness and remain separate from other AAPs. Accommodation requires job restructuring when it is "reasonable" to do so, but no agency or employer really knows what "reasonable" means. This does not, however, relieve contractors from the obligation of trying to make the law work, regardless of the degree of difficulty—subject to business necessity and financial limitation, however they may be defined. (One government source interviewed thought that financial limitations referred to a certain percentage of a contractor's federal contract to be applied toward the cost of accommodation.) It is believed that because the affected class concept will be difficult to apply in handicap employment discrimination charges, the strongest weapon will be the threat of debarment, not backpay awards.

Accommodation also has positive aspects. It allows contractors to take the first step toward resolving complaints of noncompliance. Because the concept is a general one, there is room for genuine conciliation and bargaining. The quota approach used in other affirmative action programs simply does not provide for the flexibility that could be applied toward hiring the handicapped. Although accommodation can be abused by enforcement officials, complaints from industry regarding the abuse of "goals and timetables" would suggest that this newer concept should be given a fair test.

*Architectural Barriers*

Part of the accommodation concept includes the modification or removal of architectural barriers to the handicapped at the place of employment. These provisions of the Act are contained in Section 502,[20] and contractors must take account of these barriers in their affirmative action programs. According to one expert [21] on the subject, the construction costs of eliminating architectural barriers to the handicapped are "minimal" when they are recognized early in the design phase of a plant or building. Such items as lavatories, stairs, curbs, doors and entrances, other clearances, emergency exits, warning systems, etc., all must be considered.

Older buildings present greater problems, both in terms of redesign itself and in terms of cost. Many older buildings in the larger urban areas of the country are also rented by federal contractors from an independent landlord. In this situation, it can often be very difficult for the employer to convince the landlord to modify his building at considerable expense when he may not be subject to the Act's provisions. On the other hand, there are many inexpensive modifications which can be made to existing facilities at very low cost such as ramps, curb modifications, widened parking spaces, hand rails, etc. Presumably, these problems will be studied by the committee established pursuant to Section 502.[22]

## SUMMARY OF THE ACT'S MAJOR PROVISIONS

The Rehabilitation Act of 1973 has established another group which now enjoys protected class status. Section 503 of the Act introduced the concept of accommodation into equal opportunity enforcement. This concept will vary among contractors depending upon their size, financial status, and employment needs. There is a strong emphasis upon job restructuring although such action will proceed on a case-by-case basis. In addition, the handicapped job applicant or employee must es-

---

[20] *The Rehabilitation Act of 1973*, Section 502.

[21] From a speech by Mr. Paul M. Cope, Jr., May 19, 1976.

[22] *The Rehabilitation Act of 1973*, Section 502.

tablish that he or she is qualified to meet the basic standards of the job in question.

The Department of Labor may seek general enforcement of Section 503 of the Act by processing complaints, initiating compliance reviews, and by seeking redress through litigation. The OFCCP is charged with the responsibility for initiating and publishing the regulations governing the affirmative action obligations of contractors under the Act. It may also assist the various agencies responsible for primary compliance activity by determining if charges of discrimination against a contractor are valid. If a prima facie case of discrimination is established, the OFCCP will attempt to conciliate with the contractor before proceeding to the formal legal remedies. If conciliation fails to produce the desired results, legal action may be initiated which might include a formal hearing, contract sanctions, such as debarment, litigation to enjoin the alleged discriminatory practice, or awarding monetary damages in relief to the affected individual or individuals.

CHAPTER V

# Implementing Section 503 of the
# Rehabilitation Act

The responsibility for creating and implementing the regulations under Section 503 of the Rehabilitation Act are promulgated by the Department of Labor's Office of Federal Contract Compliance Programs (OFCCP) which, as explained in the previous chapter, placed in operation a final set of regulations on May 17, 1976. They required that the handicapped be affirmatively employed by all government contractors whose contracts met a stated dollar amount; that the handicapped be hired according to affirmative action criteria which substitute accommodation for numerical hiring goals; that all job requirements be job related; that all medical examinations be job related; that the burden of proof in establishing these requirements be with the contractor; that a written handicapped worker affirmative action program (AAP) be required of all contractors who have written AAPs under Executive Order 11246; that the AAP apply only to those who have visible handicaps and to those who voluntarily identify themselves to the contractor as handicapped; but that all employees or applicants who believe they are covered by Section 503 of the Act may avail themselves of the protection afforded by the Act at any time without the requirement of pre-notification.

## ENFORCEMENT ACTIVITY

As of December 10, 1976, the OFCCP had received 1,994 complaints pursuant to Section 503 involving 33 major kinds of handicaps. Of these, 204 were settled in favor of the complainant; 366 closed because of lack of coverage, 104 complaints withdrawn, 180 no violation, 154 dismissed because complainants did not respond to government follow-up, and 29 transferred to another agency, leaving 950 still outstanding. Table V-1, supplied by U.S. Department of Labor, Office of Federal Contract Compliance Programs, summarizes these data by region and type of complaint.

## TABLE V-1
### Complaints Pursuant to the Rehabilitation Act of 1973 up to December 10, 1976

| HANDICAPPED REGION | I. COMPLAINTS | | | II. TYPE OF COMPLAINT | | | | III. REASON FOR CLOSURE | | | | | | IV. STATUS OF OPEN CASES | | | |
|---|---|---|---|---|---|---|---|---|---|---|---|---|---|---|---|---|---|
| | Received | Closed | Open | Hiring | Promotion | Discharge | Other | No Coverage | Complaint Withdrawn | No Violation | Conciliation | No Reply Over 60 Days | Transferred | Initial Stages of being Investigated | Referred to Solicitors' Office | In Negotiation for Conciliation | Total Cases Open Over 60 Days |
| I. Boston | 17 | 11 | 6 | 10 | 0 | 6 | 1 | 5 | 0 | 5 | 1 | 0 | 0 | 5 | 0 | 1 | 0 |
| II. New York | 38 | 13 | 25 | 8 | 3 | 11 | 16 | 7 | 0 | 4 | 0 | 2 | 0 | 25 | 0 | 0 | 0 |
| III. Philadelphia | 28 | 10 | 18 | 14 | 3 | 9 | 2 | 0 | 0 | 0 | 0 | 0 | 0 | 18 | 0 | 0 | 0 |
| IV. Atlanta | 24 | 4 | 20 | 10 | 1 | 11 | 2 | 3 | 1 | 0 | 0 | 0 | 0 | 20 | 0 | 0 | 0 |
| V. Chicago | 83 | 62 | 21 | 36 | 3 | 33 | 11 | 49 | 4 | 0 | 0 | 5 | 4 | 21 | 0 | 0 | 0 |
| VI. Dallas | 28 | 12 | 16 | 6 | 1 | 15 | 6 | 2 | 0 | 1 | 9 | 0 | 0 | 15 | 1 | 0 | 0 |
| VII. Kansas City | 17 | 0 | 17 | 8 | 2 | 3 | 4 | 0 | 0 | 0 | 0 | 0 | 0 | 17 | 0 | 0 | 0 |
| VIII. Denver | 15 | 4 | 11 | 10 | 1 | 2 | 2 | 2 | 1 | 0 | 1 | 0 | 0 | 9 | 2 | 0 | 0 |
| IX. San Francisco | 61 | 23 | 38 | 12 | 1 | 15 | 1 | 10 | 0 | 3 | 8 | 0 | 0 | 8 | 0 | 0 | 0 |
| X. Seattle | 24 | 6 | 18 | 5 | 1 | 8 | 10 | 5 | 0 | 0 | 1 | 0 | 0 | 18 | 0 | 0 | 0 |
| TOTAL FY to date | 335 | 145 | 190 | 119 | 16 | 113 | 55 | 83 | 6 | 13 | 20 | 7 | 4 | 156 | 3 | 1 | 0 |
| All cases to date | 1994 | 1049 | 945 | 882 | 127 | 750 | 235 | 366 | 104 | 180 | 204 | 154 | 29 | 654 | 35 | 226 | 279 |

If the OFCCP finds a potential violation after a complaint has been filed and an investigation made, the first step is conciliation. Usually, an attempt is made to return the employee to a job or to obtain the job for the employee and to secure backpay. As explained by the former director of OFCCP:

> As we have learned from other job discrimination programs, a worker who has been discriminated against cannot always be made whole without an award of back pay, where appropriate, for the time when he or she was ready and qualified for a job but was unlawfully denied the job. Accordingly, we are seeking and obtaining back pay for aggrieved individuals in appropriate situations.[1]

As of December 23, 1976, handicapped workers have been awarded more than $115,948 in backpay in settlement cases, with individual awards for workers ranging from $231 to $12,000. The handicaps involved emotional illness, diabetes, permanent leg injury, heart disorder, anemia, spinal defect, and previous mental illness.[2]

It is obvious from this summary that the Rehabilitation Act covers a broad spectrum, and that mental, as well as physical, handicaps are significant aspects of its reach. It is this part of the law that has company personnel most concerned, for they are at a loss as to how to prepare to accommodate persons with mental disabilities, how to recognize many such disabilities, and what to expect of employees with mental disabilities. Of course, the Act requires that persons who have had mental problems be restored and qualified. Medical knowledge, however, cannot predict relapses, and already employed persons may degenerate mentally as well as physically. Accommodation of the physically handicapped is often a physical or architectural matter; for the mentally handicapped, it may well be largely psychological.

As of this writing, there have been no court cases providing guidance on what is a substantial barrier to employment; how much medical information an employer may request; whether a mentally handicapped person can be given a mental test; to what health, medical and life insurance benefits a handicapped person is entitled to or whether a company must employ one whose

---

[1] "Statement of Deputy Assistant Secretary of Labor Lorber Before the Senate Labor Subcommittee on the Handicapped," *Daily Labor Report*, May 5, 1976, No. 88, p. E-2.

[2] "Handicapped Workers Awarded over $115,000 in Back Pay for Job Bias," *Daily Labor Report*, No. 6, January 10, 1977, p. A-2.

handicap is likely to make him progressively less able to work. The only court decisions pursuant to the Rehabilitation Act of March 1, 1976, involved a blind person who successfully sued pursuant to Section 501(b) to compel the U.S. Department of Housing and Urban Development to promote him.[3] Information as to the impact on the private sector, therefore, comes only from three sources: settled conciliation cases; cases litigated pursuant to state legislation; and arbitration cases.

## BACKPAY CONCILIATION CASES

The cases set forth below by region are the official OFCCP summaries of those in which it arranged backpay settlements. It appears that in some of the cases the employer settled because it was cheaper to pay damages than to litigate or to face hearings on debarment, a common occurrence in civil rights cases. Yet upon a reading of these cases, it is also apparent that failure to hire, to award a better job, or to consider carefully before discharge, can be costly if a claim of handicapped is possible.

These cases include the issue of medical costs where a disease is progressive, where there are emotional and psychiatric problems, plus where there are a variety of physical conditions. They illustrate what problems may arise, but, as already noted, provide no final answers to where the line can be drawn between permissible and proscribed conduct for the employer in dealing with the employment problems of the handicapped.

### Region I—Boston

1. A company doing research and development of medical technology products awarded a complainant, residing in the state of Massachusetts, a backpay settlement of $9,000.00. The complainant had been terminated because of a handicap, controlled epilepsy. The complainant's position, prior to termination, was junior accountant. Upon investigation, the company offered the complainant a future job when one became available. This was rejected by the complainant who preferred to make a cash settlement. In addition to the backpay settlement, the employer paid complainant's portion of the Social Security contribution for the period in question. Date executed: January 29, 1976.

---

[3] *McNutt v. Hills*, USDC, DC, CA No. 75-1422, January 31, 1977.

2. A resident of Massachusetts was awarded $326.00 by a small manufacturing company. The complainant, whose handicap was epilepsy and who had another job, did not wish to be reinstated. The complainant only requested money for the time lost while searching for another job. Date executed: October 1976.

3. A complainant residing in Massachusetts was awarded $1,365.00 by a food distribution (warehousing) company. The complainant, whose handicap was epilepsy, was employed by the company. Date executed: October 1976.

*Region III—Philadelphia*

4. A complainant residing in the state of Virginia was awarded $2,631.12 in back wages by an electric equipment testing company. Complainant was an applicant for the position of electronic equipment operator-trainee. The company felt the complainant, whose handicap was that of a manic depressive personality, would be under inordinate pressure. Complainant's psychiatrist contended that the problem remained controlled for two years with medication. Complainant accepted an alternative position with the company at the same rate of pay, plus company benefits, in addition to the backpay. Date executed: March 24, 1976.

5. A complainant residing in Pennsylvania was awarded back wages in the amount of $5,446.00 by an air brake company. The complainant, whose handicap was a back injury, was laid off and then rejected upon recall because of his back condition. Upon investigation, complainant was reinstated with full seniority plus backpay. Date executed: November 15, 1976.

6. A complainant residing in West Virginia was awarded $1,583.82 by a chemical company. The complainant was laid off because of a back injury. The company indicated there were no appropriate job openings. Several months later there *was* an appropriate job opening, however, an employee with less seniority was hired. Upon investigation, the complainant received backpay and was offered a job. Complainant did not wish to be rehired. Date executed: October 15, 1976.

*Region IV—Atlanta*

7. A complainant residing in the state of Florida was awarded backpay in the amount of $1,300.20 by a chemical company. The complainant, who was blind in the left eye, resigned his position as "pipe layer" to attend college. The company promised reinstatement upon return. When complainant reapplied (after deciding not to attend college) the company refused to hire him. Upon investigation, complainant was awarded backpay and seniority was restored. Complainant was to be reinstated in October 1976. Date executed: May 13, 1976.

8. A complainant residing in Georgia was awarded backpay in the amount of $12,000.00 by a telephone company. The complainant had been forced into early retirement because of a hearing loss. The back wages covered the period from the time complainant was forced into early retirement to the time she would normally have retired. Complainant did not wish to return to work. Date executed: October 15, 1976.

9. A complainant residing in the state of Georgia was awarded $5,957.39 in back wages by a railroad company. The company claimed the complainant, who had a visual problem, could not perform the duties required and placed her on medical retirement.

Investigation disclosed the complainant was qualified and was, therefore, reinstated to her former position with restored seniority. Date executed: November 26, 1976.

10. A complainant, a checker on the loading docks for a trucking company for fifteen years, had been discharged when the company determined that bad vision prevented him from performing the duties of his job.

Investigation proved the complainant's vision had not deteriorated for the past eight years. The complainant, a resident of the state of Georgia, was awarded backpay in the amount of $4,170.08 and was reinstated with seniority benefits. Date executed: November 26, 1976.

*Region V—Chicago*

11. A complainant residing in Chicago was awarded back wages in the amount of $4,624.51 by a heavy equipment company. The company claimed the complainant, who had

a hearing loss, could not perform the duties of the job satisfactorily.

Investigation disclosed the complainant was qualified and he was reinstated. Including back wages, the complainant received retroactive seniority to 1974, plus all benefits. Date executed: October 25, 1976.

*Region VI—Dallas*

12. A complainant, a design engineer, with a back condition, was terminated because the tool and machinery company, by which he was employed, felt he could not perform the duties required.

The company awarded the complainant $3,150.00 in back wages. The complainant, a resident of the state of Texas, had accepted a position with another company and so did not wish to be rehired. Date executed: December 7, 1976.

13. A complainant, residing in the state of Texas, felt that she was dismissed because of her handicap, a speech impairment.

The bottling company, for which the complainant worked, awarded her $2,000.00 in back wages.

Since the complainant had accepted a position with another company, she did not wish to be rehired. Date executed: November 23, 1976.

14. An industrial equipment company awarded $1,362.34 in backpay to a complainant residing in Texas. Because the complainant was mentally unstable, he had been demoted from the position of field salesman to a clerical position. In addition to back wages, he was also included in the company profit sharing. Complainant did not wish to be rehired. Date executed: April 30, 1976.

15. A complainant residing in Texas received $231.00 in back wages from a farm equipment company. The complainant, a diabetic, was a clerk/handler (sold & stocked parts). Complainant had a reaction to medication while at work and was discharged while hospitalized. Complainant did not wish to be reinstated. Date executed: March 9, 1976.

16. A copper refinery awarded $1,816.00 in backpay to a complainant residing in Texas. The complainant, who had sustained an industrial permanent injury to his right leg,

was reinstated to the position of supervisor in the mill-wright area of the refinery, retroactive to the date of separation, with no loss in service. Date executed: March 19, 1976.

17. A heavy equipment manufacturer awarded back wages in the amount of $300.00 to a complainant residing in Texas. It was determined the complainant had a congenital back defect. In addition to back wages, the complainant was considered for first available job opening as a truck driver, which was the original position he applied for. Date executed: August 9, 1976.

18. A complainant residing in Texas was awarded $419.00 in back wages. The complainant, who suffered from emotional illness, was aware that his position would be eliminated. The company terminated him sooner than expected, however, thus eliminating a Christmas bonus. Date executed: April 29, 1976.

*Region VIII—Denver*

19. A trucking company awarded $4,840.00 in back wages to a complainant residing in Colorado. The complainant, who had an enlarged heart, was laid off in wrong order of seniority, which entitled him to 4.4 months in back wages. The complainant was reinstated to his former position of dispatcher. Date executed: August 16, 1976.

*Region IX—San Francisco*

20. A maintenance worker, residing in California, was awarded $407.00 in back wages. The complainant, who has a vision problem, was hired for a temporary position. He worked the designated time. Date executed: July 2, 1976.

21. A complainant from California applied for a temporary position as clerk typist for a hospital. The hospital refused to hire alleging that the complainant would be unable to perform satisfactorily because of chronic kidney problems. A cash settlement was made of $1,500.00. Date executed: August 18, 1976.

22. A complainant residing in California and working for a cement company as a welder was terminated after having an epileptic seizure on the job. The complainant was re-

hired as a layout welder and was again terminated. Upon investigation, complainant was awarded back wages of $2,500.00. Complainant rejected re-employment. Date executed: March 6, 1976.

23. A complainant residing in Hawaii was discharged because of a back injury. Upon investigation, the company, a canning factory, awarded the complainant $2,098.00 in back wages. The complainant had accepted another position and so did not wish to be rehired. Date executed: October 1976.

24. A complainant residing in Hawaii was refused employment by an equipment company because of the complainant's congenital back problem. Upon investigation, the complainant was hired with seniority, plus fringe benefits, for a period of six months and back wages of $2,260.00. Date executed: October 1976.

25. A complainant residing in Arizona was awarded $332.52 in back wages after being terminated by an electric company because of her epilepsy. The complainant's position with the company was as a steno-secretary. Following investigation, she was reinstated with backpay. Date executed: January 9, 1976.

26. A complainant residing in California was awarded $3,946.00 in back wages by an electronics plant. The complainant, who had a mastectomy, had been terminated from her position as an electronic assembly person because of her operation. Complainant not only received back wages, but was reinstated to her former position. Date executed: December 29, 1975.

27. A hospital supply company awarded back wages in the amount of $814.45 to a complainant residing in California. The complainant, who was anemic, was an applicant for the position of a pharmacy clerk. In addition to back wages (including interest), the complainant was hired to the position she had applied for, with retroactive seniority. Date executed: July 2, 1976.

28. A school awarded back wages in the amount of $2,205.00 to a complainant who resides in Hawaii. The complainant who had a back injury, was an applicant for an assistant

welding and sheetmetal instructor's position at a school and was refused employment. The complainant was awarded a cash settlement equivalent to a semester's pay for the position. Complainant had another position and so did not seek re-employment. Date executed: July 22, 1976.

29. A complainant residing in California was awarded $1,808.56 in back wages by an Airlines Company. The complainant, whose handicap is epilepsy, was suspended for a period of time because of his handicap. Complainant agreed to back wages plus benefits. The Airlines Company also agreed to give the complainant a physical examination no later than March 30, 1977 for consideration for a position in the Air Freight Department. The complainant had originally applied for the position of ramp person. Date executed: February 27, 1976.

30. A county in California awarded back wages of $700.00 to a complainant who resides in that state. The complainant, a psychiatric social worker with a congenital spinal defect, complained she was kept in a "temporary employee" status because of her handicap. The county was found in violation after claiming to have kept complainant in such status, fearing her condition would cause excessive use of sick leave and early retirement. The complainant was awarded retroactive seniority, sick leave, and back holiday pay dating from August 1975. Date executed: June 14, 1976.

31. A county employee, a resident of California, was terminated while recovering from heart surgery. Upon investigation, the complainant was rehired and awarded back wages in the amount of $7,970.00. Date executed: October 1976.

32. A bank terminated a complainant residing in California because of the bank's concern that the complainant's handicap, cancer, would progress. The bank was also concerned about insurance costs. Upon investigation, the complainant was reinstated with full medical benefits, plus back wages of $940.00. Date executed: November 1976.

33. A complainant, employed by a city in the state of California in the position of a painter, was discharged because of psychiatric problems. Upon investigation, the complainant was rehired and awarded back wages in the amount of $4,164.00. Date executed: December 1976.

34. A complainant, a resident of the state of Arizona, was terminated from the position of computer operator by an electric and power project because of an intestinal infection. Upon investigation, the complainant was awarded $700.00 in back wages. The complainant had accepted a new position and did not wish to be reinstated. Date executed: December 1976.

35. A complainant residing in Arizona, who had previously suffered mental illness, was awarded $2,916.00 in back pay, expurgation of personnel records, and employment in a position for which he had applied, by an aircraft company. Date executed: September 10, 1976.

36. A complainant residing in California was awarded $1,425.60 and job reinstatement by a health care service agency. The complainant alleged the respondent violated their affirmative action obligation by refusing to allow him to return to work after heart surgery. Date executed: October 21, 1976.

37. A complainant residing in Hawaii, received lost wages of $2,097.21, had personnel records purged and was reemployed by a fruit company. Complainant had been considered a risk because of a back problem. Date executed: October 12, 1976.

38. A complainant residing in Hawaii was awarded back wages in the amount of $2,659.68 by an equipment company. The respondent felt that persons with congenital back problems were an increased risk, and that back pain was secondary to bending and lifting restrictions. Through investigation, it was determined the complainant had worked as warehouseman for the past eleven years, with no problem. In addition, complainant's physician indicated persons with this abnormality are not prone to back aches. In addition to back wages, complainant was reinstated and received retroactive seniority. Date executed: October 18, 1976.

## Region X—Seattle

39. A complainant residing in the state of Washington was terminated from his position as an apprentice burner repairman, because of his handicap, a hearing disability. The oil company for whom he worked awarded the complainant

$1,191.68 in back wages with reinstatement to his former position. Date executed: October 16, 1975.

40. A complainant residing in the state of Washington was discharged after having an epileptic seizure on the job. The complainant had been employed as a machine operator by a paper products and container company for five years prior to the seizure. The company awarded the complainant $9,000.00 in back wages. The complainant did not elect to return to work. Date executed: April 1976.

41. A complainant residing in the state of Washington had been employed three weeks, at which time the railroad company for which he worked gave him a medical examination. An x-ray indicated an abnormality of the spine and the complainant was discharged. The railroad company awarded the complainant back wages of $1,795.00 and reinstatement to the original position of laborer in the car repair shop. Date executed: July 9, 1976.

TOTAL AMOUNT OF BACK PAY RECORDED TO DECEMBER 23, 1976: *$115,948.00* resulting from resolution of forty-one cases.

## Comment on Back Pay Conciliation Cases

These cases illustrated how far the Rehabilitation Act of 1973 may go beyond just protecting what has commonly been known as "handicapped." Persons with back injuries, heart trouble, ulcers, etc. have not normally heretofore been considered handicapped. Once they are so considered, the use of physical examinations both in employing and terminating employees is called into question. Confronted by this Act, employers must seemingly learn to utilize the physical examinations as a technique to determine what an employee can perform, and then fit him into an available job, rather than using the physical examination to identify the person's limitation and then to eliminate him from consideration.

The implications from this assessment are in turn far-reaching. If the job found to meet the capability of the handicapped is in a line of progression, but the handicapped person cannot qualify for upgrading, can he be disqualified? Must upgrading and seniority procedures be altered? In short, how far does affirmative action reach?

It appears also from the cases summarized above that disqualification of a prospective employee, or discharge of a current one, on the basis of a physical examination may not be allowed unless the physical inadequacy is directly job related—that is directly inhibits satisfactory job performance—and unless no accommodation can reasonably be made. "Accommodation" remains, of course, a nebulous concept. It does seem to follow, nevertheless, that the Rehabilitation Act could have more impact on administration of physical examination requirements for jobs than it does on protecting those whom we have traditionally identified as handicapped.

The cases also reveal that the Rehabilitation Act is a source for employees to offset arbitrary or thoughtless action by employers. When the real motivation is different, physical or mental problems can no longer be the basis of employer action against employees. An employer who desires to discharge, or otherwise to discipline an employee must document and prove his case. If the employee is actually being penalized for poor production, uncooperative attitude, or other such reasons, physical or mental capacity can no longer be used either as an excuse for the action, or as an additional reason therefore.

In sum, it can be concluded from these cases that the potential of the statute can be more thoroughly understood by reading them and comprehending their implications than by merely familiarizing oneself with the text of the law.

## STATE AND RELATED LITIGATION

Thirty states have enacted legislation that proscribe discrimination against the handicapped.[4] These laws are of two types: separate legislation affecting handicapped only, and general civil rights legislation which includes the handicapped as a protected group. The states have concurrent jurisdiction, as in the case of age discrimination, but with a major difference. Whereas, the Age Discrimination in Employment Act provides for initial jurisdiction by existing state agencies, no such coordination ex-

---

[4] Alaska, California, Connecticut, District of Columbia, Florida, Hawaii, Illinois, Iowa, Kansas, Maine, Maryland, Massachusetts, Minnesota, Montana, Nebraska, Nevada, New Hampshire, New Jersey, New Mexico, New York, North Carolina, Oregon, Pennsylvania, Rhode Island, Texas, Vermont, Virginia, Washington, West Virginia, Wisconsin. The state laws are summarized in Appendix E.

ists in federal-state handicapped worker legislation. The federal law applies only to contractors, and enforcement is via the procurement function, thereby making respective state and federal jurisdiction and coordination more complicated and difficult.

There has been litigation concerning the handicapped in several states. Examples from such cases will not only illustrate what is expected from state legislation, but may also provide a preview of possible litigation results at the federal level. In addition, handicapped persons have made use of other statutes to contest their rights, and such cases add to our understanding of the problem.

*State Handicapped Statute Litigation*

1. In *Bevan v. New York State Teachers Retirement System*,[5] the New York trial court ordered a school board to reinstate a blind teacher whom the school board involuntarily retired without a hearing and on whose behalf the board sought disability retirement from the state teachers' retirement system. The court found unconstitutional a state law which authorized the board to enforce retirement without a prior adversary hearing for disability. In this case, the teacher was tenured and had just recently been afflicted with blindness.

2. In *Chicago, Milwaukee, St. Paul, and Pacific Railroad Company v. Wisconsin Department of Industry, Labor and Human Relations*,[6] only minimum standards of productivity were required from a handicapped employee. On March 13, 1969, Vern C. Goodwin was hired by the railroad as a laborer in the diesel house. He was given a physical at which time he disclosed a history of asthma and migraine headaches with dizziness. X-rays of Goodwin also revealed a slight disc space.

He did a variety of light and heavy cleaning jobs, performing to satisfaction for the next two weeks. On March 26, he received a discharge notice for no apparent or explained reason. He was told that he had a disqualifying back disease. When his private physician told him that he

---

[5] 7 FEP 74, (N.Y. Sup. Ct., 1973), (FEP refers to the *Fair Employment Reports*, published by the Bureau of National Affairs, Inc.).

[6] 8 FEP 938, (Wis. Sup. Ct., 1974).

was fit for work, Goodwin filed a complaint. The company physician responded that it was because of Goodwin's asthmatic condition that he had recommended that Goodwin be removed from the diesel house where fumes there would aggravate his condition.

The Wisconsin Department of Industry ordered the railroad to reinstate Goodwin to his former position with full restoration of seniority. It also ordered the railroad to cease and desist its discriminatory practices against the complainant and "like situated employees." When the railroad appealed the decision, the court found that the Department's order had been "overbroad" and limited the decision to Goodwin only. Upholding the decision regarding Goodwin, the court stated that his asthma "makes achievement unusually difficult" but that nonetheless, "the laborer was physically qualified to perform this job."

3. In *Chicago, Milwaukee, St. Paul, and Pacific Railroad v. Washington State Human Rights Commission,*[7] the railroad found itself in a different position from the previous case. The railroad had refused to hire an applicant as a brakeman because he had the "medial menisci" removed from his knees. The court found the railroad *not* guilty of discrimination because the individual was unable to perform the duties of a brakeman which involved getting on and off moving trains and operating track switches, duties which put a considerable torque on the knees. According to the court, removal of menisci makes the knees less flexible; and the court found that although the knees are neither weak nor unusable at present, there was a "significant" likelihood of degeneration in the future. The court found that the Commission had erred when it stated that the railroad had violated state law against discrimination in employment and noted that the law was void because it lacked a definition of the term "handicapped."

4. In *Holland v. The Boeing Company,*[8] an employee of twenty-three years service was terminated for poor job per-

---

[7] 11 FEP 854 (Washington Superior Court, King County, 1975).

[8] 11 EPD 10,861 (Washington Superior Court, King County, 1976). (EPD refers to Employment Practice Decisions, published by Commerce Clearing House, Inc.)

formance. The employee had been afflicted with cerebral palsy throughout his employment with the Boeing Company. His job had been one of "experimental electronics technician," requiring skill in problem solving, functional testing, and "troubleshooting" in electronics laboratory. Holland held this job from 1959 until 1974 with particular distinction in analog computer electronics.

Through a series of cut-backs in company operations and a subsequent change in job assignments, Holland found himself in a job requiring precision electronic assembly of components. Although the company did strive to keep him employed—the lab where Holland worked experienced an eighty percent reduction-in-force—the company did not do a good job in accommodating Holland's handicap. Because of his poor performance in the electrical assembly work, he was given the choice of either accepting a "storekeeper's" position or being terminated from the company. He appealed to the state agency, and the case eventually went to the state superior court which concluded:

> The Plaintiff's disability prevented him from performing many of his assignments in the facilities support area. He was unable to do the quality controlled assembly and soldering that was required of employees in that shop. He was unable to do production buildings work. Holland's inability to successfully perform in facilities support was known or should have been known to the Defendant at the time of his transfer.

Because Boeing should have accommodated work to Holland's disability, the court found the company guilty of discrimination because of his handicap. "The failure to place Plaintiff in a job *he could perform* (emphasis added) after the initial discriminatory transfer, was an unfair practice. . . ."

Boeing was ordered to grant backpay and to assign Holland to a job that he could perform which was equivalent to, or the same as, his prior electronics technician's job.

### Related Litigation

1. In *Gurmankin v. Costanzo et al.*,[9] the Philadelphia School District was ordered by the U.S. District Court for Eastern Pennsylvania to hire a "qualified" blind woman for the

---

[9] 411 F. Supp. 982 (E.D. Pa., 1976), *affirmed*, U.S. Court of Appeals, Third Circuit, April 1977.

position of high school English teacher. The plaintiff won the case on the issue of the school board's violating her due process rights under the fourteenth amendment. This was because the board had initially refused to consider *all* blind persons for teaching jobs, except for teaching jobs at a school for children with vision impairments.

Although the Rehabilitation Act of 1973 was offered by Ms. Gurmankin as grounds for having the court decide in her favor, the judge noted that "The Rehabilitation Act of 1973 is not dispositive of the plaintiff's claims in this case. The Act became effective in December of 1973; Ms. Gurmankin had been seeking a teaching position since 1969 .... Thus, Ms. Gurmankin's claim that the school district's prior policy violated her rights cannot be resolved without considering her constitutional arguments." The court then examined the question of fourteenth amendment violations and found that the school board's controlling policy of excluding all blind persons from teaching sighted students, especially in light of the fact that nationwide, over 400 blind teachers were teaching sighted students. Thus, the court found for the plaintiff because the school board's policy was not a rational policy based on fact.

2. In *Norman Atkinson v. U.S. Postal Service*,[10] it was shown that a handicapped postal worker originally hired under a special program had voluntarily resigned and, therefore, could not later allege discrimination when he was denied re-employment on the basis of a routine examination which he had not previously been required to take. The facts of this case are that Atkinson had cerebral palsy and was employed successfully as a mailhandler from July 30, 1969 to March 23, 1973. He had originally been hired under a special program for the handicapped. While employed, he sought transfer to the transportation platform, but his request was denied on the basis that it would be dangerous. He then voluntarily resigned, but later he made a series of requests asking for reinstatement. The Public Policy Program for Handicapped Persons under which he had originally been hired was discontinued, and the union now had an agreement with the Postal Service whereby applicants had to take a qualifying competitive exam. The plaintiff had

---

[10] 12 EPD 11,128 (S.D. New York 1976).

not taken the exam and the court felt that the Postal Service had acted within its discretion by not granting the transfer. The complaint was dismissed.

3. In *McNutt v. Hills*,[11] a U.S. District Court found that a blind person had been systematically passed over for promotion without any acceptable, or even stated reason by the U.S. Department of Housing and Urban Development. Since the complainant was finally promoted prior to the court's decision, the decision ordered the Department to conduct a thorough inquiry into its policies and to prepare a comprehensive report detailing how it intended to meet its obligations to the handicapped.

### State and Related Litigation—Comment

The above cases illustrate that both private and public employers must be aware not only of the Rehabilitation Act, but also of a variety of other federal and state laws and regulations that govern employment of the handicapped. An unfortunate feature of all civil rights legislation is the number of forums to which a potentially aggrieved person can address his or her complaint. This is as true for the handicapped as for other protected groups, as not only these cases but also the arbitration cases discussed below, illustrate.

### Arbitration And The Handicapped

As employees, handicapped workers have the same rights as other workers to process grievances. This has led to arbitration decisions covering many ramifications of the handicapped problem. Most of these cases focus on the question of the ability of the handicapped person to perform a job. They provide further illustration that the handicapped worker must be given the fullest consideration before a decision is made to deny him a job or a promotion.

1. In *Tennessee Corporation, Tennessee Copper Company Division and International Chemical Workers, Local 401*,[12] the grievant had been employed by the company since 1947.

---

[11] *Supra*, note 3.

[12] 70-2 ARB para. 8840, (September 10, 1970). (ARB refers to *Labor Arbitration Awards*, published by Commerce Clearing House, Inc.)

In 1962, while employed in an underground mine job, he lost vision of his right eye in an accident. He was moved to a surface job where he worked alone ninety percent of the time. He was considered very competent at the new position.

In 1968, a bidding notice for shop helper was posted by the company. Shop helper is the first job in line of progression for further promotions. Grievant bid for the shop helper job, was the senior man on the bidder list, and was disqualified solely because of his physical disability. The job was awarded to someone with less seniority. The opinion of the arbitrator was that grievant was conceded to be fully qualified for shop helper job except for limited vision. "Physical ability is an inherent requirement of any job; technical ability alone does not establish capability." The company's decision was within its management rights based on convincing evidence that grievant's physical disability would present a hazard to him, to other employees, and to the company.

2. In *Murphy Construction and Teamsters, Local 563*,[13] the arbitrator's opinion was that the employer improperly prevented an employee with a back problem from resuming her work, notwithstanding employer's contention that it had the right to rely on company doctor's assessment that, while he found the employee physically capable of returning to work, she should be placed on certain medical restrictions to prevent future injury. Arbitrator returned the employee to full employment on the condition that in the next six months, she could perform her work without any time off because of back-related problems; if she did incur any time off because of such problems, her grievance was denied.

3. In *Anaconda Aluminum Company and Aluminum Workers International Union, Local 130*,[14] the employer was attempting to comply with the Occupational Safety and Health Act (OSHA) and the arbitrator found that the employer properly refused to waive safety rules for grievant with medical ailment that prevented her from wearing ear protection. Grievant stated that ear coverings caused her

---

[13] 61 LA 503 (1975). (LA refers to *Labor Arbitration* volumes published by Bureau of National Affairs, Inc.)

[14] 64 LA 25 (1974).

dizziness and nausea. She wished to remain at her job in the punch press department without wearing ear muffs, ear plugs, or Swedish wool. Neither the arbitrator nor the company, however, felt that they had the authority to grant a waiver to the OSHA requirement. The employer gave her the option of: (1) wearing ear muffs; (2) bidding into another department with no loss of pay; (3) exercising her seniority to move into another department; and (4) being terminated. The grievant elected to take a lower paying job as a custodian in another department; she later filed this grievance and the arbitrator found her not to be entitled to pay equal to that in the punch press job.

4. In *Weber Manufacturing Company and International Woodworkers of America, Local IV-322*,[15] the arbitrator found that the employer was justified in discharging an epileptic following his second seizure while at work in the plant, notwithstanding the union's contention that the decision whether grievant can be retained safely as a loader of logs into the vat is to be determined by a qualified physician. It was found that the employer was reasonable in contending that it was unsafe for the grievant as well as others because: (1) medical testimony did not establish that grievant would not have subsequent seizures even though he took prescribed medicine (on the occasion of one seizure, the grievant had not taken his medicine while on the occasion of the other seizure, he had taken the medicine); (2) employer did not have another unit position that grievant was fit to perform without hazard.

5. In *Hyde Park Foundry and Machine Company and United Steelworkers of America*,[16] pursuant to a contract providing that "employees who have given long and faithful service in the company and who have become unable to handle heavy work to advantage, shall be given preference to such light work as they are able to perform," the company was found to have properly awarded a storekeeper job with light duties to an employee who was restricted by his doctor following a heart attack, notwithstanding the union's contention that it should have been given to a senior

---

[15] 63 LA 56 (1974).

[16] 63 LA 536 (1974).

employee. It was found that the disabled individual also had given "long and faithful service" to the company, and the arbitrator ruled that provisions relating to handicapped employees modify seniority provisions.

6. In *Masonite Corporation and International Association of Machinists and Aerospace Workers*,[17] the arbitrator found that the company was justified in refusing to reinstate a diabetic material handler whom it had placed on sick leave status after he had had a diabetic attack at work for which he was hospitalized, since (1) the employee could cause injury to himself and to other employees while performing his duties involving operation of forklift and Towmotor; (2) neither the company doctor nor personal physician had given grievant unrestricted release to work; and (3) employer did not have any other job that grievant could fill without possibly causing injury to himself or others.

## Arbitration v. Litigation

These sample arbitrations would seem to indicate that arbitrators may be more likely than administrative agencies or courts to consider company problems in deciding cases. The arbitration frame of reference is the collective agreement negotiated by the company and the union, rather than the law, although the law must be considered and cannot be disregarded. This, of course, would seem to insure greater cognizance of operating problems than would litigation obviously enacted on behalf of a disadvantaged group. On the other hand, it would appear that an employee may not only eschew the grievance-arbitration route and file his claim with a state or federal agency instead, but may even utilize the latter route after failing to achieve his objective by utilizing the former.[18]

## Problems Involving Handicapped Employment

In a survey of "Fortune 500" companies in mid-1976, the author recorded a number of situations involving problems and potential litigations. These are summarized in this section.

---

[17] 62 LA 558 (1974).

[18] This seems to be the meaning of the U.S. Supreme Court's decision in *Alexander v. Gardner-Denver Company*, 415 U.S. 36 (1974), in which the court noted that "The arbitrator . . . has no general authority to invoke public laws that conflict with the bargain between the parties. . . ."

1. A company declined to hire a person later found to be a diabetic after it made the individual an offer, and advised him that he would be hired by a certain date. No physical examination was given at that point. Several days later, an applicant deemed to be more qualified was actually placed in the job. The firm was then charged with handicapped discrimination by the rejected applicant. The case is still open.

2. An individual with a heart condition applied for work in a plant that uses nitroglycerin. The applicant was refused work on grounds of safety and the potential of a violation of the Occupational, Safety and Health Act. The individual appealed to the appropriate state agency which found the company guilty of discrimination. The case is on appeal.

3. A craftsman who lost an arm in an accident was accommodated and found a job in the toolroom. His complaint centered on his reduced pay, and he sued to keep his old craft rate even though he was holding a lower-rated job. The case is pending.

4. An epileptic falsified his employment application. He subsequently enlisted in an apprenticeship program which had climbing requirements, among others. The company terminated him from the program for safety reasons and for falsification of his application after it learned of his handicap. The employee sued to be reinstated into the program. The case is still open.

5. A company salesman with fifteen years service who had suffered a heart attack was no longer able to perform satisfactorily. Under the company's "de-selection" policy, the salesman chose separation pay rather than a lower-rated position. After his release from service, he filed both age and handicapped discrimination complaints against the company with a state agency. The company won the case.

6. This firm has had one complaint by a handicapped person —a former employee who was terminated for poor work performance and attendance. This particular individual was afflicted with chronic bone spurs which, during recurrences, required extensive treatments, operations, and medical leaves. The case is currently being handled by the Department of Labor (OFCCP) and appears headed for litigation.

In addition to being handicapped, this individual is a Vietnam-era veteran as well as a black. In its complaint, OFCCP has cited both the Rehabilitation Act of 1973 and the Vietnam Era Veterans Readjustment Assistance Act of 1974. Although no formal note of his race has been mentioned to date, the company believes that, if his complaint proves unsuccessful, a charge of race discrimination could be filed.

7. A company hired a draftsman with a good employment record elsewhere and with sound references. He was, however, suffering from a disease that progressively restricted, and would eventually eliminate, his vision. He was terminated from the company. A state agency found probable cause and the case is currently in litigation.

8. This employer has experienced several handicap charges dealing mostly with the company's restriction regarding physical disabilities and heavy, strenuous jobs. One case involved a mill-wright who had had several back operations and consequent lifting restrictions imposed on him by his physician. He was placed in another, lower-rated job and claimed discrimination because of his handicap. The case was dismissed after OFCCP investigation.

9. This case involved a small company retail unit of two employees. A new employee was hired for the job, which, among other tasks, involved driving a truck. A physical examination given after his actual employment began, found that he suffered from epilepsy. The firm terminated the employee for safety reasons. The case went before a state agency which ruled that the company rule barring an epileptic from driving a company vehicle was discriminatory, even though the accident potential was rather obvious.

*Problem Areas*

The aforementioned survey also uncovered a number of problem areas in handling handicapped worker problems, including conflicts with other social legislation and with union contractual arrangements, which the previous cases have already touched upon. In particular, companies are seriously concerned about problems resulting from possible violations of the federal Occupational, Safety and Health Act. In addition, conflicts with union-management collective agreements were frequently noted by respondents.

1. For example, one company has punch presses which require two hands to operate—start buttons located at arm's length on each side of the machine—for compliance with OSHA standards. If a one-armed individual were assigned to this operation,

the machine would present a hazard to co-workers and violate OSHA.

Also, the state of Ohio has recently passed legislation amending its equal employment law. This law makes it illegal for an employer to "elicit or attempt to elicit any information" concerning a handicap from any applicant for employment as well as making it unlawful to make or keep any records of an empolyee's or applicant's handicap. This may be in direct conflict with other laws which require handicap information, such as OSHA, the Rehabilitation Act, and Worker's Compensation Acts, not to mention the impact on employment physicals, engineering and plant modifications for accommodation, forms, employment applications, and medical records.

2. Although it is too early to determine which area of handicapped discrimination might present this firm with the most problems, there has been some recent experience with the problem of the handicapped employee during layoffs. For example, one of their production complexes has approximately 400 people with special work restrictions because of physical disabilities who had to be laid off when jobs available for them according to seniority could not be performed or accommodated. This added friction in union relations because of the large amount of bumping that took place. The union situation also removes a large degree of flexibility that would be necessary to accommodate this problem. Seniority simply cannot be overlooked and remains the single biggest obstacle to accommodation. For example, it now takes approximately twenty years' seniority, in this particular company's facility, to reach a job that has the worker sitting full-time instead of standing.

3. This large company has had approximately twenty-six handicap charges, but it states that most have involved handicapped employees trying to use the law to obtain a less demanding and/or more lucrative job. The company fought the union hard on the right to maintain the flexibility of job assignments. Now, more "handicapped" employees are challenging this company prerogative. The company believes that accommodation, because of the huge cost potential and conflicts with OSHA, are the main difficulties with the Rehabilitation Act.

For example, the firm had a plant which had a press accommodated for a one-armed employee, i.e., it had one of its two "on" buttons locked out for this individual on his shift. One day, he forgot to unlock his locked-out "on" button, and when the second shift began work, the employee working the machine assumed it had been properly set up for him as had been done in previous months. This was not the case, however, and in the course of operations, the second shift employee lost three fingers as a direct result of this accommodation, coupled with the carelessness of both employees.

4. This company commented on the problem of employing people who are terminally ill. It is difficult for employers because on the one hand, the Department of Labor regulations require that these people be employed if they apply and are qualified. On the other hand, employers are barred from changing benefit or insurance policies to ease their burden and therefore will be forced actually to buy insurance claims. A reasonable accommodation may be to employ these people without any insurance whatsoever.

5. This company has a small office in one location, which had a second floor for working space and first floor for employee parking. There was no elevator, only stairs and a service hoist. The facility employed one individual who was wheelchair-bound. He was carried up and down the office stairs by other employees, the only accommodation necessary, as the cost of putting in a special ramp or elevator for just one person at a single small office would be prohibitive. During an OSHA inspection, the government agent advised the company either to provide an elevator or terminate the handicapped employee so that he would not be a hazard in the event of an emergency.

6. One case involved an employee with one eye who was restricted from working at any job in an eye hazard area or where the company felt that the probability of his losing his only eye was high. The pertinent state agency ruled that the employee, not the company, should be allowed to decide if the risk were too great. This, of course, is a spurious argument because under law, the employee cannot transfer a risk of that nature onto himself from the company. The company therefore had the employee sign a release form, but it feels that the chances of its validity in court if the other eye is lost would be slim.

7. Workers' compensation legislation and handicapped problems appear to conflict in many states. If the employer cannot determine the extent of a prospective employee's handicap—or must employ him in any case—to what relief is he entitled if injuries or disease relating to the handicap result? Must the affirmative action employer assume the burden for any aggrava-

tions to the handicap related, even remotely, to employment? In some states, e.g., Illinois, this is apparently so. Obviously, a fundamental conflict in social purpose exists here, with the employer in the middle of a potentially costly situation.

*Handicapped Awareness and Employment*

Although litigation pursuant to the Rehabilitation Act and pertinent state laws has been minimal, it may well increase because of the growing awareness of the handicapped problems both by the handicapped themselves and by the public at large. An increasing number of newspaper and magazine articles [19] have depicted not only the plight of the handicapped struggling to overcome barriers to employment, but also their increasing willingness to settle for nothing less than full acceptance into all facets of society. This has included legal challenges by specific handicapped groups against both private and public sector employers who have refused to hire the handicapped in addition to pressure applied against the governmental authorities that have responsibility for such functions as housing, transit, enforcement of local antidiscrimination laws, and development and operation of rehabilitation centers.

On the other hand, the handicapped are a very diverse minority with widely differing skills, needs, and problems. Accom-

----

[19] See for example "Handicapped Campaign for Rights to Mobility, Jobs, and Education," *The New York Times*, December 13, 1976, p. 26. The article illustrated the attitude of "militant" handicapped individuals who claimed that "they don't have the traditional attitude of the handicapped accepting (discrimination) and staying at home behind closed doors." See also, "Deaf Professionals Open Fight Against Job Discrimination," *Fair Employment Report*, February 23, 1976, p. 30. That group launched a class action suit with the National Center for Law charging the Minnesota School for the Deaf with discrimination in hiring against deaf applicants. Other articles include: Jonathon Kwitny, "Patients Who Recover (from serious illness) Often Can't Regain Spot in Work Force," *The Wall Street Journal*, July 20, 1976, p. 1; Joann S. Lublin, "Lowering Barriers—Pressured Companies Decide The Disabled Can Handle More Jobs," *The Wall Street Journal*, January 27, 1976, p. 1; Jeffrey A. Tannenbaum, "New Crusaders—Angry Blind Militants, Seeking Equal Rights, Try Tougher Tactics," *The Wall Street Journal*, July 10, 1975, p. 1; Jane E. Brody, "Equal Opportunity Job Laws for Disabled Have Little Effect," *The New York Times*, May 3, 1975, p. 14; "Jobs for the Handicapped," *Focus*, April 7, 1976; Roy R. Silver, "Handicapped Get L.I. (Limb-Impaired) Driver Course," *The New York Times*, August 8, 1974; Dorothy Barclay Thompson, *Guide to Job Placement of the Mentally Restored*, The Presidents Committee on Employment of the Handicapped (Washington, D.C.: U.S. Government Printing Office, 1969); and Terri Schultz, "The Handicapped, A Minority Demanding Its Rights," *The New York Times*, February 13, 1977, Section 4, p. 8.

modation to one type of handicap often means little to an individual with a different type of handicap. A person who has lost an eye, an arm, or a leg is clearly in a different position than one totally blind, or without both arms or legs, and in turn, all these are differently situated than a person with a growing disabling illness or those mentally deficient or with mental instability. Moreover, handicapped is often a personal, or psychological situation. One person with a missing eye or arm may have overcome the loss without regard to any identity with, or psychology of, being handicapped; another may feel and act quite differently. Group identity under such diversity is, therefore, difficult and probably unlikely.

On the other hand, the existence of federal legislation is likely to be a coalescing force. This could be particularly evident if a dramatic court case on the order of *Standard Oil of California* occurred. In discussing the problem of regulations and policies with federal enforcement officials, one cannot escape the conclusion that they are waiting for such a major case to spur interest in the handicapped legislation as *Standard Oil of California* did for the age discrimination law. Since the number of handicapped in any one company is unlikely to be sufficient to generate a monetary settlement approaching that of a case involving older workers in a large company, litigation results for the handicapped may not be dramatic. On the other hand, a few well-publicized cases barring, or threatening to bar, federal contracts could undoubtedly generate many more, as well as settle some of the unanswered questions about the meaning of the law, the duties of employers and the rights of the handicapped.

## The Handicapped as Employees

Because the handicapped include such a diverse group, the generalizations about their performance and productivity are hazardous. Companies which have had a program designed to employ the handicapped have, however, found the handicapped to be excellent employees. DuPont began its program in response to the problems of returning veterans of World War II. It has kept excellent records since then, surveying its handicapped population in 1958 and again in 1973, both studies including over 1,000 employees. DuPont's 1,452 handicapped employees covered in the latter survey found that:

Handicapped employees are engaged in a wide range of occupations at DuPont. Craftsmen comprise the largest segment with 562; professional, technical and managerial are next with 334; followed by operators at 233; and office and clerical workers at 224. The remainder is divided between service workers at 83 and laborers at 16.

The nature of the handicap is divided into nine categories for the study, ranging from nonparalytic orthopedic, the largest group, with 415 include: heart disease, 380; vision impairment, 277; amputees, 163; paralyses, 106; epilepsy, 56; hearing impairment, 43; and total deafness, 14. Some employees have more than one handicap.

Among the findings of the survey of the DuPont handicapped were:

1. Insurance
   No increase in compensation costs and no lost-time injuries.

2. Physical Adjustments
   Minimal with most requiring no special work arrangements.

3. Safety
   96 percent rated average-or-better on and off the job with more than half above average.

4. Special Privileges
   Disabled want to be treated as a normal employee.

5. Job Performance
   91 percent rated average or better.

6. Job Stability
   93 percent rated average-or-better.

7. Attendance
   79 percent rated average-or-better.[20]

Many other companies have long records of successful employment of the handicapped, but like DuPont's experience, generalization from theirs must be done with care. DuPont, for example, began its program to take care of its own employees who were wounded in World War II, and since then, its handicapped workers have been a carefully selected group. This is not in anyway meant to derogate what DuPont and others have accomplished. By effective affirmative action and the best of business social policy, they have successfully brought numerous handicapped persons into the mainstream of work and life.

---

[20] Joe Wolfe, "Disability Is No Handicap for DuPont," reprint from *The Alliance Review*, (Winter 1973-74), n. p.

There is, however, serious question whether such experience presents the same problem as employing persons with mental illness, progressively impairing diseases, disablements accompanied by serious psychological problems, or handicapped persons with little or no training or skills. Careful, selective employment seems to be a key to the excellent records of DuPont and other companies that have pioneered in this field.

On the other hand, it is encouraging that companies have had such success in employment of the handicapped. The DuPont experience is indicative of what constructive efforts can accomplish in this field of social endeavor.

## CONCLUSION

The Rehabilitation Act of 1973 has without any doubt filled a need for individuals in the handicapped community. There is no question that for years, the majority of employers would not consider hiring or promoting handicapped individuals. There have been notable, successful exceptions, but they remained exceptions until the passage of the Act. Now other problems are emerging. Employers are generally anxious to hire qualified handicapped individuals, partly because there is much natural sympathy for this affected class, but at the same time they are seriously concerned about the extent and potential costs of their obligations.

The cases discussed in this chapter including Department of Labor conciliations state and related litigation, and those referred to in the employer survey, all emphasize the expanded definition of handicapped, and its application to persons heretofore considered by common usage not handicapped. Some cases also illustrate the use of the statute as a grievance procedure to overcome employer action considered arbitrary or unfair—something that is common with all anti-discrimination legislation. And we have already commented about the potential of this law to alter the use of physical examinations and to alter upgrading and seniority procedures.

The Act is vague and the regulations not much more precise. Problems in defining who is handicapped both physically and mentally and therefore eligible for the statute's protection will continue to be a burden for employers. The same may be said about the concept of accommodation. No one knows what to do or how much an employer must spend to meet the needs of public policy. What is rquired is more definitive answers in this area, but to date the regulatory agencies have preferred to wait for court decisions to answer these questions.

Major problems also exist in the relationship of the Rehabilitation Act to other civil rights enforcement mechanisms, to union contractual arrangements, and above all, to the Occupational Safety and Health Act and to state workers' compensation laws. What legislation has priority if two are in conflict? Should safety measures be waived in order to employ the handicapped, or should handicapped employment be foregone in order to insure safety? If an epileptic is declared eligible to drive a truck and has an accident on the highway, who is responsible and liable? Who pays the costs of an aggravated injury caused by the required employment of the handicapped? Would it not be wiser to follow the paths of the successful employers of the handicapped and concentrate on constructive selective employment?

Thus far, the attitude of the compliance authorities, state and federal, is that the employer complies with all laws, however, contradictory and impossible that might appear to be, and pays whatever costs are necessary. It remains to be determined what the burdens and costs will be, and whether such attempts to force industry to shoulder costs and contradictory requirements will increase the employment of the handicapped, or so reduce profit margins that net employment—including that of the handicapped—is adversely affected.

# PART FOUR

*Affirmative Action for Veterans*

# CHAPTER VI

# Vietnam Era Veterans' Readjustment Assistance Act of 1974

The United States of America has always been determined to acknowledge the debt that it owes its servicemen. Beginning with the Selective Training and Service Act during World War II, Congress has converted this sentiment into a matter of public policy by legislating protection of veterans' re-employment rights. Laws detailing the reabsorption of veterans into the work force extended re-employment benefits to those who had left their jobs for military service. Thus, the country codified a social climate so that the veteran could resume his "rightful place."

Post World II and Korean conflict Congresses continued to reaffirm this position regarding veterans through further legislation which reiterated the wartime law. These Acts, including the Servicemen's Readjustment Act of 1944, the Veteran's Readjustment Assistance Act of 1952, the Veteran's Readjustment Benefits Act of 1966, and the Universal Military Training and Service Act of 1967, granted veterans who had been employed either by the federal government or by private employers, the right to be re-employed in their former positions or one of like seniority, status, and pay, provided the private employer's situation had not changed so much as to make re-employment either impossible or unreasonable. The exserviceman was also entitled to participate in any insurance programs or other benefit packages extended to workers during his absence. Post-war legislation extended the provisions to cover both reservists and the National Guard.

Subsequent court cases and action by the Department of Labor liberally construed the law in the veterans' favor, ruling on such issues as reinstatement, missed promotions, and pay progression. In 1946, the United States Supreme Court explicitly interpreted the law as assuring the veteran that those changes and promotions in status that would have accrued to him simply through continued employment would not be refused him because of his induction into the armed forces. "Thus he does not step back on the seniority escalator at the point he stepped off. He steps back on at the precise point he would have occupied had he kept his position continuously during the war." [1]

## SPECIAL VIETNAM-ERA CIRCUMSTANCES

This entire body of legislation and court precedent was not, however, considered sufficient to handle the unique problems arising out of the Vietnam War, a conflict which caused anguish throughout the nation not only by its divisive nature, but also by the serious economic dislocations peculiar to the era. Although a smooth and easy transition for returning veterans into the civilian labor force has never been notably easy after any war in this century, the Vietnam conflict produces several problems which aggravated this situation.

Among these problems was unprecedented difficulty generated by trying to turn the nation from a partial wartime to a peacetime economy. The "Great Society" years, combined with the needs of the war, contributed to serious economic repercussions, including inflation. The duration of the war—more than ten years of military involvement—produced a substantial number of veterans who were in need of post-service employment. Moreover, a large percentage of the draft-age population managed to postpone or to avoid altogether, the obligation of military service. Employers although experiencing a tight labor market for many of the war years, were not subject to anything comparable to the drastic labor force changes which occurred during World War II.

As the war became increasingly unpopular, the special status of being a veteran began to evaporate in the nation as a whole, an experience with which previous generations of returning veterans did not have to contend. This, in turn, eased the social pressure upon employers to extend themselves as they had done after the World War II and Korean conflicts.

Finally, the changing nature of the labor force placed an emphasis upon education and/or the acquisition of special skills. Those who avoided military service had either valuable skills, educational commitments (college deferments, etc.), or initially, family obligations. Although those who served often did obtain valuable

---

[1] *Fishgold v. Sullivan Drydock and Repair Corporation*, 328 U.S. 275 (1946).

training, much of it was not readily transferable to the civilian labor market.

## Number of Vietnam Veterans

Congressional interest in Vietnam veterans has also undoubtedly been sustained by the numbers involved who have returned to civilian life. Table VI-1 shows that more than eight million persons were included in this category as of June 30, 1976, as compared with 15.4 million from World War II and 5.6 million from the Korean conflict.

## Veteran Unemployment, 1970-1974

Of special concern was the unemployment rate of veterans. A study conducted by the U.S. Bureau of Labor Statistics found that veterans returning in 1973 and 1974 "continued to have greater problems finding work than non-veterans. By contrast, veterans discharged earlier were doing about as well or better in the job market as non-veterans." [2]

Figure VI-1 compares the unemployment rate of Vietnam-era veterans with that of non-veterans by age groups, 1970-1974. It shows that the younger veterans, 20-24, were having a particularly difficult time obtaining jobs in comparison with this age group's non-veterans. Black veterans' unemployment in these years generally averaged twice that of white veterans—a comparable situation to the black-white non-veteran unemployment ratio. [3]

These facts, combined by pressure from war supporters who were both angered by the attention given to war protestors by Congress and the media and determined to aid those who did fight, and encouraged by others hoping to soothe their guilt feelings, led Congress to take prior legislation one step further in order to meet the special needs of returning Vietnam veterans. Thus, for the first time in the long history of veteran employment legislation, Congress, in 1974, passed legislation requiring employers to take "affirmative action" to employ veterans and disabled veterans. In addition, the re-employment rights of veterans were strengthened. We shall first discuss Section 402 of the Act and its regulations and then Section 404 which pertains to re-employment rights.

---

[2] Kathryn R. Gover and Beverly J. McEaddy, "Job Situation of Vietnam-era Veterans," *Monthly Labor Review*, Vol. 97 (August 1974), p. 17.

[3] *Ibid.*, p. 18.

## TABLE VI-1

ESTIMATED NUMBER OF VIETNAM ERA VETERANS IN CIVIL LIFE

(thousands)

| End of Month | Total | With Service in Korean Conflict | With No Service in Korean Conflict |
|---|---|---|---|
| 1964 September | 98 | 6 | 92 |
| December | 212 | 9 | 203 |
| 1965 June | 456 | 22 | 434 |
| December | 700 | 46 | 654 |
| 1966 June | 962 | 78 | 884 |
| December | 1,242 | 108 | 1,134 |
| 1967 June | 1,493 | 123 | 1,370 |
| December | 1,848 | 137 | 1,711 |
| 1968 June | 2,234 | 159 | 2,075 |
| December | 2,760 | 196 | 2,564 |
| 1969 June | 3,169 | 213 | 2,956 |
| December | 3,679 | 240 | 3,439 |
| 1970 June | 4,173 | 255 | 3,918 |
| December | 4,642 | 280 | 4,362 |
| 1971 June | 5,138 | 301 | 4,837 |
| December | 5,597 | 334 | 5,263 |
| 1972 June | 5,976 | 350 | 5,626 |
| December | 6,268 | 381 | 5,887 |
| 1973 June | 6,557 | 406 | 6,151 |
| December | 6,826 | 435 | 6,391 |
| 1974 June | 7,088 | 460 | 6,628 |
| December | 7,382 | 488 | 6,894 |
| 1975 June | 7,597 | 503 | 7,094 |
| December | 7,875 | 516 | 7,359 |
| 1976 June | 8,070 | 517 | 7,553 |

Source:  Semi-Annual reports of VETERAN POPULATION—BY AGE, REGIONAL OFFICE, PERIOD OF SERVICE AND STATE OF RESIDENCE, Research Division, Reports and Statistics Service, Office of Controller, Veterans Administration, Washington, D.C.

Comment:  The Vietnam era veteran population, which had been increasing at a peak average rate of 84,000 per month during fiscal year 1970, increased during fiscal year 1976 at an average rate of 39,000 per month.

## *SECTION 402 AND ITS REGULATIONS*

The Vietnam Era Veterans' Readjustment Assistance Act of 1974 [4] (hereinafter referred to as the "Act") is an amendment to the Vietnam Era Veterans' Readjustment Assistance Act of 1972. Section 402 requires that government contractors take affirmative action to hire and to promote both disabled veterans and veterans

---

[4] *Vietnam Era Veterans' Readjustment Assistance of 1974,* Public Law 93-508 93 U.S.C., H.R. 12628, December 3, 1974. Sections 402 and 404 are reproduced in Appendix F.

## FIGURE VI-1

**Unemployment rates of Vietnam-era veterans and nonveterans 20 to 34 years old, 1970–74**
[Seasonally adjusted quarterly averages]

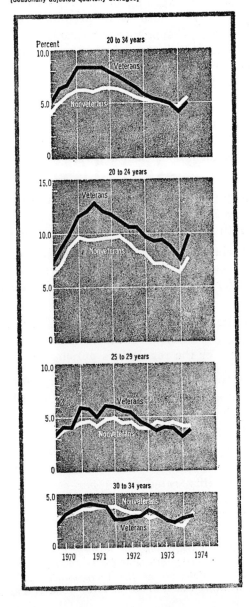

Source: *Monthly Labor Review*, Vol. 97 (August 1974), p. 18.

of the Vietnam War. In addition, it requires that all "appropriate" job openings be listed with the state employment services and that quarterly reports be filed regarding the employment of disabled veterans and veterans of the Vietnam era. The regulations follow closely the wording of the regulations to the Rehabilitation Act of 1973. Both were promulgated by the Office of Federal Contract Compliance Programs (OFCCP) of the Department of Labor and are enforced pursuant to the government's procurement process.

## Definitions

There are several definitions in the regulations which are crucial to understanding who is covered under the Act. A "Veteran of the Vietnam era" means a person who:

1. served on active duty for a period of more than 180 days, any part of which occurred between August 5, 1964 and May 7, 1975, and was discharged or released therefrom with *other than a dishonorable* discharge; or

2. was discharged or released from active duty for a service-connected disability if any part of such active duty was performed between August 5, 1964 and May 7, 1975; and

3. was so discharged or released *within 48 months preceding* the alleged violation of the Act, the affirmative action clause and/or the regulations pursuant to the Act.[5]

The regulations thus place stringent time limitations upon non-disabled veterans as there are relatively few months of coverage left for the majority of Vietnam-era veterans. Thus in 1979 coverage for this group expires completely.

A "disabled veteran" means a person entitled to disability compensation under laws administered by the Veterans Administrations for disability rated at *30 per centum or more,* or a person whose discharge or release from active duty was for a disability incurred or aggravated in the line of duty.[6]

---

[5] U.S. Department of Labor, Office of Federal Contract Compliance Programs, *Affirmative Action Obligations of Contractors and Subcontractors for Disabled Veterans and Veterans of the Vietnam Era* (Washington, D.C.: U.S. Government Printing Office, June 25, 1976) Title 41 Part 60.250.2.

[6] *Ibid.*

A "qualified disabled veteran" means a disabled veteran as defined above who is capable of performing a particular job, with *reasonable accommodation* to his or her disability.[7]

This definition is derived from the handicap regulations of the Rehabilitation Act, with the concept of accommodation being the controlling theme upon which the regulation has been drafted. Accommodation applies in the same fashion for qualified disabled veterans as it does for the handicapped, inheriting the same problems of vagueness and general uncertainty as to the precise requirements that will be demanded of employers. The employer still must meet the burden of proof of financial costs and expenses and business necessity once a prima facie case of discrimination has been established.

## Coverage and Affirmative Action

As in the handicap regulations, government contractors for $10,000 or more are covered under the Act. Those contracts which are for $50,000 or more and have 50 or more employees working for the contractor require a written affirmative action program. Each affirmative action plan (AAP) developed under the contractor's program must be left on file at his place of business so that it may be inspected by employees or interested applicants. In addition, the program must be updated annually if there are any significant changes. A contractor has 120 days from the commencement of the initial contract to develop the AAP.

Like the handicap regulations, the Vietnam-era veteran regulations ask contractors to "invite" all disabled veterans and veterans of the Vietnam era who wish to benefit under the AAP to identify themselves. After this is done, the employer's liability for not adhering to the requirements of the statute may nevertheless remain intact. The OFCCP's "Synopsis of Obligations . . ." states that a contractor should, as part of his affirmative action program, "balance [the] need to know who is entitled to affirmative action under Section 402 with the individual worker's right to privacy . . . the affirmative action obligations apply only to those with clearly visible disabilities and to those who voluntarily come forward and identify themselves as disabled veterans or veterans of the Vietnam era" (See Appendix D for complete text).

---

[7] *Ibid.*

Contractors are required to undertake all of the steps necessary in affirmative action similar to the handicap program with several important adaptations unique to the veterans program. In particular, the contractor "shall consider only that portion of the military record, including discharge papers, relevant to the specific job qualifications for which the veteran is being considered." [8] This policy is designed to minimize any adverse record which a veteran might possess. Except in a few circumstances, it is difficult to imagine how many types of bad conduct short of major crimes could be considered job-related in any meaningful sense of the term. Of course, the new amnesty policy may make the discharge qualification obsolete.

Another aspect of affirmative action for disabled veterans is the use of the preemployment physical examination to "screen in" prospective applicants rather than using it to "screen them out." This screening in of "qualified disabled veterans" applies in exactly the same fashion as it does for the qualified handicapped under the Rehabilitation Act regulations. It includes all disabilities, with special attention given to job qualifications as established by the contractor. The only way a contractor may reject "qualified" disabled veterans is by establishing—that is by meeting the burden of proof—that the job requirements are consistent with business necessity and the safe performance of the job. [9]

## Internal Dissemination of Policy

All contractors are required as part of affirmative action to have their "outreach" program balanced by an effective policy of internal communications for disabled veterans and veterans of the Vietnam era. Such a program includes a large number of items which the regulations list in detail—for example, special information meetings, posting of the policy, employee orientation talks, and inclusion of the policy in all union agreements. By requiring the policy to be included in all union agreements, the regulations essentially call for a unilateral move on the part of contractors without a corresponding action by unions. Although many unions have been, and are, cooperating in helping to insure that disabled veterans and veterans of the Vietnam-era are affirmatively employed and promoted, unions are essentially

---

[8] *Ibid.*, part 60-250.6 (b).

[9] *Ibid.*, Part 60-250.6 (2).

not reached by the procurement enforcement process, which follows the questionable procedure of enforcing such a requirement through the contractor alone. As in the Rehabilitation Act regulations, the OFCCP has required that collective bargaining agreements be revised in order to provide for a new affirmative action program, neglecting the issue that this is potentially in conflict with the Taft-Hartley Act. The regulations, emphasizing the Deparement of Labor's recognized impotence to deal with unions obstructing the program, require the OFCCP director to "use his or her best efforts" to secure union cooperation.[10]

### Complaint Procedures and Enforcement

As in the handicap regulations, the OFCCP has established a complaint procedure which allows for conciliation with the alleged discriminator. What is different from other regulations for disabled veterans and veterans of the Vietnam-era is the channel through which the complaints are processed:

> any applicant for employment with a contractor of any employee of a contractor may, personally or by an authorized representative, file a written complaint with the Veterans' Employment Service of the Department of Labor through the Local Veteran's Employment Representative (LVER) or his designee at the local State employment office. . . .[11]

The local Veteran's Employment Representative (LVER) is charged with assisting veterans in preparing their complaints and is responsible for forwarding those complaints to the Department of Labor. There is a 180 day limit for filing discrimination complaints with the Department of Labor, but unlike the Age Discrimination in Employment Act's notice requirements, this limit is clearly directional not jurisdictional. The secretary specifically has reserved the right to extend the filing period for "good cause."

The conciliation period itself is scheduled to last up to 60 days after which the Department of Labor will be given the complaint by the LVER—who is responsible for initial conciliation—for a determination under the government's contract compliance enforcement mechanism. This covers the full panoply of actions for non-compliance including backpay where applicable. The veteran who alleges discrimination must provide the De-

---

10 *Ibid.*, Part 60-250.9(b).

11 *Ibid.*, Part 60-250.26.

partment of Labor with the form DD-214, and, where applicable, appropriate Veterans Administration certification indicating the percent of disability, updated within one year prior to the date that the complaint is filed. These forms are the proof of veteran status and proof of the extent of disability which was incurred while on active duty. If the required information furnished to the Department of Labor is incomplete, the veteran has 60 days in which to complete his case file. If that deadline is missed, the Department may close the case. The Department may also enter into conciliation for a "reasonable period of time" (even though the conciliation of the LVER has already occurred and presumably failed) after which, if the results are "unsatisfactory," the actions for non-compliance may commence. These procedures are identical to other contract compliance enforcement procedures and have been detailed in the previous discussion of the Rehabilitation Act regulations.

## Enforcement Activities

The affirmative action obligation of government contractors under the Vietnam Era Veterans' Readjustment Assistance Act is quite new. Although the Act was passed in 1974, the regulations issued pursuant to the Act were not effective until June 1976. As a result, there have been no known court cases filed pursuant to Section 402 of the Act. As of December 10, 1976, Table VI-2 shows that 1,229 complaints had been filed with the Department of Labor, virtually all of which were in the New York and Denver regions. Moreover, almost all these cases were caused by the failure of employers to list jobs with the employment service as required by the regulations. By that date, only one case had been referred to the Solicitor's office for possible court action, and no significant number of conciliations had been involved.

The requirement that job openings be listed with, and that at least quarterly reports on all veteran hiring activities be sent to, state employment services poses a possible conflict particularly between the Vietnam-era legislation and the Age Discrimination in Employment Act. As of June 30, 1976, the average age of Vietnam-era veterans in civilian life was 30.3 years.[12] An employer that lists his jobs with the state employ-

---

[12] *Data on Vietnam Era Veterans June 1976* (Washington, D.C.: Veterans Administration, Office of Controller, Reports and Statistics Service, 1976), p. 3.

## TABLE VI-2
### Complaints Pursuant To Vietnam-Era Veterans Readjustment Assistance Act Up To December 10, 1976

| VETERANS REGION | I. COMPLAINTS | | | II. TYPE OF COMPLAINT | | | | III. REASON FOR CLOSURE | | | | | | IV. STATUS OF OPEN CASES | | | |
|---|---|---|---|---|---|---|---|---|---|---|---|---|---|---|---|---|---|
| | Received | Closed | Open | Hiring | Promotion | Discharge | Other | No Coverage | Complaint Withdrawn | No Violation | Conciliation | No Reply Over 60 Days | Transferred | Initial Stages of being Investigated | Referred to Solicitors' Office | In Negotiation for Conciliation | Total Cases Open Over 60 Days |
| I. Boston | 0 | 0 | 0 | 0 | 0 | 0 | 0 | 0 | 0 | 0 | 0 | 0 | 0 | 0 | 0 | 0 | 0 |
| II. New York | 809 | 13 | 796 | 10 | 1 | 4 | *794 | 4 | 2 | 2 | 3 | 1 | 1 | 796 | 0 | 0 | 0 |
| III. Philadelphia | 1 | 0 | 1 | 0 | 0 | 1 | 0 | 0 | 0 | 0 | 0 | 0 | 0 | 1 | 0 | 0 | 0 |
| IV. Atlanta | 2 | 0 | 2 | 1 | 0 | 1 | 0 | 0 | 0 | 0 | 0 | 0 | 0 | 2 | 0 | 0 | 0 |
| V. Chicago | 6 | 0 | 6 | 4 | 0 | 2 | 0 | 0 | 0 | 0 | 0 | 0 | 0 | 6 | 0 | 0 | 0 |
| VI. Dallas | 1 | 0 | 1 | 1 | 0 | 0 | 0 | 0 | 0 | 0 | 0 | 0 | 0 | 1 | 0 | 0 | 0 |
| VII. Kansas City | 5 | 0 | 5 | 3 | 0 | 0 | 2 | 0 | 0 | 0 | 0 | 0 | 0 | 5 | 0 | 0 | 0 |
| VIII. Denver | 296 | 1 | 295 | 1 | 0 | 0 | *295 | 1 | 0 | 0 | 0 | 0 | 0 | 295 | 0 | 0 | 0 |
| IX. San Francisco | 0 | 0 | 0 | 0 | 0 | 0 | 0 | 0 | 0 | 0 | 0 | 0 | 0 | 0 | 0 | 0 | 0 |
| X. Seattle | 1 | 1 | 0 | 1 | 0 | 0 | 0 | 1 | 0 | 0 | 0 | 0 | 0 | 0 | 0 | 0 | 0 |
| TOTAL FY to date | 1121 | 15 | 1106 | 21 | 1 | 8 | 1091 | 6 | 2 | 2 | 3 | 1 | 1 | 1106 | 0 | 0 | 0 |
| All cases to date | 1229 | 48 | 1181 | 70 | 11 | 23 | 1125 | 17 | 8 | 9 | 6 | 4 | 4 | 1172 | 1 | 8 | 11 |

*State ES Referrals of Failure to List Jobs.

Source: U.S. Department of Labor, Office of Federal Contract Compliance Programs.

ment services and affirmatively employs veterans may find that
he is closing opportunities to older workers, and thus is risking
a charge pursuant to the ADEA.

*Reasons for Dearth of Cases*

There are a number of reasons in addition to the newness of
the law that explain the dearth of cases under Section 402 of
this law. Persons who are aggrieved are more likely to file under
other legislation if they qualify to do so. Thus, a black female
veteran has Title VII of the Civil Rights Act available for
complaints; the older veterans now use the ADEA; and disabled veterans can file under the Rehabilitation Act. The Department of Labor advised the Industrial Research Unit that
the last was quite important in explaining why the Department
had virtually no Section 402 cases, including conciliation experiences. Disabled veterans have learned that by filing under
the Rehabilitation Act, they receive faster action because this
skips a procedure. The complaint goes directly to the Department for conciliation without prior activity by the Veteran's
Employment Service.[13] Many of the conciliation cases described
in Chapter V involved veterans, who for this reason filed their
complaints under the handicapped rather than the veterans legislation.

## VETERANS RE-EMPLOYMENT RIGHTS

As was noted in the introduction to this chapter, the reemployment rights of veterans have long been guaranteed by the
Selective Service Act (now known as the Military Selective
Service Act [14]). There is a substantial body of law concerning
returning veteran's rights to seniority, vacations, pensions, promotions, dismissals, etc., which is not discussed here. Rather,
we have highlighted only a few key cases in order better to
understand the new rights prescribed in Section 404 of the Vietnam Act, discussed below. Thus, the U.S. Supreme Court has
consistently interpreted the Act "to assure that benefits and
advancements that would necessarily have accrued by virtue of
continued employment would not be denied the veteran merely

---

[13] Telephone interview, March 1, 1977.

[14] 50 U.S.C. App. 459, Section 9.

because of his absence in the military service." [15] In *Accardi v. Pennsylvania Railroad Co.,*[16] for example, the court ruled that severance pay based upon length of service must be calculated to include time spent in the military service. Similarly, in *Edgar v. Magma Copper Co.,*[17] the court ruled that an employee was entitled to vacation and holiday pay where he would have met the conditions for same if he had remained on the payroll instead of served in the military.

Where, however, the vacation clause of the collective agreement requires an employee to work a minimum time in one year in order to earn full vacation benefits, the Supreme Court found that "the benefit in question was intended as a form of compensation . . . where the work requirement constitutes a bona fide effort to compensate for work actually performed, the fact that it correlates only loosely with the benefit is not enough to make the statutory guarantee." Accordingly, the court ruled that the Selective Service Act did not require a full vacation payment in any year to a returning veteran who did not meet the work requirement.[18]

Similar to the above decision, the courts have ruled that where an apprenticeship program requires a set hours of work before journeyman status and pay accordingly are achieved, the returning veteran must put in these hours before being eligible for journeyman pay.[19] Likewise, returning veterans are not entitled to credit for time spent in the military service either for the calculation of the amount of their company pension, or for the vesting of their pension rights where 1) a year's credit required a fixed number of hours work, and 2) credit was given for work related but not for non-work related absences.[20]

### Section 404 of the Vietnam Act

Section 404 of the Vietnam Era Veterans' Readjustment Assistance Act of 1974 both reaffirms the prior legislation concerning

---

[15] *Foster v. Dravo Corporation,* 420 U.S. 92 (1975). See also *Fishgold v. Sullivan Drydock and Repair Company,* 328 U.S. 275 (1946); and *McKimey v. Missouri-Kansas-Texas R. Co.,* 35.7 U.S. 265 (1958).

[16] 383 U.S. 225 (1966).

[17] 389 U.S. 323 (1967).

[18] *Foster v. Dravo Corporation, supra,* note 15.

[19] *Hilton et al. v. Thriftimart, Inc.,* 77 LC 10,925 (D.C. California, 1975).

[20] *LaPinta v. Ohio Crankshaft Division,* 77 LC 11,156 (N.D. Ohio, 1975).

returning veterans to their "rightful place," and in addition requires former employers affirmatively to find a job for veterans no longer able to perform their former work. Thus Section 404 essentially provides that a returning veteran be entitled, if still qualified to perform the duties of such position, to restoration by his former employer to the position, or a position similar to the one which he had before he went on active duty. In addition, his seniority status, and pay are to be counted for the period of time the individual was in military service so that upon returning, any increases in seniority status, and pay due to that position will be given to him. This part of Section 404 reiterates the obligations of the Military Selective Service Act and does not appreciably change them.

Section 404, however, adds another requirement. If the returning veteran is not qualified to return to his former job by reason of a disability sustained while in the service, the employer is obligated to offer the disabled veteran a position which he is *qualified to perform*. In addition, the seniority and former pay of the returning veteran should be considered when the employer makes the job offer. Section 404 is thus essentially an affirmative *re-employment* obligation for employers but concerns only those employees who served in the military and desire to return to their former employment. Section 402, as discussed earlier in the chapter, is an affirmative employment obligation for all covered employment in so far as any Vietnam-era veteran is involved.

## SECTION 404 CONCILIATION AND LITIGATION

The Department of Labor is responsible for the initial enforcement of Section 402 disputes, attempts to resolve the issues involving Section 404 by conciliation. The Department of Labor, however, does not have the authority to issue administrative rulings pertaining to Section 404 which have the force of law, as it does for Section 402. Rather the Department of Justice handles all litigation brought pursuant to Section 404. Although the end of the Vietnam conflict has greatly lessened the impact of Section 404, there is an active and developed case law as well as a number of significant Department of Labor conciliations. Some key cases are summarized below by type of issue.

## Discharge and Pay Rates

1. In one case, the grievant was employed by a shipbuilding company in Virginia in a position requiring manual labor; he left to enter military service. While in the service, he incurred a service-connected heart condition. Upon release from the service, he was reinstated, because of his heart, by his former employer in a clerical position. He worked from April 1974 to July 1974, and during that time, he was "admonished" for absenteeism, clerical errors because of his poor handwriting, etc. He was recommended for a transfer which he refused to consider because he would have to return to manual labor. He was retained in the clerical position with a warning, but was finally discharged for unsatisfactory work. He filed a claim with the Department of Labor stating that, he had been entitled to a rate of $3.26 per hour, rather than $2.46 per hour; he claimed that he was not given enough time to learn the job and that he had been pressured in it. The union felt that he should have been transferred rather than discharged. It was the Department of Labor's contention that the employer had not tried to find a suitable position for him upon his return and that they could have found another clerical position that was not as demanding. The Department of Labor recommended the case for litigation, but the Department of Justice was able to obtain a $500 settlement, which the grievant accepted.

2. This case was settled May 15, 1976 for $1,500. While in the service, a veteran had suffered a service-connected injury which resulted in an early arthritic condition of the spine. The Veterans Administration doctor recommended not lifting anything over forty pounds; he returned to employment, which involved physically demanding work and he suffered severe back discomfort. Also, during his absence, a junior employee had been promoted to "Heat Treat Helper," a less demanding position. The grievant was then terminated. The Department of Labor first obtained reinstatement to a legally proper position with proper seniority and pay on December 8, 1974. The company, however, refused to compensate the veteran for his wage losses for the period July 26, 1974 to December 8, 1974. The Department of Labor found that he had been "improperly restored" to his former position and obtained the backpay for him.

*Reinstatement*

1. This case was settled for $500 in March of 1976. The grievant had been employed by a Baltimore Hospital. He had enlisted in the Maryland National Guard. The hospital failed to reinstate him timely. After the Department of Labor conciliation failed, the Department of Justice won the settlement before going to court.

2. Grievant was employed from October 21, 1969 until March 26, 1970, when he left the position for military service. He was discharged from the service on January 1, 1974; he timely reapplied for work on February 25, 1974. The defendant corporation, however, refused to reinstate him until the Department of Labor intervened; grievant was reinstated on July 1, 1974, but lost wages were refused. The case was recommended for litigation and the Department of Justice was able to secure a settlement of $1,000, which the grievant accepted. Actual net lost wages were $1,460.97 after subtracting what he earned at a temporary position with another company.

3. This case was settled in U.S. District Court, Washington, D.C., prior to hearing. Grievant was employed at an "other than temporary" position from April 30, 1974 to May 17, 1974. He entered the service for inactive duty from May 17, 1974 to May 19, 1974, obtaining a leave of absence from his company. On May 20, 1974, he tried to return to work, but was refused and discharged. The company was charged with discrimination against grievant solely because of his military obligation. The case was settled on September 15, 1975 with grievant receiving $7,500 and a job.

4. A veteran worked for a Pittsburgh corporation from May 20, 1972 until October 30, 1972, when he entered the military service. Upon his release October 25, 1974, he re-applied for work, but defendant company refused to reinstate him until February 4, 1975. The Department of Labor conciliation won a backpay settlement of $1,200 to make up for his lost wages.

5. The grievant was employed by a West Virginia company from July 31, 1968 until April 24, 1969, when he was inducted for military service. He was discharged from the service on January 23, 1973, re-applied for work, but was refused. The company claimed his position was temporary and that he had originally been hired as a favor to his father who was a long-term employee. Grievant claimed that he had been doing work of auto glass installer; company maintained that the grievant

had actually been doing manual labor (janitorial work) and that his position had been abolished during the time he was in the service. The Department of Labor inspected company records, however, and found that grievant had, as he claimed, actually been doing work as a glass installer, despite company's claim that this was an apprenticeship position. Grievant was offered a laborer position in another location; company claimed that in order to rehire him, it would have to "bump" a married man with two children. The case was settled for $2,500, and the veteran was employed elsewhere on September 8, 1973.

6. *Thomas J. O'Grady v. U.S. Steel Corporation.*[21] The plaintiff enlisted on July 17, 1967, while employed at United States Steel plant. He was discharged on July 31, 1967, but did not seek reinstatement until October 23, 1967. He took on a temporary position with an engineering firm for August and September. Upon discharge from the military, he applied for reinstatement with the company. The court found that "the employee was entitled to reemployment and damages as a returned veteran because his employer sought to evade its statutory obligations by discharging him before he was to report to active duty—the veteran contended that he was discharged by his employer because he was called to active duty." The court said that the Act should be "liberally construed" in protecting veterans' rights.

*Seniority and Pay Rates*

1. Grievant had been employed by a Maryland company on August 31, 1970 and had subsequently been put on layoff status. While laid off, he entered the military. Upon his discharge, he was re-employed on January 1, 1975, but at a pay rate that did not give him credit for military service. Progression to higher pay rates and job levels was also delayed because of this. He settled for $300 after Department of Labor conciliation.

2. *Scott v. Atchison, Topeka, and Santa Fe Railway.*[22] The defendant claimed he was wrongfully denied an appropriate wage upon his discharge from military service. Scott worked as a class D signal helper, and then was offered a promotion to class C assistant signalman which required a transfer; he declined the promotion, however, and his request was granted. He was

---

[21] 78 LC 11,304 (N.D. Illinois, 1973).

[22] 78 LC 11,291 (D.C. Central California, 1976).

drafted in February 1968, and discharged from the military in March 1971. He made a timely re-application for work on June 10, 1971; he was reinstated to class D signal helper and with seniority date of May 17, 1967 and pay of $3.4884 per hour. On September 3, 1971, he entered the student signalman training program for class B position. His seniority was always back-dated to reflect military time credit, but he did not receive class B pay rate until March 16, 1973, the date of his actual promotion.

He initiated action in February, 1975; he felt that he would have been at class B level by June 14, 1971 except for the military service time. He felt he was entitled to the pay difference from June 14, 1971 to March 15, 1973. The issue was: Was it reasonably certain that advancement in the plaintiff's case would have occurred if he had remained in the continuous employment of the defendant? The court found that advancement is not dependent on the mere passage of time and that where advancement depends upon satisfactory completion of a comprehensive training program, a returning veteran cannot show that he would have enjoyed advancement simply by virtue of continuing employment during the time he was in military service.

3. *Wilson v. Toledo Apprenticeship Committee.*[23] In May 1970, the plaintiff took an apprenticeship qualification exam to be a sheetmetal worker. He received a score of 91 and placed seventh on the eligibility list. In the meantime, he continued to work in his current job of "roofer" which he left in December 1970, for military service. He was honorably discharged in January 1973. During his time in the service, one person was called from the list in 1971 and thirteen persons, in 1972. Plaintiff was not placed on the 1973 list because he was not available for work when the list was made up. He claimed that he should have been No. 1 on the list and claimed retroactive seniority as if he were apprenticed in 1972. The court agreed with the defendant that the Act does not cover the plaintiff because he was not "employed" and therefore did not leave a "position." The plaintiff was, however, re-employed by the company with an equitable position and wage scale.

4. *David L. Watkins v. Consumers Power Company.*[24] This case is apparently a key one in regard to statute of limitations problems. It determined that state statutes of limitations **do**

---

[23] 78 LC 11,280 (D.C. Ohio, 1976).

[24] 78 LC 11,449 (D.C. Michigan, 1976).

not apply to Section 404. Plaintiff was re-employed by the defendant after military service at his pre-service position in October 1971. He was laid off in February of 1975, but would not have been laid off if he had been properly credited with seniority due him when he was originally reinstated. The court agreed with the plaintiff, despite company's claim that he was not filing a timely claim.

*Section 404—Final Comment*

Section 404's obligation for employers to reinstate returning veterans continues the obligations in effect since World War II. The additional obligations to re-employ in a suitable position disabled veterans who can no longer perform their former jobs is not likely to loom large in the future now that the Vietnam era is closed. Moreover, such disabled veterans can, if they so desire, file their complaints under the Rehabilitation Act.

## ARBITRATION OF VETERANS EMPLOYMENT RIGHTS

Since the issues concerned in veterans' employment rights following military service necessarily involve issues of what the late Professor Sumner H. Slichter termed "industrial jurisprudence" [25]—hiring, seniority, promotion, lay-offs, job wage rates, etc.—and since veterans employment rights are frequently written into collective agreements, it is not surprising that they are frequently the subject of arbitration. The *Todd Shipyards* case,[26] described below, is one of the few cases, however, which involves the conflict between affirmative action requirements and obligations arising out of the collective agreements, an increasingly familiar situation in civil rights controversies.

In this situation, Todd was required by its union contract to employ through the union hiring hall. It was also, however, subject to the affirmative action requirements of Section 402 of the Vietnam Era Veterans Readjustment Assistance Act. The difficulty arose when a "qualified" Vietnam era veteran applied to the company for work that fell within the union's jurisdiction.

---

[25] Sumner H. Slichter, et al., *The Impact of Collective Bargaining Upon Management* (Washington, D.C.: The Brookings Institution, 1960).

[26] 65 LA 1019 (1975).

Not wanting to violate the provisions of the Act, Todd referred the Vietnam-era veteran to the union hiring hall. The union, however, refused to refer the veteran claiming that it had more individuals on its waiting list who had seniority over the veteran, who already were union-members, and who should be employed before the veteran pursuant to the union contract. Todd chose to fulfill its affirmative action obligation over the collectively bargained obligation with the union by hiring the veteran outside of the hiring hall mechanism, thus deciding to risk the union's displeasure rather than to risk contract debarment.

As a result of the company's unilateral action, the union requested arbitration. The findings of the arbitrator were as follows:

1. There is a clear line of authority developing in discrimination cases that when conflict arises between federal anti-discrimination rules and collective bargaining agreements, federal law will prevail in seniority matters and presumably in hiring practices;

2. the union has acquiesced in past practices of hiring persons directly off the street who were not union members, after which they were referred to the union for dispatch and the union then dispatched them.

Thus, the arbitrator determined, that the combination of past practice and anti-discrimination law overruled the obligations of the company to adhere to the provisions of its collective bargaining agreement.

The *Todd* case illustrates a very crucial issue that procurement enforced anti-discrimination legislation ignores. The regulations covering Section 402 enforce the provisions of the Act through the contractor only—not the union. The union is obligated by the Taft-Hartley Act—to represent its membership fairly and in the most responsible manner possible. By insisting in the instant case that the more senior members be employed at Todd before the Vietnam era veteran, the union was discharging its statutory obligations even though they were in direct conflict with some of the employer's statutory obligations.

The employer, by contrast, was compelled to choose between acting unilaterally thereby possibly violating the Taft-Hartley Act and a certain violation of the collective agreement and a violation of the Vietnam Era Veterans' Readjustment Assistance Act of 1974. Assessing the economic impact of both, Todd chose to violate the former and go to arbitration rather than to risk losing its government contracts. The failure of Congress to accommodate new laws to existing legislation not only places employers and unions in a position where they must choose which law to obey, but also by generating such conflicts adds unnecessarily to costly litigation.

## VIETNAM-ERA VETERAN STATUS, 1976-1977

The first act of the Carter Administration was to pardon Vietnam-era military draft evaders. According to one national news magazine, "It was an effort to offset criticism of his pardon of draft evaders, say insiders, that was behind Carter's last-minute 1.3-billion-dollar plan to find jobs for Vietnam veterans." [27]

Whatever the reason, employment problems have indeed existed for some Vietnam-era veterans. Table VI-3 shows that the overall unemployment rate for these veterans was lower in January 1977 than the rate for non-veterans—7.6 percent compared with 8.2 percent. Moreover, Vietnam-era veterans age 30-34 had an unemployment rate of 3.6 percent as compared with a non-veteran rate for the same age group of 4.2 percent. In the 25-29 year age group the non-veteran rate of 7.7 percent was slightly lower than the veteran rate of 7.9 percent.

In the 20-24 age group, however, the unemployment rate for Vietnam-era veterans was 16.8 percent as compared with 10.6 percent for non-veterans. The 558,000 unemployed Vietnam-era veterans are concentrated in this age group. The Carter program proposes to place 140,000 of these unemployed in public service jobs and to place 50,000 to 60,000 more in major corporations for training and employment. According to Secretary of Labor F. Ray Marshall, the Vietnam-era Veterans' Readjustment Assistance Act of 1974 would be applied "to the fullest extent—

---

[27] "Washington Whispers," *U.S. News and World Report*, February 7, 1977, p. 8. At a press conference following his swearing in, Secretary of Labor F. Ray Marshall stressed the veteran program. "Asked if the veterans jobs program would help blunt the criticisms of veterans groups to the President's pardoning of Vietnam draft evaders, Marshall said he didn't know but added that the program was drawn up in consultation with major veterans organizations." *Daily Labor Report*, No. 19, January 27, 1977, p. A-11.

## TABLE VI-3

**Employment status of male Vietnam-Era veterans and nonveterans 20 to 34 years of age**

[Numbers in thousands]

| Employment status | Not seasonally adjusted | | | Seasonally adjusted | | | | | |
|---|---|---|---|---|---|---|---|---|---|
| | Jan. 1976 | Dec. 1976 | Jan. 1977 | Jan. 1976 | Sept. 1976 | Oct. 1976 | Nov. 1976 | Dec. 1976 | Jan. 1977 |
| **VETERANS[1]** | | | | | | | | | |
| **Total, 20 to 34 years:** | | | | | | | | | |
| Civilian noninstitutional population[2] | 6,629 | 6,828 | 6,847 | 6,629 | 6,735 | 6,765 | 6,797 | 6,828 | 6,847 |
| Civilian labor force | 6,235 | 6,433 | 6,492 | 6,221 | 6,364 | 6,309 | 6,436 | 6,456 | 6,486 |
| Employed | 5,615 | 5,930 | 5,881 | 5,723 | 5,795 | 5,832 | 5,891 | 5,918 | 5,995 |
| Unemployed | 620 | 503 | 611 | 498 | 569 | 557 | 545 | 538 | 491 |
| Unemployment rate | 9.9 | 7.8 | 9.4 | 8.0 | 8.9 | 8.7 | 8.5 | 8.3 | 7.6 |
| **20 to 24 years** | | | | | | | | | |
| Civilian noninstitutional population[2] | 1,103 | 1,089 | 1,086 | 1,103 | 1,073 | 1,078 | 1,083 | 1,089 | 1,086 |
| Civilian labor force | 926 | 952 | 975 | 912 | 937 | 951 | 965 | 956 | 964 |
| Employed | 717 | 794 | 772 | 745 | 757 | 770 | 803 | 795 | 802 |
| Unemployed | 209 | 158 | 203 | 167 | 180 | 181 | 162 | 161 | 162 |
| Unemployment rate | 22.6 | 16.6 | 20.8 | 18.3 | 19.2 | 19.0 | 16.8 | 16.8 | 16.8 |
| **25 to 29 years** | | | | | | | | | |
| Civilian noninstitutional population[2] | 3,453 | 3,165 | 3,141 | 3,453 | 3,227 | 3,206 | 3,186 | 3,165 | 3,141 |
| Civilian labor force | 3,296 | 2,985 | 2,981 | 3,291 | 3,046 | 3,019 | 3,021 | 3,010 | 2,972 |
| Employed | 3,005 | 2,756 | 2,689 | 3,056 | 2,804 | 2,780 | 2,760 | 2,749 | 2,736 |
| Unemployed | 291 | 229 | 292 | 235 | 242 | 239 | 261 | 261 | 236 |
| Unemployment rate | 8.8 | 7.7 | 9.8 | 7.1 | 7.9 | 7.9 | 8.6 | 8.7 | 7.9 |
| **30 to 34 years** | | | | | | | | | |
| Civilian noninstitutional population[2] | 2,073 | 2,574 | 2,620 | 2,073 | 2,435 | 2,481 | 2,528 | 2,574 | 2,620 |
| Civilian labor force | 2,013 | 2,496 | 2,536 | 2,018 | 2,381 | 2,419 | 2,450 | 2,490 | 2,550 |
| Employed | 1,893 | 2,380 | 2,420 | 1,922 | 2,234 | 2,282 | 2,328 | 2,374 | 2,457 |
| Unemployed | 120 | 116 | 116 | 96 | 147 | 137 | 122 | 1,116 | 93 |
| Unemployment rate | 6.0 | 4.6 | 4.6 | 4.8 | 6.2 | 5.7 | 5.0 | 4.7 | 3.6 |
| **NONVETERANS** | | | | | | | | | |
| **Total, 20 to 34 years:** | | | | | | | | | |
| Civilian noninstitutional population[2] | 16,349 | 17,036 | 17,116 | 16,349 | 16,911 | 16,954 | 17,008 | 17,036 | 17,116 |
| Civilian labor force | 14,478 | 15,339 | 15,312 | 14,601 | 15,230 | 15,372 | 15,487 | 15,562 | 15,460 |
| Employed | 12,952 | 14,019 | 13,818 | 13,307 | 13,980 | 14,004 | 14,053 | 14,141 | 14,198 |
| Unemployed | 1,526 | 1,320 | 1,494 | 1,294 | 1,250 | 1,368 | 1,434 | 1,421 | 1,262 |
| Unemployment rate | 10.5 | 8.6 | 9.8 | 8.9 | 8.2 | 8.9 | 9.3 | 9.1 | 8.2 |
| **20 to 24 years** | | | | | | | | | |
| Civilian noninstitutional population[2] | 7,802 | 7,981 | 8,018 | 7,802 | 7,968 | 7,976 | 7,989 | 7,981 | 8,018 |
| Civilian labor force | 6,427 | 6,750 | 6,729 | 6,575 | 6,718 | 6,816 | 6,878 | 6,948 | 6,905 |
| Employed | 5,522 | 5,982 | 5,896 | 5,781 | 6,013 | 6,007 | 6,046 | 6,083 | 6,174 |
| Unemployed | 905 | 768 | 833 | 794 | 705 | 809 | 832 | 865 | 731 |
| Unemployment rate | 14.1 | 11.4 | 12.4 | 12.1 | 10.5 | 11.9 | 12.1 | 12.4 | 10.6 |
| **25 to 29 years** | | | | | | | | | |
| Civilian noninstitutional population[2] | 4,708 | 5,188 | 5,211 | 4,708 | 5,141 | 5,157 | 5,175 | 5,188 | 5,211 |
| Civilian labor force | 4,409 | 4,878 | 4,879 | 4,388 | 4,863 | 4,880 | 4,884 | 4,882 | 4,849 |
| Employed | 4,015 | 4,514 | 4,412 | 4,072 | 4,515 | 4,507 | 4,499 | 4,529 | 4,475 |
| Unemployed | 394 | 364 | 467 | 316 | 348 | 373 | 385 | 353 | 374 |
| Unemployment rate | 8.9 | 7.5 | 9.6 | 7.2 | 7.2 | 7.6 | 7.9 | 7.2 | 7.7 |
| **30 to 34 years** | | | | | | | | | |
| Civilian noninstitutional population[2] | 3,839 | 3,867 | 3,887 | 3,839 | 3,802 | 3,821 | 3,844 | 3,867 | 3,887 |
| Civilian labor force | 3,642 | 3,711 | 3,704 | 3,638 | 3,649 | 3,676 | 3,725 | 3,732 | 3,706 |
| Employed | 3,415 | 3,523 | 3,510 | 3,454 | 3,452 | 3,490 | 3,508 | 3,529 | 3,549 |
| Unemployed | 227 | 188 | 194 | 184 | 197 | 186 | 217 | 203 | 157 |
| Unemployment rate | 6.2 | 5.1 | 5.2 | 5.1 | 5.4 | 5.1 | 5.8 | 5.4 | 4.2 |

[1] Vietnam-era veterans are those who served between August 5, 1964, and April 30, 1975.

[2] Since seasonal variations are not present in the population figures, identical numbers appear in the unadjusted and seasonally adjusted columns.

Source: *Employment and Earnings*, Vol. 24 (February 1977), p. 52.

especially the affirmative action provision which calls for the hiring of veterans by firms with federal contracts." [28]

As of March 1977, the program envisioned by Secretary Marshall had not been implemented, and results would obviously not

---

[28] "Marshall Unveils: $1.3 Billion Jobs Plan to Put 200,000 Vietnam Vets Back to Work," *Daily Labor Report*, No. 19, Jan. 27, 1977, p. A-10. The full text of Secretary Marshall's statement is found on pp. A-11-13.

be available till after this monograph has been published. It is clear, however, that as the veterans progress in age, they appear not only to suffer less unemployment, as does the general population, but in addition these veterans also improve their relative standings so that, as noted, both overall and in the higher age groups, their unemployment rate is below that of non-veterans.[29]

## Disabled Veterans

Unemployment data do not reflect the special problems of the disabled veteran. In June 1976, 458,111 Vietnam-era veterans were receiving disability compensation, and 8,954 were receiving pensions.[30] It is not known how many of these were handicapped in terms of employment. Although there are no Department of Labor census data on disabled veterans, the Department has commissioned several studies on the topic. One study found that:

> Except for the college graduated, severely disabled veterans, whether defined by age, race, education, or marital status, have more difficulty than the slightly disabled veterans in finding a job, and, if working, are working for lower pay. Among college graduates under 30 years of age, the differences between slightly and severely disabled veterans in employment . . . are minimal.[31]

Even though the severely disabled veterans qualify under the Rehabilitation Act and are equivalent to most other severely disabled citizens, they differ in one important aspect. Before the war, now disabled veterans were basically without handicaps. Therefore, the experience of the disabled veteran is different from most of the general handicapped population in terms of previous experiences, such as education. As the study reports, the well-educated are best able to overcome their handicaps while those with the least education tend to find labor market acceptance difficult. One of the programs announced by the Carter Administration is to establish "outreach units" staffed by ap-

---

[29] The Secretary's remarks have consistently referred to higher unemployment rates for Vietnam-era veterans, both totally and relatively, than the data in Table VI-3, reproduced from a U.S. Department of Labor publication, show.

[30] *Veterans Administration Data on Vietnam Era Veterans*, p. 35.

[31] Thurlow R. Wilson, John A. Richards, and Deborah H. Bercini, *Disabled Veterans of The Vietnam Era: Employment Problems and Programs* (Alexandria, Virginia: Human Resources Research Organization, 1975), p. vi.

proximately 2,500 disabled veterans in the employment service offices in the country's 100 largest cities at a cost of $20 million. The function of these personnel will be to identify disabled veterans needing job assistance, and then in utilizing job training programs and assist them to find jobs.[32]

Veterans rated 10 percent or more disabled for compensation purposes may be provided the training that they require to overcome the handicapping effect of their disability. As of June 30, 1976, 73,327 had entered training and 11,872 were in training.[33] This training effort thus involves 18.5 percent of the 458,111 veterans rated for compensation. The outreach program is designed to increase such training where needed.

### Veterans and Education

Table VI-4 shows that over five million Vietnam-era veterans have entered training, and nearly three million have done training in institutions of higher learning (colleges). This augurs well for the employment prospects of these veterans and is undoubtedly a major reason why the employment status of veterans improves so dramatically as their years of age advance. Earlier studies found that a greater percentage of Vietnam-era veterans have gone to school under the GI Bill and a greater proportion are in college than was true of veterans of World War II and of the Korean conflict.[34]

## EMPLOYER COMMENTS

The survey of major employers, made during July and August 1976, and referred to in earlier chapters, found that there was virtually no experience either with Section 402 or 404 of the Vietnam Era Veterans Readjustment Assistance Act of 1975. The newness of the law and the general practice of looking favorably upon veterans employment, which major companies have long done, undoubtedly accounted for this lack of experience. Two companies did, however, have related experiences which are set forth below:

---

[32] *Daily Labor Report,* No. 19, January 27, 1977, p. A-10. The first such employment of disabled veterans began in Kansas in March 1977. *Daily Labor Report,* no. 63, March 31, 1977, p. A-5.

[33] *Veterans Administration Data on Vietnam Era Veterans,* p. 40.

[34] Gover and McEaddy, "Job Situation of Vietnam-era Veterans," p. 25.

### TABLE VI-4

EDUCATIONAL ASSISTANCE FOR VIETNAM ERA VETERANS [a]
(Chapter 34, Title 38, U.S.C.)

June 30, 1976

| Item | Number |
|------|--------|
| Applications received to date | 5,505,669 |
| Entered training to date | 5,131,170 |
|    Institutions of higher learning | 2,916,655 |
|    Other schools | 1,801,737 |
|    On-job training | 412,778 |
| In training | 789,901 |
|    Institutions of higher learning | 448,475 |
|    Other schools | 274,904 |
|    On-job training | 66,522 |
|    Included in above | |
|       Cooperative farm training | (14,848) |
|       Educational disadvantaged | (20,440) |
|       Flight training | (14,054) |
|       Training by correspondence | (164,668) |
| Terminated | 4,341,269 |
| Entitlement exhausted | NA |

[a] Includes service personnel.

Source: Semi-Annual reports of VETERAN POPULATION—BY AGE, REGIONAL OFFICE, PERIOD OF SERVICE AND STATE OF RESIDENCE, Research Division, Reports and Statistics Service, Office of Controller, Veterans Administration, Washington, D.C.

1. In one case, an applicant filed a charge with the Equal Employment Opportunity Commission claiming that he was discriminated against and not employed because he was a black Vietnam war veteran. The company found that not only was the applicant not a veteran, but he had been in jail for selling drugs during the time period he claimed veteran (service) status. In addition, he had falsified his employment application. Nevertheless the EEOC had not dismissed the case.

2. In another situation, the company involved expressed alarm over pressure from local Comprehensive Employment and Training Act (CETA) sponsoring agencies trying to induce it to accept trainees, some of whom were veterans, when the company had a strong veterans employment program and good relations with the state employment service. The company's

collective labor agreement provided for the employment of veterans with anything other than a dishonorable discharge, and its salaried employment policy affirmatively sought veterans with job related records. It was felt that a CETA relationship would be diversionary rather than helpful. Other experiences of this nature may occur since the Carter Administration is planning to utilize CETA agencies in its special veterans program.

## CONCLUDING REMARKS

The Vietnam Era Veterans Readjustment Assistance Act of 1974 has not apparently had much direct impact. The Act seems to be the result of the nation's conscience toward a group whose patriotism often seemed to be less rewarded than those who evaded service, legally and illegally. The recent Carter Administration program appears to be an amplification of the same motives.

When comparing the educational and employment data of veterans and non-veterans, an overall picture emerges. That picture is of a group who are generally far from helpless, striving to improve, and in many instances, actually ahead of their non-veteran counterparts. The exception is found in the severely disabled non-college educated veteran, and the young minority veteran without work and job skills. Their stories are poignant and deserving of attention. A separate statute such as this Act, however, does appear to be both unnecessary and duplicative. Almost to a man (and to a woman) each Vietnam-era veteran who could claim a special need has already been covered under one or more other statutes, and sometimes this includes local and state laws as well as federal.

# PART FIVE

*Concluding Comments*

# CHAPTER VII

# Some General Observations

Since the New Deal of Franklin D. Roosevelt in the 1930s, public policy in the form of federal, state and municipal legislation has attempted to address the grievances of various groups in our society. The Age Discrimination in Employment Act of 1967, the Rehabilitation Act of 1973 and the Vietnam Era Veterans Readjustment Assistance Act of 1974 are each designed to support a particular constituency. The number of so-called protected groups including those under the jurisdiction of Title VII of the Civil Rights Act of 1964, as amended, thus, encompasses a growing majority of the nation's labor force.

The expansion of nondiscrimination legislation and regulations to include those in the 40-65 age group, the handicapped, and the disabled, and Vietnam-era veterans has had, and will continue to have, a notable impact upon companies, union, and many members of society, as well as those protected. It cannot be denied that many individuals have been helped by these laws when they became the victims of unwitting or purposeful discrimination. This is certainly the result contemplated by Congress when such legislation is enacted. But these laws also have costs associated with them; although to measure the real costs—as well as the benefits—with any degree of acceptable accuracy is difficult if not impossible. Nevertheless, it would appear that there are very substantial costs associated with all nondiscrimination laws, and the three laws examined in this study are no exception.

## COSTS AND BENEFITS

Before the passage of the age, handicapped, and disabled, and Vietnam era veterans laws, many companies did discriminate against one or more of these groups. But discrimination has a cost. Not only are those hurt who have been denied an opportunity to utilize their skills and make a maximum contribution to industry and to society; in addition, the employer artificially limits his labor market and thereby is likely to employ someone less able and productive than someone he would hire if merit were the guiding employment criterion.

On the other hand, the substitution of "affirmative action" for equal or merit employment tends to move society toward status or quota representation. By adding older workers, the handicapped, and Vietnam-era veterans to minorities and women, those for whom affirmative action is required, Congress has required American companies to be as concerned about their employment "mix" as they are about employee capacity and efficiency. The company labor force must mirror the various race, sex, age, veteran, and normality aspects of the contiguous labor force, or the company faces severe economic consequences. Yet there is no rational or statistical reason why labor demand and supply should be so equated in a given area; in fact, the different obligations can even be quite contradictory. The conflict between affirmative action requirements for older workers, for women, and for Vietnam-era veterans are clear examples. Even more important is the indisputable fact that affirmative action in behalf of these groups requires favoring them in employment and promotion and thus clearly discriminates against unprotected personnel. When the latter are denied opportunity in order to meet affirmative action requirements, the costs to the individuals and to society are no different than when discrimination affected those now protected. As Professor Thomas Sowell has written:

> The grand assumption that body count proves discrimination proceeds as if people would be evenly distributed in the absence of deliberate barriers. There is not a speck of evidence for this assumption and there is a mountain of evidence against it . . . .[1]

Although Professor Sowell's remarks were directed at affirmative action goals for women and minorities, they are equally applicable to older workers, to the handicapped, and to Vietnam-era veterans.

## Age Discrimination

Older workers now have the protection not only of the Act itself but of a sizable body of court precedent as well. It now ap-

---

[1] Thomas Sowell, "A Black Conservative Dissents," *The New York Times Magazine*, August 8, 1976, p. 14.

pears that many problems of interpretation of the Act have been resolved, but one key issue still requires definitive interpretation.

The key unsettled issue is the question of mandatory retirement. This is a crucial issue for employers and employees alike. It may have the most profound affect on a wide range of issues depending upon the outcome either of present litigation or future congressional legislation.

Mandatory retirement affects not only the employee who reaches 65, but actually reaches through the whole economy. It allows those responsible for evaluating a firm's pension system to calculate the future plan costs with a high degree of accuracy even where the pension permits retirement at various ages, but requires retirement no later than a given age.[2]

It also allows companies to retain the flexibility needed to cope with changing economic circumstances or the movement of population demographics. Although age 65 is generally the accepted year for normal retirement, it is not cast in stone by legislative or judicial decree, and this is the crucial point. Flexibility allows many companies to institute retirement at earlier ages than 65 with benefits equal to those originally reserved for persons reaching 65. In fact, many firms have instituted special early retirement programs without reduced benefits because of the increased demand for early retirement by their own employees. This appears to be especially strong among the organized ranks in basic industry, and the trend is also evident elsewhere.

The issue of mandatory retirement has also come under attack from unexpected quarters. According to a study by The Conference Board,[3] the federal government "is beginning to press for an end to early retirement policies in order to prevent the loss of payments with social security by workers who retire early." The report also cited other factors impacting upon the mandatory retirement issue. They included such items as escalating company costs, the likelihood of lawsuits under the Age Discrimination in Employment Act, and recurring recessions. The study said in part:

> Up to now, both federal and state legislation and the courts have looked favorably upon the practice of mandatory retirement

---

[2] See Dan M. McGill, *Fundamentals of Private Pensions*, 3rd Ed., (Homewood, Ill.: Richard D. Irwin, Inc., 1975), pp. 323-324.

[3] "Pre-Retirement Counseling On The Rise, Conference Board Survey Says," *Daily Labor Report*, (Number 65) April 4, 1977, pp. A-2-4.

at age 65. Indications are that they will go on doing so as long
as current economic conditions prevail. Emerging developments,
however, such as the steady increase in the numbers of social security beneficiaries and the corresponding decrease in the number of
social security taxpayers, could eventually change present legislative and judicial attitudes.[4]

While the report does offer some valuable insights into several
aspects of the mandatory retirement problem, there are other
difficulties which need to be examined before legislation eliminating mandatory retirement can be seriously considered.

First, and probably foremost, is the question of where organized
labor fits into the equation. Labor spokesmen have repeatedly
been on record as saying they do not desire any unilateral
changes in mandatory retirement programs or laws. In fact, organized labor has been at the forefront of the trend in reducing the ages at which employees may retire prior to age 65 with
full benefits. This has continued to be one of their key bargaining topics, and any move to change this or remove it from labor's
control altogether would surely meet stiff opposition. In addition, the current studies and legislative bearings have paid no sub-
stantive attention to the problem an employer would face if
mandatory retirement were outlawed. By seeking to enforce
such a policy through the employer while ignoring the consequences
of bargaining relationships would place unfair burdens upon
employers. Furthermore, those companies which have pension
plans find that most employee presure is exerted towards earlier
retirement, not increasing the retirement age, because as long
as adequate benefits are available, a given group of employees will
opt for retirement.

The pressure by some groups and some older employees and
retirees to eliminate mandatory retirement is, in many respects,
a result of the same factors which have induced women in unprecedented numbers to enter the labor market. Improved medical treatment, inflation, the general absence of physical strain
in the majority of jobs, the increasing educational levels of the
general population, the desire for more income, smaller and
less closely-knit family structure, and the proclivity of Congress
to pass nondiscrimination legislation for almost every conceivable
group have all played a part in this process.

The other key issue, the nature of BFOQ, appears to be well
on the way toward resolution. Its construction is narrow, but not

---

[4] *Ibid.*, p. A-3.

so narrow as to place clearly impossible or unfair burdens of proof upon employers.

## Handicapped Discrimination

The disabled face many unknowns in the pursuit of their employment rights as do employers who must somehow cope with the vagueness of who is covered under the Act and how they must be accommodated. Although the Department of Labor has given practical examples of inexpensive accommodations to employers, they are limited in number and do not address obviously fundamental problems. As written, both the Act and the regulations are open-ended and do not consider cumulative costs. Accommodation is required for every qualified handicapped applicant or employee, including those with mental handicaps. Although the spirit of enforcement today is generally constructive— witness the absence of litigation—that may change in the future, especially if the Department of Labor adopts the philosophy of extending the Act to its farthest limits, which Congress seems to have mandated in the 1974 amendments. That such a policy has been followed with other laws under the Department's jurisdiction only lends support to the apprehension that currently exists among covered employers.

A key feature of the handicapped legislation is its impact on physical examination and other screening devices. Companies utilizing this traditional form of entry requirement may well be doing so at their peril. The broad definition of handicap hiring within the Act's coverage covers a large range of personnel heretofore considered physically and mentally normal. This was the work of Congress, overruling a more manageable interpretation by the Department of Labor. As a result, the less handicapped, those only slightly disadvantaged, may well have been given more protection by this law than those more severely handicapped.

## Disabled and Vietnam Era Veterans Discrimination

This legislation appears to be the least needed of any Civil Rights laws that now exist. The disabled veteran uses the Rehabilitation Act; many veterans are more qualified than their civilian counterparts; and those who do need assistance are more likely to be better served by other nondiscrimination laws, job-training programs, or education aid. About the only positive aspect of this law is that it will result in government hiring and public service job creation for disabled veterans and veterans of the Vietnam era. This is expensive, but as a Vietnam-era veteran, this writer can empathize with the spirit behind the program while questioning its need.

## THE QUESTION OF AGENCY OVERLAP

The laws discussed in this monograph add still another administrative burden which must adversely affect the profitability, competitiveness, and, therefore, job creating potential of industry. There has been no effective coordination among agencies in enforcing equal employment matters. Even agencies within the U.S. Department of Labor do not seem to cooperate effectively. This has resulted in monumental amounts of paperwork, including duplications in affirmative action plan preparation, inspections by various state, federal agencies, and even municipal agencies, plus thousands of hours of managerial and executive time wasted by re-preparing for, and explaining the same information to various bureaucracies.

The litigation costs are also enormous, and made more so, by the attempts of enforcement agencies to stretch the laws to their utmost boundaries, or even, as the Court of Appeals, Third Circuit, aptly noted, "rather than proposing an amendment to Congress, as Congress had instructed . . . [seek] to change the Act by court decision or administrative fiat." [5] Again the burden on enterprise is severe, and the impact on employment, including the employment of those the laws seek to protect, cannot be anything but adverse.

### Superagency

The confused and diffuse anti-bias regulatory situation has lent support to proposals to create a "superagency" to enforce government antidiscrimination programs and to lodge all such activity

---

[5] *Zinger v. Blanchette,* —— F.2d —— (3rd Cir. 1977). In the same vein, the U.S. Supreme Court rebuked the Equal Employment Opportunity Commission in a recent case: "The EEOC guideline in question does not fare well. . . . It is not a contemporaneous interpretation of Title VII, since it was first promulgated eight years after the enactment of that Title. More importantly the 1972 guideline fully contradicts the position which the agency has enunciated at an earlier date, closer to the enactment of the governing statute." *General Electric Company v. Gilbert,* —— U.S. ——, 45 U.S.L.W. 4031 (1976).

therein, including the enforcement mechanisms pertaining to old age, handicapped, and Vietnam-era veterans. On the face, this is appealing since it presumably would bring some uniformity and consistency to the situation. The word "presumably" is used advisedly; thus far, even different agencies within the Department of Labor have been neither consistent nor cooperative with each other. Since each enforcement agency in government has its own bureaucracy, structure and constituency, putting them within a single umbrella organization would not, by itself, bring unity in approach or consistency in action.

The Rehabilitation Act and the Vietnam Era Veterans' Readjustment Assistance Act are both enforced through the government's procurement process, a mechanism which is both unfair and incomplete in application. It is unfair chiefly because the covered contractor must bear the full brunt of responsibility for compliance while other parties, particularly unions, may escape the reach of enforcement activitiy. It is also unfair because the contract compliance procedure assumes that doing business with the government is a privilege. Therefore, the enforcing agency is under a correspondingly reduced burden to follow due process as required under other civil rights laws. This enforcement process can become a form of implicit coercion as the government seeks to gain compliance from contractors with vague, often difficult-to-interpret laws, such as the Rehabilitation Act, by threatening to take away business.

Affirmative action is required by the Department of Labor regardless of any showing of past or present discrimination. The contractor must, in effect, provide a "fair share" of work to the affected group. In practice, this would seem to require favoritism of the minority involved. Sanctions are severe even though actual formal debarment is rare. All OFCCP is required to do is to hold the contractor "nonresponsible" because, for example, the contracting officer decides that an affirmative action plan is unsatisfactory. If this occurs, the contractor will be blacklisted. Obviously, where considerable business is at stake, the companies will agree to actions and programs which may well be totally unwarranted rather than suffer great economic loss. To permit such arbitrary and capricious authority to exist is certainly questionable; to transfer it to a superagency and, thereby, probably to enhance its use would seem intolerable.

The contract compliance mechanism is incomplete because many businesses are not government contractors or subcontractors.

Certainly those businesses which have a marginal dollar volume with the government have every incentive to eliminate that business, not because they want to discriminate, but because the overhead costs of compliance are very high.

## FINAL COMMENT

The basic assumption underlying much of the discussion of equal employment opportunity enforcement is often quite simplistic. It assumes that if any inequality exists, the reason is that enforcement mechanisms have failed. Past history, inadequate training and education, the varying natures of industrial job structures, and the desires of the various affected groups are largely ignored while the alleged discrimination which may or may not exist is given all the attention. It is, of course, proper that discrimination and all its attendant evils be eliminated, but as Professor Charles Killingsworth noted almost a decade ago, "There appears to be a reasonable basis for doubting that this factor [discrimination] is the principal present source of economic disadvantage . . . ." [6]

If this is so, he pointed out, then we are diverting attention and effort from effective remedial action. Would it not be wise, therefore, to utilize training, education, and real conciliation to work for improvement of opportunities for the groups discussed in this study and concurrently to lessen the emphasis upon litigation designed to expand legal boundaries? If this could be done, if public policy were aimed at creating real *opportunity* for all protected groups, then the confusion over numbers might dissipate, and the emphasis could be placed upon expanding the labor market opportunities for all. Possibly then, employers would find themselves in a more agreeable situation—an expanded labor market filled increasingly with highly trained and skilled people from all protected groups.

---

[6] Charles C. Killingsworth, *Jobs and Incomes for Negroes* (Washington, D.C.: National Manpower Policy Task Force and University of Michigan, 1968), p. 31.

# Appendix A

## THE AGE DISCRIMINATION IN EMPLOYMENT ACT

Public Law 90-202
90th Congress, S. 830
December 15, 1967

## An Act

To prohibit age discrimination in employment.

81 STAT. 602

*Be it enacted by the Senate and House of Representatives of the United States of America in Congress assembled,* That this Act may be cited as the "Age Discrimination in Employment Act of 1967".

Age Discrimination in Employment Act of 1967.

### STATEMENT OF FINDINGS AND PURPOSE

SEC. 2. (a) The Congress hereby finds and declares that—

(1) in the face of rising productivity and affluence, older workers find themselves disadvantaged in their efforts to retain employment, and especially to regain employment when displaced from jobs;

(2) the setting of arbitrary age limits regardless of potential for job performance has become a common practice, and certain otherwise desirable practices may work to the disadvantage of older persons;

(3) the incidence of unemployment, especially long-term unemployment with resultant deterioration of skill, morale, and employer acceptability is, relative to the younger ages, high among older workers; their numbers are great and growing; and their employment problems grave;

(4) the existence in industries affecting commerce, of arbitrary discrimination in employment because of age, burdens commerce and the free flow of goods in commerce.

(b) It is therefore the purpose of this Act to promote employment of older persons based on their ability rather than age; to prohibit arbitrary age discrimination in employment; to help employers and workers find ways of meeting problems arising from the impact of age on employment.

### EDUCATION AND RESEARCH PROGRAM

SEC. 3. (a) The Secretary of Labor shall undertake studies and provide information to labor unions, management, and the general public concerning the needs and abilities of older workers, and their potentials for continued employment and contribution to the economy. In order to achieve the purposes of this Act, the Secretary of Labor shall carry on a continuing program of education and information, under which he may, among other measures—

(1) undertake research, and promote research, with a view to reducing barriers to the employment of older persons, and the promotion of measures for utilizing their skills;

(2) publish and otherwise make available to employers, professional societies, the various media of communication, and other interested persons the findings of studies and other materials for the promotion of employment;

(3) foster through the public employment service system and through cooperative effort the development of facilities of public and private agencies for expanding the opportunities and potentials of older persons;

(4) sponsor and assist State and community informational and educational programs.

(b) Not later than six months after the effective date of this Act, the Secretary shall recommend to the Congress any measures he may deem desirable to change the lower or upper age limits set forth in section 12.

Recommendation to Congress.

48-081 O

Pub. Law 90-202     - 2 -     December 15, 1967
81 STAT. 603

PROHIBITION OF AGE DISCRIMINATION

Sec. 4. (a) It shall be unlawful for an employer—

(1) to fail or refuse to hire or to discharge any individual or otherwise discriminate against any individual with respect to his compensation, terms, conditions, or privileges of employment, because of such individual's age;

(2) to limit, segregate, or classify his employees in any way which would deprive or tend to deprive any individual of employment opportunities or otherwise adversely affect his status as an employee, because of such individual's age; or

(3) to reduce the wage rate of any employee in order to comply with this Act.

(b) It shall be unlawful for an employment agency to fail or refuse to refer for employment, or otherwise to discriminate against, any individual because of such individual's age, or to classify or refer for employment any individual on the basis of such individual's age.

(c) It shall be unlawful for a labor organization—

(1) to exclude or to expel from its membership, or otherwise to discriminate against, any individual because of his age;

(2) to limit, segregate, or classify its membership, or to classify or fail or refuse to refer for employment any individual, in any way which would deprive or tend to deprive any individual of employment opportunities, or would limit such employment opportunities or otherwise adversely affect his status as an employee or as an applicant for employment, because of such individual's age;

(3) to cause or attempt to cause an employer to discriminate against an individual in violation of this section.

(d) It shall be unlawful for an employer to discriminate against any of his employees or applicants for employment, for an employment agency to discriminate against any individual, or for a labor organization to discriminate against any member thereof or applicant for membership, because such individual, member or applicant for membership has opposed any practice made unlawful by this section, or because such individual, member or applicant for membership has made a charge, testified, assisted, or participated in any manner in an investigation, proceeding, or litigation under this Act.

(e) It shall be unlawful for an employer, labor organization, or employment agency to print or publish, or cause to be printed or published, any notice or advertisement relating to employment by such an employer or membership in or any classification or referral for employment by such a labor organization, or relating to any classification or referral for employment by such an employment agency, indicating any preference, limitation, specification, or discrimination, based on age.

(f) It shall not be unlawful for an employer, employment agency, or labor organization—

(1) to take any action otherwise prohibited under subsections (a), (b), (c), or (e) of this section where age is a bona fide occupational qualification reasonably necessary to the normal operation of the particular business, or where the differentiation is based on reasonable factors other than age;

(2) to observe the terms of a bona fide seniority system or any bona fide employee benefit plan such as a retirement, pension, or insurance plan, which is not a subterfuge to evade the purposes of this Act, except that no such employee benefit plan shall excuse the failure to hire any individual; or

(3) to discharge or otherwise discipline an individual for good cause.

### STUDY BY SECRETARY OF LABOR

SEC. 5. The Secretary of Labor is directed to undertake an appropriate study of institutional and other arrangements giving rise to involuntary retirement, and report his findings and any appropriate legislative recommendations to the President and to the Congress.  *Reports to President and Congress.*

### ADMINISTRATION

SEC. 6. The Secretary shall have the power—

(a) to make delegations, to appoint such agents and employees, and to pay for technical assistance on a fee for service basis, as he deems necessary to assist him in the performance of his functions under this Act;

(b) to cooperate with regional, State, local, and other agencies, and to cooperate with and furnish technical assistance to employers, labor organizations, and employment agencies to aid in effectuating the purposes of this Act.

### RECORDKEEPING, INVESTIGATION, AND ENFORCEMENT

SEC. 7. (a) The Secretary shall have the power to make investigations and require the keeping of records necessary or appropriate for the administration of this Act in accordance with the powers and procedures provided in sections 9 and 11 of the Fair Labor Standards Act of 1938, as amended (29 U.S.C. 209 and 211).

(b) The provisions of this Act shall be enforced in accordance with the powers, remedies, and procedures provided in sections 11(b), 16 (except for subsection (a) thereof), and 17 of the Fair Labor Standards Act of 1938, as amended (29 U.S.C. 211(b), 216, 217), and subsection (c) of this section. Any act prohibited under section 4 of this Act shall be deemed to be a prohibited act under section 15 of the Fair Labor Standards Act of 1938, as amended (29 U.S.C. 215). Amounts owing to a person as a result of a violation of this Act shall be deemed to be unpaid minimum wages or unpaid overtime compensation for purposes of sections 16 and 17 of the Fair Labor Standards Act of 1938, as amended (29 U.S.C. 216, 217): *Provided,* That liquidated damages shall be payable only in cases of willful violations of this Act. In any action brought to enforce this Act the court shall have jurisdiction to grant such legal or equitable relief as may be appropriate to effectuate the purposes of this Act, including without limitation judgments compelling employment, reinstatement or promotion, or enforcing the liability for amounts deemed to be unpaid minimum wages or unpaid overtime compensation under this section. Before instituting any action under this section, the Secretary shall attempt to eliminate the discriminatory practice or practices alleged, and to effect voluntary compliance with the requirements of this Act through informal methods of conciliation, conference, and persuasion.

*52 Stat. 1065, 1066; 63 Stat. 916.*

*52 Stat. 1069; 75 Stat. 74.*

*52 Stat. 1068.*

(c) Any person aggrieved may bring a civil action in any court of competent jurisdiction for such legal or equitable relief as will effectuate the purposes of this Act: *Provided,* That the right of any person to bring such action shall terminate upon the commencement of an action by the Secretary to enforce the right of such employee under this Act.

(d) No civil action may be commenced by any individual under this section until the individual has given the Secretary not less than sixty days' notice of an intent to file such action. Such notice shall be filed—

(1) within one hundred and eighty days after the alleged unlawful practice occurred, or

(2) in a case to which section 14(b) applies, within three hundred days after the alleged unlawful practice occurred or within thirty days after receipt by the individual of notice of termination of proceedings under State law, whichever is earlier.

Upon receiving a notice of intent to sue, the Secretary shall promptly notify all persons named therein as prospective defendants in the action and shall promptly seek to eliminate any alleged unlawful practice by informal methods of conciliation, conference, and persuasion.

61 Stat. 87,89.
29 USC 255, 259.

(e) Sections 6 and 10 of the Portal-to-Portal Act of 1947 shall apply to actions under this Act.

## NOTICES TO BE POSTED

SEC. 8. Every employer, employment agency, and labor organization shall post and keep posted in conspicuous places upon its premises a notice to be prepared or approved by the Secretary setting forth information as the Secretary deems appropriate to effectuate the purposes of this Act.

## RULES AND REGULATIONS

80 Stat. 381.

SEC. 9. In accordance with the provisions of subchapter II of chapter 5 of title 5, United States Code, the Secretary of Labor may issue such rules and regulations as he may consider necessary or appropriate for carrying out this Act, and may establish such reasonable exemptions to and from any or all provisions of this Act as he may find necessary and proper in the public interest.

## CRIMINAL PENALTIES

SEC. 10. Whoever shall forcibly resist, oppose, impede, intimidate or interfere with a duly authorized representative of the Secretary while he is engaged in the performance of duties under this Act shall be punished by a fine of not more than $500 or by imprisonment for not more than one year, or by both: *Provided, however,* That no person shall be imprisoned under this section except when there has been a prior conviction hereunder.

## DEFINITIONS

SEC. 11. For the purposes of this Act—

(a) The term "person" means one or more individuals, partnerships, associations, labor organizations, corporations, business trusts, legal representatives, or any organized groups of persons.

(b) The term "employer" means a person engaged in an industry affecting commerce who has twenty-five or more employees for each working day in each of twenty or more calendar weeks in the current or preceding calendar year: *Provided,* That prior to June 30, 1968, employers having fewer than fifty employees shall not be considered employers. The term also means any agent of such a person, but such term does not include the United States, a corporation wholly owned by the Government of the United States, or a State or political subdivision thereof.

81 STAT. 606

(c) The term "employment agency" means any person regularly undertaking with or without compensation to procure employees for an employer and includes an agent of such a person; but shall not include an agency of the United States, or an agency of a State or political subdivision of a State, except that such term shall include the United States Employment Service and the system of State and local employment services receiving Federal assistance.

(d) The term "labor organization" means a labor organization engaged in an industry affecting commerce, and any agent of such an organization, and includes any organization of any kind, any agency, or employee representation committee, group, association, or plan so engaged in which employees participate and which exists for the purpose, in whole or in part, of dealing with employers concerning grievances, labor disputes, wages, rates of pay, hours, or other terms or conditions of employment, and any conference, general committee, joint or system board, or joint council so engaged which is subordinate to a national or international labor organization.

(e) A labor organization shall be deemed to be engaged in an industry affecting commerce if (1) it maintains or operates a hiring hall or hiring office which procures employees for an employer or procures for employees opportunities to work for an employer, or (2) the number of its members (or, where it is a labor organization composed of other labor organizations or their representatives, if the aggregate number of the members of such other labor organization) is fifty or more prior to July 1, 1968, or twenty-five or more on or after July 1, 1968, and such labor organization—

(1) is the certified representative of employees under the provisions of the National Labor Relations Act, as amended, or the Railway Labor Act, as amended; or

61 Stat. 136.
29 USC 167.

(2) although not certified, is a national or international labor organization or a local labor organization recognized or acting as the representative of employees of an employer or employers engaged in an industry affecting commerce; or

44 Stat. 577.
45 USC 151-188.

(3) has chartered a local labor organization or subsidiary body which is representing or actively seeking to represent employees of employers within the meaning of paragraph (1) or (2); or

(4) has been chartered by a labor organization representing or actively seeking to represent employees within the meaning of paragraph (1) or (2) as the local or subordinate body through which such employees may enjoy membership or become affiliated with such labor organization; or

(5) is a conference, general committee, joint or system board, or joint council subordinate to a national or international labor organization, which includes a labor organization engaged in an industry affecting commerce within the meaning of any of the preceding paragraphs of this subsection.

(f) The term "employee" means an individual employed by any employer.

(g) The term "commerce" means trade, traffic, commerce, transportation, transmission, or communication among the several States; or between a State and any place outside thereof; or within the District of Columbia, or a possession of the United States; or between points in the same State but through a point outside thereof.

(h) The term "industry affecting commerce" means any activity, business, or industry in commerce or in which a labor dispute would hinder or obstruct commerce or the free flow of commerce and includes

STAT. 607

Stat. 519.
USC 401
e.

any activity or industry "affecting commerce" within the meaning of the Labor-Management Reporting and Disclosure Act of 1959.

(i) The term "State" includes a State of the United States, the District of Columbia, Puerto Rico, the Virgin Islands, American Samoa, Guam, Wake Island, the Canal Zone, and Outer Continental Shelf lands defined in the Outer Continental Shelf Lands Act.

### LIMITATION

SEC. 12. The prohibitions in this Act shall be limited to individuals who are at least forty years of age but less than sixty-five years of age.

### ANNUAL REPORT

port to Congress.

SEC. 13. The Secretary shall submit annually in January a report to the Congress covering his activities for the preceding year and including such information, data, and recommendations for further legislation in connection with the matters covered by this Act as he may find advisable. Such report shall contain an evaluation and appraisal by the Secretary of the effect of the minimum and maximum ages established by this Act, together with his recommendations to the Congress. In making such evaluation and appraisal, the Secretary shall take into consideration any changes which may have occurred in the general age level of the population, the effect of the Act upon workers not covered by its provisions, and such other factors as he may deem pertinent.

### FEDERAL-STATE RELATIONSHIP

SEC. 14. (a) Nothing in this Act shall affect the jurisdiction of any agency of any State performing like functions with regard to discriminatory employment practices on account of age except that upon commencement of action under this Act such action shall supersede any State action.

(b) In the case of an alleged unlawful practice occurring in a State which has a law prohibiting discrimination in employment because of age and establishing or authorizing a State authority to grant or seek relief from such discriminatory practice, no suit may be brought under section 7 of this Act before the expiration of sixty days after proceedings have been commenced under the State law, unless such proceedings have been earlier terminated: *Provided*, That such sixty-day period shall be extended to one hundred and twenty days during the first year after the effective date of such State law. If any requirement for the commencement of such proceedings is imposed by a State authority other than a requirement of the filing of a written and signed statement of the facts upon which the proceeding is based, the proceeding shall be deemed to have been commenced for the purposes of this subsection at the time such statement is sent by registered mail to the appropriate State authority.

### EFFECTIVE DATE

SEC. 15. This Act shall become effective one hundred and eighty days after enactment, except (a) that the Secretary of Labor may extend the delay in effective date of any provision of this Act up to an additional ninety days thereafter if he finds that such time is necessary in permitting adjustments to the provisions hereof, and

December 15, 1967      - 7 -          **Pub. Law 90-202**
81 STAT. 608

(b) that on or after the date of enactment the Secretary of Labor is authorized to issue such rules and regulations as may be necessary to carry out its provisions.

## APPROPRIATIONS

Sec. 16. There are hereby authorized to be appropriated such sums, not in excess of $3,000,000 for any fiscal year, as may be necessary to carry out this Act.

**Approved December 15, 1967.**

---

LEGISLATIVE HISTORY:

HOUSE REPORT No. 805 accompanying H. R. 13054 (Comm. on Education & Labor).
SENATE REPORT No. 723 (Comm. on Labor & Public Welfare).
CONGRESSIONAL RECORD, Vol. 113 (1967):
    Nov. 6: Considered and passed Senate.
    Dec. 4: Considered and passed House, amended, in lieu of H. R. 13054.
    Dec. 5: Senate concurred in House amendment with amendments.
    Dec. 6: House concurred in Senate amendments.

## SLIP SHEET

## AGE DISCRIMINATION IN EMPLOYMENT ACT OF 1967

The Age Discrimination in Employment Act of

1967 is amended by Public Law 93-259, Fair

Labor Standards Amendments of 1974, effective

May 1, 1974, as follows:

SEC. 28. (a)(1) The first sentence of section 11(b) of the Age Discrimination in Employment Act of 1967 (29 U.S.C. 630(b)) is amended by striking out "twenty-five" and inserting in lieu thereof "twenty".

(2) The second sentence of section 11(b) of such Act is amended to read as follows: "The term also means (1) any agent of such a person, and (2) a State or political subdivision of a State and any agency or instrumentality of a State or a political subdivision of a State, and any interstate agency, but such term does not include the United States, or a corporation wholly owned by the Government of the United States.".

(3) Section 11(c) of such Act is amended by striking out ", or an agency of a State or political subdivision of a State, except that such term shall include the United States Employment Service and the system of State and local employment services receiving Federal assistance".

(4) Section 11(f) of such Act is amended to read as follows:

"(f) The term 'employee' means an individual employed by any employer except that the term 'employee' shall not include any person elected to public office in any State or political subdivision of any State by the qualified voters thereof, or any person chosen by such officer to be on such officer's personal staff, or an appointee on the policymaking level or an immediate adviser with respect to the exercise of the constitutional or legal powers of the office. The exemption set forth in the preceding sentence shall not include employees subject to the civil service laws of a State government, governmental agency, or political subdivision.".

(5) Section 16 of such Act is amended by striking out "$3,000,000" and inserting in lieu thereof "$5,000,000".

(b)(1) The Age Discrimination in Employment Act of 1967 is amended by redesignating sections 15 and 16, and all references thereto, as sections 16 and 17, respectively.

(2) The Age Discrimination in Employment Act of 1967 is further amended by adding immediately after section 14 the following new section:

"SEC. 15. (a) *All personnel actions affecting employees or applicants
for employment (except with regard to aliens employed outside the
limits of the United States) in military departments as defined in
section 102 of title 5, United States Code, in executive agencies as defined in section 105 of title 5, United States Code (including employees and applicants for employment who are paid from nonappro-
priated funds), in the United States Postal Service and the Postal
Rate Commission, in those units in the government of the District of
Columbia having positions in the competitive service, and in those
units of the legislative and judicial branches of the Federal Government having positions in the competitive service, and in the Library of
Congress shall be made free from any discrimination based on age.*

"*(b) Except as otherwise provided in this subsection, the Civil
Service Commission is authorized to enforce the provisions of subsection (a) through appropriate remedies, including reinstatement or
hiring of employees with or without backpay, as will effectuate the
policies of this section. The Civil Service Commission shall issue such
rules, regulations, orders, and instructions as it deems necessary and
appropriate to carry out its responsibilities under this section. The
Civil Service Commission shall—*

"*(1) be responsible for the review and evaluation of the operation of all agency programs designed to carry out the policy of
this section, periodically obtaining and publishing (on at least a
semiannual basis) progress reports from each department, agency,
or unit referred to in subsection (a);*

"*(2) consult with and solicit the recommendations of interested
individuals, groups, and organizations relating to nondiscrimination in employment on account of age; and*

"*(3) provide for the acceptance and processing of complaints of
discrimination in Federal employment on account of age.*

*The head of each such department, agency, or unit shall comply with
such rules, regulations, orders, and instructions of the Civil Service
Commission which shall include a provision that an employee or applicant for employment shall be notified of any final action taken on any
complaint of discrimination filed by him thereunder. Reasonable exemptions to the provisions of this section may be established by the
Commission but only when the Commission has established a maximum age requirement on the basis of a determination that age is a
bona fide occupational qualification necessary to the performance of
the duties of the position. With respect to employment in the Library
of Congress, authorities granted in this subsection to the Civil Service
Commission shall be exercised by the Librarian of Congress.*

"*(c) Any person aggrieved may bring a civil action in any Federal
district court of competent jurisdiction for such legal or equitable
relief as will effectuate the purposes of this Act.*

"*(d) When the individual has not filed a complaint concerning age
discrimination with the Commission, no civil action may be commenced by any individual under this section until the individual has
given the Commission not less than thirty days' notice of an intent to
file such action. Such notice shall be filed within one hundred and
eighty days after the alleged unlawful practice occurred. Upon receiving a notice of intent to sue, the Commission shall promptly notify
all persons named therein as prospective defendants in the action and
take any appropriate action to assure the elimination of any unlawful
practice.*

"*(e) Nothing contained in this section shall relieve any Government agency or official of the responsibility to assure nondiscrimination on account of age in employment as required under any provision
of Federal law.*"

*Appendix B*

# SUMMARY OF STATE LAWS PERTAINING TO AGE DISCRIMINATION

TABLE B-1

Summary of provisions under State laws pertaining to discrimination in employment because of age, December 1, 1976

| State | Coverage | | Prohibited practices | Penalties | Enforcement agency |
|---|---|---|---|---|---|
| | Law applies to-- | Age limits* : Exclusions and exemptions ** | | | |
| Alabama | No law. | | | | |
| Alaska | Employers; labor organizations; employment agencies. | None : Nonprofit social clubs; fraternal, charitable, educational, or religious organizations, associations, or corporations; domestic service. | Employer: To refuse or bar from employment; to discriminate in compensation, terms, conditions or privileges of employment. Employer and employment agency: To advertise, publish or to use application forms which suggest age limitations. Labor organization: To exclude, expel or discriminate in any way. All three: To discharge, expel, or otherwise discriminate against a person who has opposed unlawful practices, filed a charge, testified, or assisted in any proceeding under the law. Any person: To print, publish, broadcast, or otherwise circulate a statement, inquiry, or advertisement directly expressing a limitation, specification, or discrimination. State, employer, labor organization, and employment agency: Failure to maintain confidential age records required by civil rights agencies for administrative and statistical evaluation. | Up to $500 fine, up to 30 days in jail, or both. | Commission for Human Rights |
| American Samoa | No law. | | | | |
| Arizona | No law. | | | | |

See footnotes at end of table.

TABLE B-1 (Continued)

Summary of provisions under State laws pertaining to discrimination in employment because of age. December 1, 1976
(Continued)

| State | Law applies to-- | Coverage Age limits* | Exclusions and exemptions ** | Prohibited practices | Penalties: | Enforcement agency |
|-------|------------------|---------------------|------------------------------|----------------------|------------|--------------------|
| Arkansas | No law. | | | | | |
| California | Employers; State and local governments; labor organizations; employment agencies. | 40 to 64 | Employers of fewer than 5; domestic service; family employment; non-profit social clubs, fraternal, educational or religious associations or corporations. | To refuse to hire or employ, to discharge, dismiss, reduce, suspend or demote. | Up to $500 fine, up to 6 months in jail, or both. | Department of Industrial Relations |
| Canal Zone | No law. | | | | | |
| Colorado | Any person, firm, association, or corporation conducting business in the State. | 18 to 60 | None | To discharge. | No less than $100 or more than $250 fine. | None |

See footnotes at end of table.

TABLE B-1 (Continued)

Summary of provisions under State laws pertaining to discrimination in employment because of age, December 1, 1976
(Continued)

| State | Coverage | | Prohibited practices | Penalties | Enforcement agency |
| | Law applies to-- | Age limits* | Exclusions and exemptions ** | | |
|---|---|---|---|---|---|---|
| Connecticut | Employers; State and political subdivisions; employment agencies; labor organizations. | None | Employers of fewer than 3; domestic service; family employment. | Employer: To refuse, bar, or discharge from employment; to discriminate in compensation, terms, conditions or privileges of employment. Labor organization: To exclude, expel or discriminate in any way. Employment agency: To fail or refuse to classify properly or refer or otherwise discriminate. All three: To advertise in such a manner that restricts employment so as to discriminate; discriminate for opposing unfair practices, filing a complaint or testifying or assisting in proceedings. Person: To aid, abet; incite, compel, or coerce the doing or attempting to do an unlawful act under the law. | Contempt of court citations. | Commission on Human Rights and Opportunities. |
| Delaware | Employers; State and political subdivisions; employment agencies; labor organizations; joint labor-management committees. | 40 to 65 | Employers of fewer than 4; domestic service; agriculture; family employment; any employee residing in the personal residence of the employer. | Employer: To refuse, bar or discharge from employment; to discriminate in compensation, terms, conditions, or privileges of employment. Employment agency: To fail or refuse to refer for employment or otherwise discriminate. Labor organization: To exclude, expel or discriminate in any way. Employer, labor organization, joint labor-management committee: To discriminate in apprenticeship, or other training and retraining, including on-the-job training programs. | Contempt of court citations. | Department of Labor |

See footnotes at end of table.

TABLE B-1 (Continued)

Summary of provisions under State laws pertaining to discrimination in employment because of age, December 1, 1976
(Continued)

| State | Coverage | | Prohibited practices | Penalties | Enforcement agency |
| | Law applies to-- | Age limits* | Exclusions and exemptions ** | | | |
|---|---|---|---|---|---|---|
| District of Columbia | Employers; employ- ment agencies; labor organiza- tions; government agency. | 18 to 65 | Domestic service; family employment; working in or about employer's household; religious or politi- cal organizations or any organizations operated for chari- table or educational purposes; profes- sional associations. | Employer: To fail or refuse to hire; to discharge or otherwise discriminate in compensation, terms, conditions, or privileges of employment, including promotion; to limit, segregate, or classify; to deprive of opportunities or otherwise adversely affect employ- ment status. Employment agency: To fail or refuse to refer for employ- ment, or to classify or refer for employment, or otherwise discriminate. Labor organization: To exclude, ex- pel, or otherwise discriminate; to limit, segregate, classify, fail or refuse to refer for employment. All three: To discriminate for complaints or assistance in complaints; to print or publish notices or advertisement in- dicating age preference; to discrim- inate in admission to or employment in apprenticeship or other training or retraining programs. Person: To aid, abet, incite, compel or coerce for do- ing or attempting to do an unlawful act under the law; to retaliate. | Up to $300 fine, up to 10 days in jail, or both. | Office of Human Rights and Commission on Human Rights |

See footnotes at end of table.

TABLE B-1 (Continued)

Summary of provisions under State laws pertaining to discrimination in employment because of age, December 1, 1976
(Continued)

| State | Coverage | | | | |
| | Law applies to-- | Age limits* | Exclusions and exemptions ** | Prohibited practices | Penalties | Enforcement agency |
|---|---|---|---|---|---|---|
| Florida | State, county, municipality, special district or any subdivision or agency thereof; employment agencies servicing covered employers, including also State and local employment services receiving Federal assistance; labor organizations. | None | Law enforcement agency; firefighting agency. | Employer: To fail or refuse to hire, to discharge or mandatorily retire, or otherwise discriminate in compensation, terms, conditions or privileges of employment; to limit, segregate, or classify; to deprive of opportunities or otherwise adversely affect employment status; to reduce wage rate, terms or conditions, without employee consent, in order to comply with act. Employment agency: To fail or refuse to refer for employment or otherwise discriminate; to classify or refer for employment on age basis. Labor organization: To exclude or expel from membership, or otherwise discriminate; to limit, segregate or classify its membership; to fail or refuse to refer for employment; to deprive of opportunities or otherwise adversely affect status as employee or applicant; to cause employer to discriminate. All three: To discriminate against a person who has made a charge, testified, or assisted in any proceeding; to print or publish notice or advertisement indicating age preference. | None | Career Service Commission for career service system employees, and civil suit for others. Department of Commerce, on posting duty only |

See footnotes at end of table.

TABLE B-1 (Continued)

Summary of provisions under State laws pertaining to discrimination in employment because of age, December 1, 1976
(Continued)

| State | Coverage | | Prohibited practices | Penalties | Enforcement agency |
| | Law applies to-- | Age limits* | Exclusions and exemptions ** | | | |

| State | Law applies to-- | Age limits* | Exclusions and exemptions ** | Prohibited practices | Penalties | Enforcement agency |
|---|---|---|---|---|---|---|
| Georgia | Persons, firms, associations, or corporations. | 40 to 65 | None | Employer: To refuse to hire, employ, license, or bar or discharge from employment. | Not less than $100 or more than $250 fine. | None |
| Guam | Employers; employment agencies; labor organizations. | None | None | Employer: To refuse to hire; to bar or discharge from employment; to discriminate in compensation, terms, conditions, or privileges of employment. Employer and employment agency: To advertise, print, circulate material or use application forms which suggest limitations, specifications or discrimination. Labor organization: To exclude, expel, or otherwise discriminate. All three: To discriminate because of complaint or assistance in complaints. Person: To aid in or cause forbidden discrimination practices. | Not more than $200 fine for first offense, not more than $500 fine for second and subsequent offenses, or up to 90 days in jail, or both. | Department of Labor |

See footnotes at end of table.

TABLE B-1 (Continued)

Summary of provisions under State laws pertaining to discrimination in employment because of age, December 1, 1976
(Continued)

| State | Coverage | | Prohibited practices | Penalties | Enforcement agency |
| | Law applies to-- | Age limits* | Exclusions and exemptions ** | | |
|---|---|---|---|---|---|---|
| Hawaii | Employers; employment agencies; labor organizations. | None | None | **Employer:** To refuse, bar, or discharge from employment; to discriminate in compensation, terms, conditions or privileges of employment. **Employer and employment agency:** To print or circulate any statement, advertisement, or publication, or use any job application or make preemployment inquiry expressing limitations, specifications or discrimination. **Employer or labor organization:** To refuse to enter into an apprenticeship agreement. **Labor organization:** To exclude, expel or discriminate in any way. **All three:** To discharge, expel or otherwise discriminate for opposition to any practice forbidden by this act, for filing a complaint, testifying or assisting in proceedings. **Person:** To aid, abet, incite, compel or coerce the doing or attempting to do any practices forbidden by this act. | First conviction, up to $200 fine, subsequent convictions, up to $500 fine, up to 90 days in jail, or both. | Department of Labor and Industrial Relations |

See footnotes at end of table.

TABLE B-1 (Continued)

Summary of provisions under State laws pertaining to discrimination in employment because of age, December 1, 1976

(Continued)

| State | Coverage | | Prohibited practices | Penalties | Enforcement agency |
| | Law applies to-- | Age limits* | Exclusions and exemptions ** | | | |
|---|---|---|---|---|---|---|
| Idaho | Employers. | Under 60 | None | To refuse to hire, bar, or discharge or to otherwise discriminate in compensation, hire, tenure, terms, conditions or privileges of employment. | Not less than $100 or more than $500 fine, up to 30 days in jail, or both. | Commissioner of Labor |
| Illinois | Employers; governmental units in State; labor organizations. | Over 45 | None | Employer: To refuse, bar, or discharge from employment; to discriminate in compensation, terms, conditions, or privileges of employment; to utilize any employment agency, placement service, training school or center, labor organization or any other source of unreasonable discrimination. Labor organization: To limit, segregate or classify; to in any way affect adversely wages, hours, or conditions of employment. Employer and labor organization: To discharge, expel or otherwise discriminate for opposing unlawful employment practices; or filing a charge, testifying, participation or assistance in proceedings under the law. | Not less than $50 or more than $100 fine. | None |

See footnotes at end of table.

TABLE B-1(Continued)

Summary of provisions under State laws pertaining to discrimination in employment because of age, December 1, 1976
(Continued)

| State | Law applies to-- | Coverage Age limits* | Exclusions and exemptions ** | Prohibited practices | Penalties | Enforcement agency |
|---|---|---|---|---|---|---|
| Indiana | Employers; labor organizations; State and political subdivisions. | 40 to 65 | Nonprofit social, fraternal, charitable, educational, religious or sectarian organizations, associations or corporations; domestic service; farm labor. | Employer: To dismiss, refuse to employ or rehire, to discharge for furnishing evidence in connection with a complaint. Labor organization: To deny full and equal membership rights; to fail or refuse to classify or refer for employment. | None | Commissioner of Labor |
| Iowa | Employers; employment agencies; labor organizations; State and political subdivisions. | None | Employers of fewer than 4; family employment; domestic service; employees rendering personal service to employer; religious institutions. | Employer: To refuse to hire, accept, register, classify, or refer; to discharge or otherwise discriminate. Labor organization: To refuse to hire or admit for membership, to expel or otherwise discriminate. Employer, employment agency and labor organization: To advertise or in any other manner indicate or publicize not welcome, objectionable, not acceptable, or not solicited for employment or membership. Person: To aid, abet, compel, or coerce to engage in unfair practices; to discriminate for opposing or obeying practices, or filing a complaint, testifying or assisting in proceedings under the law. | Contempt of court citations. | Civil Rights Commission |
| Kansas | No law. | | | | | |

See footnotes at end of table.

TABLE B-1 (Continued)

Summary of provisions under State laws pertaining to discrimination in employment because of age, December 1, 1976

(Continued)

| State | Law applies to-- | Coverage Age limits* | Exclusions and exemptions ** | Prohibited practices | Penalties | Enforcement agency |
|-------|------------------|---------------------|------------------------------|----------------------|-----------|--------------------|
| Kentucky | Employers; employment agencies; labor organizations; licensing agency (public and private); joint labor-management committees; State and political subdivisions. | 40 to 65 | Employers of fewer than 8; domestic service; family employment. | *Employer:* To fail or refuse to hire or discharge or otherwise discriminate in compensation, terms, conditions, or privileges of employment; to limit, segregate, or classify; to deprive of employment opportunities or otherwise adversely affect employment status. *Employment agency:* To fail or refuse to refer to employment or otherwise discriminate; to classify or refer on the basis of age; to refuse, bar, or terminate licensing to individuals. *Labor organization:* To exclude or expel or otherwise discriminate; to limit, segregate, or classify; or refuse to refer so as to deprive of employment opportunities or otherwise affect status; to cause or attempt to cause an employer to discriminate. *Employer, labor organization, licensing agency or employment agency:* To print or publish notice or advertisement indicating preference, limitations, specifications or discrimination of any kind. *Licensing agency:* To refuse to license, or to bar or terminate from licensing. *Employer, labor organization, joint labor-management committee:* To discriminate in admission or employment in apprenticeship or | Contempt of court citations. | Commission on Human Rights |

See footnotes at end of table.

TABLE B-1 (Continued)

Summary of provisions under State laws pertaining to discrimination in employment because of age, December 1, 1976
(Continued)

| State | Law applies to-- | Coverage Age limits* | Exclusions and exemptions ** | Prohibited practices | Penalties | Enforcement agency |
|---|---|---|---|---|---|---|
| Kentucky (continued) | | | | other training programs. Person: To retaliate for opposition to unlawful practice or for making a charge, filing a complaint, testifying, assisting or participating in any investigation under the law; to aid, abet, incite, compel or coerce to engage in an unlawful practice; to resist or interfere with the Commission on Human Rights or its representatives in performance of its duty under the act. | | |
| Louisiana | Employers | Under 50 | Employers of fewer than 25; bus drivers. 1/ | To adopt rules for discharge or rejection of applications for employment. | Up to $500 fine, up to 90 days in jail, or both. | None |

See footnotes at end of table.

## TABLE B-1 (Continued)

Summary of provisions under State laws pertaining to discrimination in employment because of age, December 1, 1976
(Continued)

| State | Law applies to-- | Coverage Age limits* | Exclusions and exemptions ** | Prohibited practices | Penalties | Enforcement agency |
|---|---|---|---|---|---|---|
| Maine | Employers; employment agencies; labor organizations; State agencies. | None | Nonprofit religious or fraternal corporations or associations employing own members; family employment. | Employer and labor organization: To fail or refuse to hire, to discharge or otherwise discriminate in hiring, tenure, promotion, transfer, compensation, terms, conditions, or privileges; to use employment agency which discriminates. Employment agency: To fail or refuse to classify properly, or to refer, or otherwise discriminate; to comply with an employer's request, if request indicates no full and equal employment opportunities will be afforded. Labor organization: To exclude from apprenticeship or membership or to deny full and equal membership rights; to discriminate in representation, or in grievance whether or not authorized by contract, collective agreement or, bylaws or constitution; to fail or refuse to classify or refer for employment. All three: To discriminate because of opposition to any violation of the act; or to make a charge, give testimony or assistance in proceedings under the act. Person: To aid, abet, coerce, incite, compel to perform unlawful acts under the law; obstruct or prevent from complying with act; punish, penalize for seeking to exercise civil rights. | Damages, not more than $100 for first unlawful act; not more than $250 for second; not more than $1,000 for third and subsequent violations. | Human Rights Commission |

See footnotes at end of table.

TABLE B-1 (Continued)

Summary of provisions under State laws pertaining to discrimination in employment because of age, December 1, 1976
(Continued)

| State | Law applies to-- | Coverage Age limits* | Exclusions and exemptions ** | Prohibited practices | Penalties | Enforcement agency |
|---|---|---|---|---|---|---|
| Maryland | Employers; employment agencies; labor organizations; joint labor-management committees; State. | None | Employers of fewer than 15; private clubs; religious corporations. | Employer: To fail or refuse to hire, to discharge or otherwise discriminate in compensation, terms, conditions, or privileges of employment; to limit, segregate, or classify employees to deprive of employment opportunities or otherwise adversely affect status. Employment agency: To refuse or fail to refer or to classify or refer for employment. Labor organization: To exclude, expel or otherwise discriminate; to limit, segregate or classify; to cause employer to discriminate. Employer, employment agency, labor organization: To discriminate for opposition to unlawful practices, filed charges, testimony, or assistance in any proceeding under the law; to print or publish any notice or advertisement indicating preference, limitation, specification or other discrimination. Employer, labor organization, joint labor-management committee: To discriminate in admission to or employment in any training program. | Contempt of court citations. | Commission on Human Relations |

See footnotes at end of table.

## TABLE B-1 (Continued)

Summary of provisions under State laws pertaining to discrimination in employment because of age, December 1, 1976
(Continued)

| State | Law applies to-- | Coverage Age limits* | Exclusions and exemptions ** | Prohibited practices | Penalties | Enforcement agency |
|---|---|---|---|---|---|---|
| Massachusetts | Employers; State and political subdivisions; employment agencies; labor organizations. | 40 to 65 | Employers of fewer than 6; nonprofit social, religious, fraternal clubs, organizations, associations, or corporations; domestic service; family employment. | Employer: To refuse, bar, or discharge from employment; to discriminate in compensation, terms, conditions, or privileges of employment. Employer and employment agency: To print or circulate any statement, advertisement, or publication or to use an application form or to make any inquiry or record expressing limitations, specifications, or discrimination. Labor organization: To exclude, expel or discriminate in any way. Person, employer, labor organization, employment agency: To discharge, expel or otherwise discriminate for opposition to any practice forbidden by law, or for filing a complaint, testifying or assisting in any proceeding; to aid, abet, incite, compel or coerce a person to do or attempt an act forbidden by this law. | Up to $500 fine, up to one year in jail, or both. | Commission Against Discrimination |

See footnotes at end of table.

TABLE B-1 (Continued)

Summary of provisions under State laws pertaining to discrimination in employment because of age, December 1, 1976
(Continued)

| State | Law applies to-- | Coverage Age limits* | Exclusions and exemptions ** | Prohibited practices | Penalties | Enforcement agency |
|---|---|---|---|---|---|---|
| Michigan | Employers; State and civil or political subdivisions; employment agencies; labor organizations. | 18 to 60 | Employers of fewer than 8; domestic service. | Employer: To refuse or to otherwise discriminate in hiring, tenure, terms, conditions, or privileges of employment. Employment agency: To fail or refuse to properly classify, refer or otherwise discriminate. Labor organization: To discriminate, limit, segregate, or qualify in any way; to adversely affect employment status, wages, hours, or conditions of work. All three: To, prior to employment or admission to membership, print or publish any notice or advertisement indicating preference, limitation, specification, or discrimination; to establish or announce a policy of denying or limiting opportunities, through a quota system or otherwise; to utilize in recruitment or hiring an agency, service, school or any other labor-referring source known to discriminate. | Contempt of court citations; not less than $100 or more than $500 fine for failure to post required notices. | Civil Rights Commission |
| Minnesota | No law. | | | | | |

See footnotes at end of table.

## TABLE B-1 (Continued)

Summary of provisions under State laws pertaining to discrimination in employment because of age, December 1, 1976
(Continued)

| State | Law applies to-- | Coverage — Age limits* | Exclusions and exemptions ** | Prohibited practices | Penalties | Enforcement agency |
|---|---|---|---|---|---|---|
| Mississippi | No law. | | | | | |
| Missouri | No law. | | | | | |
| Montana | Employers; labor organizations; joint labor-management committees; employment agencies; State and political subdivisions. | None | Nonprofit fraternal, charitable or religious associations or corporations. | Employer: To refuse employment; to discriminate in compensation or in terms, conditions or privileges of employment. Labor organization or joint labor-management committee: To exclude or expel from its membership, apprenticeship, or training program; or to discriminate in any way against a member or applicant. Employment agency: To fail or refuse to classify or otherwise discriminate. Employer or employment agency: To print, circulate a discriminatory statement, advertisement, publication, or job application. Person: To discharge, expel, blacklist, or otherwise discriminate for opposing any forbidden practice, or for filing a complaint, testifying or assisting in any proceeding under the law. State, employer, labor organization, employment agency: To fail to maintain records required by civil rights agencies for administrative and statistical evaluation. | Up to $500 fine, or up to 6 months in jail, or both. | Commission for Human Rights |

See footnotes at end of table.

TABLE B-1 (Continued)

Summary of provisions under State laws pertaining to discrimination in employment because of age, December 1, 1976
(Continued)

| State | Law applies to-- | Coverage Age limits* | Exclusions and exemptions** | Prohibited practices | Penalties | Enforcement agency |
|---|---|---|---|---|---|---|
| Nebraska | Employers; labor organizations. | 40 to 65 | Employers of fewer than 25; peace officers; firefighters. | Employer: To refuse to hire, discharge or otherwise discriminate in terms, conditions, or privileges of employment; to utilize any labor organization or employment agency which discriminates. Labor organization: To discriminate or to limit, segregate or classify membership. Employer and labor organization: To discharge, expel, or discriminate for opposing, filing charges, testifying or assisting in proceedings. | Up to $100 fine, up to 30 days in jail, or both, for second or subsequent convictions. | Equal Opportunity Commission |
| Nevada | Employers; employment agencies; labor organizations; joint labor-management committees; State and political subdivisions. | None | Employers of fewer than 15; private membership clubs; religious corporations, associations, or societies. | Employer: To refuse to hire, to discharge or to otherwise discriminate in compensation, terms, conditions or privileges of employment; to limit, segregate or classify employees; to deprive of employment opportunities or otherwise adversely affect status. Employment agency: To refer or to classify on basis of age or otherwise discriminate. Labor organization: To exclude, expel or otherwise discriminate; to limit, segregate, classify or refuse to refer; to cause employer to discriminate. All three: To discriminate because of complaints or assistance in complaints; to advertise indicating preference, limitation, specification, or discrimination. Employer, labor organization, or joint labor-management committee: To discriminate in admission or employment in any apprenticeship or other training program. | Contempt of court citations. | Equal Rights Commission |

See footnotes at end of table.

## TABLE B-1 (Continued)

Summary of provisions under State laws pertaining to discrimination in employment because of age, December 1, 1976
(Continued)

| State | Law applies to-- | Coverage Age limits* | Exclusions and exemptions ** | Prohibited practices | Penalties | Enforcement agency |
|---|---|---|---|---|---|---|
| New Hampshire | Employers; State and political subdivisions; employment agencies. | Less than 65 | Employers of fewer than 6; family employment; domestic service; and nonprofit social, fraternal, charitable, educational, or religious associations or corporations. | Employer: To refuse, bar, discharge or otherwise discriminate in compensation, terms, conditions or privileges of employment. Employer and employment agency: To print and circulate any material, to use application forms, or to make inquiries or records with limitation, specification or discrimination. Person: To discriminate against persons who oppose forbidden practices, file a complaint, testify or assist in any proceeding under the law; to aid, abet, incite, compel or coerce a person to do or attempt an act forbidden by this law. | Up to $500 fine, up to 6 months in jail, or both. | Commission for Human Rights |
| New Jersey | Employers; employment agencies; labor organizations. | Over 21 | Nonprofit social clubs, fraternal, charitable, educational, or religious organizations, associations, or corporations; domestic service; family employment. | Employer: To refuse, bar, or discharge from employment or to discriminate in compensation, terms, conditions, or privileges of employment. Employer and employment agency: To advertise, print or circulate any material, or use application forms which suggest age limitations. Labor organization: To exclude, expel or discriminate in any way; to discriminate against persons in apprenticeship or other training programs. Person: To take reprisals for opposition to any practices or acts forbidden under the law or because of testimony, complaint, or assistance in any proceedings under the law; to aid, abet, incite, compel, or coerce any discrimination. | Up to $500 fine, up to one year in jail, or both. | Division on Civil Rights |

See footnotes at end of table..

TABLE B-1 (Continued)

Summary of provisions under State laws pertaining to discrimination in employment because of age, December 1, 1976
(Continued)

| State | Coverage — Law applies to-- | Coverage — Age limits* | Exclusions and exemptions ** | Prohibited practices | Penalties | Enforcement agency |
|---|---|---|---|---|---|---|
| New Mexico | Employers; State and political subdivisions. | None | Employers of fewer than 4. | Employer: To refuse to hire or to promote, to discharge or demote, or to discriminate in matters of compensation. Person and employer: To aid, abet, incite, compel or coerce the doing of any act forbidden by the law; to engage in threats, reprisals, or discrimination for opposition to unlawful practices, for filing a complaint, testifying or participating in any proceeding under the law. | Damages up to $1,000. | Human Rights Commission |
| New York | Employers; employment agencies; labor organizations; licensing agencies. | 18 to 65 | Employers of fewer than 4; domestic service; family employment. | Employer: To refuse, bar, or discharge from employment; to discriminate in compensation, terms, conditions, or privileges of employment. Employment agency: To discriminate in receiving, classifying, disposing or otherwise acting upon applications for service, or in referring applicants to employers. Employer, employment agency and licensing agency: To advertise, publish or use application forms which suggest age limitations. Labor organization: To exclude, expel or discriminate in any way. Licensing agency, employer: To refuse to hire, employ or license and to discriminate in promotion, compensation or terms, conditions, or privileges of employment. Employer, employment agency, licensing agency: To encourage or compel the accomplishment of any forbidden action under the law, or because individual has opposed, complained, testified or assisted in any proceeding. | Up to $500 fine, up to one year in jail, or both. | Division of Human Rights |

See footnotes at end of table.

TABLE B-1 (Continued)

Summary of provisions under State laws pertaining to discrimination in employment because of age, December 1, 1976
(Continued)

| State | Law applies to-- | Coverage Age limits* | Exclusions and exemptions ** | Prohibited practices | Penalties | Enforcement agency |
|---|---|---|---|---|---|---|
| North Carolina | State, and political subdivisions. | 40 to 65 | None | <u>Department or agency</u>: To deny equal employment opportunity. | None | None |
| North Dakota 2/ | Employers. | 40 to 65 | None | To refuse to hire, employ, or license; to bar or discharge. | Up to $25 fine, up to one day in jail, or both. | None |
| Ohio 3/ | Employers; State and political subdivisions. | None | Employers with gross annual sales of less than $95,000; baby-sitters, live-in companions. Certain employees of political subdivisions: Police, fire protection agencies, or students in part-time or seasonal work. | <u>Employer</u>: To discriminate in payment of wages or against persons complaining, instituting or testifying in proceedings. | Minor misdemeanor. | Department of Industrial Relations |
| Oklahoma 4/ | State. | 40 to 65 | None | To discriminate. | None | None |

See footnotes at end of table.

TABLE B-1 (Continued)

Summary of provisions under State laws pertaining to discrimination in employment because of age, December 1, 1976
(Continued)

| State | Coverage | | Prohibited practices | Penalties | Enforcement agency |
|---|---|---|---|---|---|
| | Law applies to-- | Age limits* : Exclusions and exemptions ** | | | |
| Oregon | Employers; State and political subdivisions; employment agencies; labor organizations. | 18 to 65 : Domestic service; family employment; nonprofit religious institutions; correctional institutions; State and city police, sheriffs; employees of Liquor Control Commission and State Agriculture Department; firefighters; weighmasters of the State Department of Transportation. | Employer: To refuse, bar, discharge, dismiss, reduce, suspend, or demote. Employer and employment agency: To advertise, publish, use application forms, or make inquiry about prospective employment which suggest limitations, specifications or discrimination. Employer, employment agency, labor organization: To discharge, expel or discriminate against persons who oppose forbidden practice, complain, testify, or assist in any proceeding under the law; to encourage or compel any forbidden action. Public employer: To disqualify or discriminate in any civil service entrance, appointment, or promotion; to refuse to hire or reemploy; or to bar, discharge, reduce, suspend, or demote. | Up to $500 fine, up to one year in jail, or both. | Bureau of Labor (except for public employment) |
| Outer Continental Shelf Lands | No law. | | | | |

See footnotes at end of table.

TABLE B-1 (Continued)

Summary of provisions under State laws pertaining to discrimination in employment because of age, December 1, 1976
(Continued)

| State | Coverage Law applies to-- | Coverage Age limits* | Exclusions and exemptions ** | Prohibited practices | Penalties | Enforcement agency |
|---|---|---|---|---|---|---|
| Pennsylvania | Employers; State and political subdivisions; employment agencies; labor organizations. | 40 to 62 | Employers of fewer than 4; domestic service; family employment; agriculture; live-in workers. | Employer: To refuse, bar, discharge from employment or to otherwise discriminate in compensation, hire, tenure, terms, conditions, or privileges of employment. Employment agency: To fail or refuse to classify properly, refer, or to otherwise discriminate. Employer, employment agency, and labor organization: To advertise, publish or use application forms that suggest limitations, specifications or discrimination. Labor organization: To exclude, expel or discriminate in any way. All three: To discriminate against any person who has opposed forbidden practice or has made a charge, testified or assisted in any investigation or proceeding under the law; to aid, abet, incite, compel or coerce the doing of an unlawful act under the law; to deny or limit employment or membership through a quota system; to confine or limit recruitment or hiring to an employee-referring source serving persons in predominantly the same age group. Any individual: To publish any advertisement expressing preferences or limitations for a prospective employer. | Not less than $100 nor more than $500 fine, not more than 30 days in jail, or both. | Human Relations Commission |

See footnotes at end of table.

TABLE B-1 (Continued)

Summary of provisions under State laws pertaining to discrimination in employment because of age, December 1, 1976
(Continued)

| State | Coverage Law applies to-- | Age limits* | Exclusions and exemptions ** | Prohibited practices | Penalties | Enforcement agency |
|---|---|---|---|---|---|---|
| Puerto Rico | Employers; agencies and instrumentalities of the Commonwealth operated as private businesses or enterprises; employment agencies; labor organizations. | 30 to 65 | None | Employer: To discharge, suspend, demote, reduce the salary, impose more burdensome working conditions, or refuse to employ or reemploy, to advertise, publish, or use application forms which suggest age limitations. Employment agency: To make inquiries, establish limitations or exclusions; to publish or circulate statement, advertisement or notice expressing limitations or exclusions. Labor organization: To limit, divide, or classify membership. | Various civil and criminal penalties including double damages, up to $1,000 fine, up to 90 days in jail, or both. | Department of Labor |
| Rhode Island | Employers; State and political subdivisions; employment agencies; labor organizations. | 45 to 65 | Nonprofit social clubs; fraternal, charitable, educational or religious organizations, associations, or corporations; domestic service; farm labor. | Employer: To dismiss or refuse to employ or rehire; to discharge for furnishing evidence on a complaint. Employment agency: To fail or refuse to classify or refer. Employer and employment agency: To advertise, publish, or use application forms, to make inquiry which expresses intent to dismiss, or refuse to employ or rehire. Labor organization: To deny full and equal membership, or fail or refuse to classify or refer for employment. | None | Department of Labor |

See footnotes at end of table.

*Appendix B*

TABLE B-1 (Continued)

Summary of provisions under State laws pertaining to discrimination in employment because of age, December 1, 1976
(Continued)

| State | Coverage: Law applies to-- | Coverage: Age limits* | Exclusions and exemptions ** | Prohibited practices | Penalties | Enforcement agency |
|---|---|---|---|---|---|---|
| South Carolina | State and political subdivisions. | None | None | Department or agency: To fail or refuse to hire, bar, discharge; to advertise, publish or use application forms suggesting age limitations. Person: To aid, abet, incite, compel or coerce the doing of a forbidden act; to retaliate, discharge, expel or discriminate because person has opposed, filed a complaint, testified or assisted in any investigation, proceeding, or hearing. | None | Human Affairs Commission |
| South Dakota | State. | 18 to 65 | None | To discriminate. | None | None |
| Tennessee | No law. | | | | | |
| Texas | State and political subdivisions. | 21 to 65 | Law enforcement personnel; peace officers; firefighters; institutions of higher education. | To deny employment. | None | None |

See footnotes at end of table.

## TABLE B-1 (Continued)

Summary of provisions under State laws pertaining to discrimination in employment because of age, December 1, 1976
(Continued)

| State | Coverage Law applies to-- | Age limits* | Exclusions and exemptions ** | Prohibited practices | Penalties | Enforcement agency |
|---|---|---|---|---|---|---|
| Utah | Employers; employment agencies; labor organizations; joint apprenticeship committees; vocational schools. | 40 to 65 | Family employment. | Employer: To refuse to hire or promote, discharge or demote, or discriminate in compensation. Employment agency: To refuse to list, classify, or refer; to comply with an employer's discriminatory request. Labor organization: To exclude, or expel from membership or otherwise discriminate. Employer, labor organization, joint apprenticeship committee and vocational school: To deny or withhold admission or participation in training programs; discriminate in terms, conditions, or privileges. All five: To print, circulate, advertise, publish or to use application forms expressing discrimination. Person: To aid, abet, incite, compel or coerce the doing of a forbidden act; to obstruct or prevent compliance; or to commit a discriminatory act. | None | Industrial Commission |
| Vermont | No law. | | | | | |
| Virginia | No law. | | | | | |

See footnotes at end of table.

TABLE B-1 (Continued)

Summary of provisions under State laws pertaining to discrimination in employment because of age, December 1, 1976 (Continued)

| State | Coverage | | Exclusions and exemptions ** | Prohibited practices | Penalties | Enforcement agency |
|---|---|---|---|---|---|---|
| | Law applies to-- | Age limits* | | | | |
| Virgin Islands | Employers; employment agencies. | None | None | Employer: To refuse to hire; to bar or discharge from employment; to discriminate in compensation, terms, conditions, or privileges of employment. Employer and employment agency: To advertise, publish, or use application forms which suggest age limitations. | Up to $200 fine for first offense; up to $500 for second and subsequent offenses. | Department of Labor |
| Wake Island | No law. | | | | | |
| Washington | Employers; State and political subdivisions; employment agencies; labor organizations; licensing agencies. | 40 to 65 | Employers of fewer than 8; nonprofit religious or sectarian organizations; domestic service; family employment. | Employer and licensing agency: To refuse, discharge, or bar from employment or licensing; to discriminate in compensation or other terms, or conditions of employment. Employer, licensing agency and employment agency: To advertise, publish or use application forms, make inquiry suggesting limitations, specifications or discrimination. Labor organization: To deny membership or full membership rights, expel or discriminate in any way. All three: To expel or otherwise discriminate against a person because he has opposed a forbidden practice or because he has filed a charge, testified or assisted in any proceeding under the law. | Misdemeanor. | Human Rights Commission |

See footnotes at end of table.

**TABLE B-1** (Continued)

Summary of provisions under State laws pertaining to discrimination in employment because of age, December 1, 1976
(Continued)

| State | Coverage | | Prohibited practices | Penalties | Enforcement agency |
|---|---|---|---|---|---|
| | Law applies to-- | Age limits* | Exclusions and exemptions ** | | |
| West Virginia | Employers; State and political subdivisions; employment agencies; labor organizations; joint labor-management committees. | 40 to 65 | Employers of fewer than 12; private clubs; family employment; domestic service. | Employer: To discriminate with respect to compensation, hire, tenure, terms, conditions, or privileges of employment. Employment agency: To fail or refuse to classify properly, refer for employment or otherwise discriminate. Labor organization: To deny full and equal membership rights or otherwise discriminate in hiring, tenure, terms, conditions or privileges of employment. All three: To elicit information, keep records, use forms, print or publish advertisements showing preference, limitation, specification or discrimination; to deny or limit employment or membership through a quota system; to engage in reprisal or otherwise discriminate against individual who has opposed a forbidden practice, filed a complaint, testified or assisted in any proceeding under the law. Employer, labor organization, employment agency or joint labor-management committee: To select trainees on any basis other than qualifications; to discriminate in right to be admitted to and to participate in the pursuit of such training, in terms, conditions or privileges of such program; to print or publish any statement, advertisement or publication which expresses discrimination or any intent to discriminate. | Not less than. $100. or more than $500 fine, up to 30 days in prison, or both. | Human Rights Commission |

See footnotes at end of table.

## TABLE B-1 (Continued)

Summary of provisions under State laws pertaining to discrimination in employment because of age, December 1, 1976
(Concluded)

| State | Law applies to-- | Coverage Age limits* | Exclusions and exemptions ** | Prohibited practices | Penalties | Enforcement agency |
|---|---|---|---|---|---|---|
| Wisconsin | Employers; licensing agencies; employment agencies; labor organizations. | 40 to 65 | Nonprofit social clubs; fraternal, or religious associations; family employment; hazardous occupations; law enforcement or fire-fighting personnel. | Employer, labor organization and licensing agency: To refuse to hire, employ, admit, license, bar, or terminate or to discriminate in promotion, compensation, or in terms, conditions or privileges of employment. Employer, employment agency and licensing agency: To advertise, publish or use application forms which suggest age limitations or to discharge or otherwise discriminate against person who has opposed discriminatory practices or because he has made a complaint, testified or assisted in any proceeding under the law. | None | Department of Industry, Labor, and Human Relations |
| Wyoming | No law. | | | | | |

*Age limits refer to birthdays.
**In addition to the listed exclusions and exemptions, many laws are also inapplicable to other specified persons or circumstances, such as, the establishment of bona fide occupational qualifications, the operation of a bona fide retirement or pension plan, persons immediately eligible for retirement benefits, apprenticeship programs, and other situations.
1/ Louisiana: An attorney general's opinion declared that bus drivers are engaged in hazardous work, therefore exempt.
2/ North Dakota: Under the personnel system law, age discrimination is prohibited in all appointments and promotions in the State classified service.
3/ Ohio: In 1975, Ohio added age discrimination to its equal pay law, reported in the table, which deals only with discrimination in pay. Under another law dealing with age discrimination in other employment conditions, an employer is prohibited from refusing an opportunity for an interview or from discharging persons 40 to 65; there is no enforcement agency designated under this law.
4/ Oklahoma: A resolution declares it to be the legislative intent and purpose that departments and agencies of the State government conform as nearly as practicable to the Federal "Age Discrimination in Employment Act."

Note: Data for American Samoa, Wake Island, the Canal Zone, and the Outer Continental Shelf Lands are as of February 1, 1974.

*Appendix C*

EXCERPTS FROM THE REHABILITATION ACT
OF 1973

**EMPLOYMENT OF HANDICAPPED INDIVIDUALS**

SEC. 501. (a) There is established within the Federal Government an Interagency Committee on Handicapped Employees (hereinafter in this section referred to as the "Committee"), comprised of such members as the President may select, including the following (or their designees whose positions are Executive Level IV or higher) : the Chairman of the Civil Service Commission, the Administrator of Veterans' Affairs, and the Secretaries of Labor and Health, Education, and Welfare. The Secretary of Health, Education, and Welfare and the Chairman of the Civil Service Commission shall serve as co-chairmen of the Committee. The resources of the President's Committees on Employment of the Handicapped and on Mental Retardation shall be made fully available to the Committee. It shall be the purpose and function of the Committee (1) to provide a focus for Federal and other employment of handicapped individuals, and to review, on a periodic basis, in cooperation with the Civil Service Commission, the adequacy of hiring, placement, and advancement practices with respect to handicapped individuals, by each department, agency, and instrumentality in the executive branch of Government, and to insure that the special needs of such individuals are being met; and (2) to consult with the Civil Service Commission to assist the Commission to carry out its responsibilities under subsections (b), (c), and (d) of this section. On the basis of such review and consultation, the Committee shall periodically make to the Civil Service Commission such recommendations for legislative and administrative changes as it deems necessary or desirable. The Civil Service Commission shall timely transmit to the appropriate committees of Congress any such recommendations.

(b) Each department, agency, and instrumentality (including the United States Postal Service and the Postal Rate Commission) in the executive branch shall, within one hundred and eighty days after the date of enactment of this Act, submit to the Civil Service Commission

*[margin notes:]* Interagency Committee on Handicapped Employees, establishment. 83 Stat. 864. 5 USC 5315 note.

Committee functions.

Federal agencies, affirmative action program plans.

and to the Committee an affirmative action program plan for the hiring, placement, and advancement of handicapped individuals in such department, agency, or instrumentality. Such plan shall include a description of the extent to which and methods whereby the special needs of handicapped employees are being met. Such plan shall be updated annually, and shall be reviewed annually and approved by the Commission, if the Commission determines, after consultation with the Committee, that such plan provides sufficient assurances, procedures and commitments to provide adequate hiring, placement, and advancement opportunities for handicapped individuals.

**Rehabilitated individuals, employment.** (c) The Civil Service Commission, after consultation with the Committee, shall develop and recommend to the Secretary for referral to the appropriate State agencies, policies and procedures which will facilitate the hiring, placement, and advancement in employment of individuals who have received rehabilitation services under State vocational rehabilitation programs, veterans' programs, or any other program for handicapped individuals, including the promotion of job opportunities for such individuals. The Secretary shall encourage such State agencies to adopt and implement such policies and procedures.

**Report to congressional committees.** (d) The Civil Service Commission, after consultation with the Committee, shall, on June 30, 1974, and at the end of each subsequent fiscal year, make a complete report to the appropriate committees of the Congress with respect to the practices of and achievements in hiring, placement, and advancement of handicapped individuals by each department, agency, and instrumentality and the effectiveness of the affirmative action programs required by subsection (b) of this section, together with recommendations as to legislation which have been submitted to the Civil Service Commission under subsection (a) of this section, or other appropriate action to insure the adequacy of such practices. Such report shall also include an evaluation by the Committee of the effectiveness of the Civil Service Commission's activities under subsections (b) and (c) of this section.

**Unpaid Federal work experience.** (e) An individual who, as a part of his individualized written rehabilitation program under a State plan approved under this Act, participates in a program of unpaid work experience in a Federal agency, shall not, by reason thereof, be considered to be a Federal employee or to be subject to the provisions of law relating to Federal employment, including those relating to hours of work, rates of compensation, leave, unemployment compensation, and Federal employee benefits.

**Federal agency cooperation.** (f) (1) The Secretary of Labor and the Secretary of Health, Education, and Welfare are authorized and directed to cooperate with the President's Committee on Employment of the Handicapped in carrying out its functions.

(2) In selecting personnel to fill all positions on the President's Committee on Employment of the Handicapped, special consideration shall be given to qualified handicapped individuals.

### ARCHITECTURAL AND TRANSPORTATION BARRIERS COMPLIANCE BOARD

**Establishment; membership.** SEC. 502. (a) There is established within the Federal Government the Architectural and Transportation Barriers Compliance Board (hereinafter referred to as the "Board") which shall be composed of the heads of each of the following departments or agencies (or their designees whose positions are Executive Level IV or higher):

**83 Stat. 864.**
**5 USC 5315 note.**
    (1) Department of Health, Education, and Welfare;
    (2) Department of Transportation;
    (3) Department of Housing and Urban Development;
    (4) Department of Labor;

September 26, 1973     - 37 -      Pub. Law 93-112

                                                         87 STAT. 392

(5) Department of the Interior;
(6) General Services Administration;
(7) United States Postal Service; and
(8) Veterans' Administration.

(b) It shall be the function of the Board to: (1) insure compliance with the standards prescribed by the General Services Administration, the Department of Defense, and the Department of Housing and Urban Development pursuant to the Architectural Barriers Act of 1968 (Public Law 90–480), as amended by the Act of March 5, 1970 (Public Law 91–205); (2) investigate and examine alternative approaches to the architectural, transportation, and attitudinal barriers confronting handicapped individuals, particularly with respect to public buildings and monuments, parks and parklands, public transportation (including air, water, and surface transportation whether interstate, foreign, intrastate, or local), and residential and institutional housing; (3) determine what measures are being taken by Federal, State, and local governments and by other public or nonprofit agencies to eliminate the barriers described in clause (2) of this subsection; (4) promote the use of the International Accessibility Symbol in all public facilities that are in compliance with the standards prescribed by the Administrator of the General Services Administration, the Secretary of Defense, and the Secretary of Housing and Urban Development pursuant to the Architectural Barriers Act of 1968; (5) make to the President and to Congress reports which shall describe in detail the results to its investigations under clauses (2) and (3) of this subsection; and (6) make to the President and to the Congress such recommendations for legislation and administration as it deems necessary or desirable to eliminate the barriers described in clause (2) of this subsection.          *82 Stat. 718;*   *84 Stat. 49.*   *42 USC 4151.*   *International Accessibility Symbol, promotion.*   *Reports to President and Congress.*

(c) The Board shall also (1) (A) determine how and to what extent transportation barriers impede the mobility of handicapped individuals and aged handicapped individuals and consider ways in which travel expenses in connection with transportation to and from work for handicapped individuals can be met or subsidized when such individuals are unable to use mass transit systems or need special equipment in private transportation, and (B) consider the housing needs of handicapped individuals; (2) determine what measures are being taken, especially by public and other nonprofit agencies and groups having an interest in and a capacity to deal with such problems, (A) to eliminate barriers from public transportation systems (including vehicles used in such systems), and to prevent their incorporation in new or expanded transportation systems and (B) to make housing available and accessible to handicapped individuals or to meet sheltered housing needs; and (3) prepare plans and proposals for such further actions as may be necessary to the goals of adequate transportation and housing for handicapped individuals, including proposals for bringing together in a cooperative effort, agencies, organizations, and groups already working toward such goals or whose cooperation is essential to effective and comprehensive action.      *Transportation barriers.*

(d) In carrying out its functions under this section, the Board shall conduct investigations, hold public hearings, and issue such orders as it deems necessary to insure compliance with the provisions of the Acts cited in subsection (b). The provisions of subchapter II of chapter 5, and chapter 7 of title 5, United States Code, shall apply to procedures under this section, and an order of compliance issued by the Board shall be a final order for purposes of judicial review.      *5 USC 551, 701.*

87 STAT. 393

(e) The Board is authorized to appoint as many hearing examiners as are necessary for proceedings required to be conducted under this section. The provisions applicable to hearing examiners appointed under section 3105 of title 5, United States Code, shall apply to hearing examiners appointed under this subsection.

80 Stat. 415.

(f) The departments or agencies specified in subsection (a) of this section shall make available to the Board such technical, administrative, or other assistance as it may require to carry out its functions under this section, and the Board may appoint such other advisers, technical experts, and consultants as it deems necessary to assist it in carrying out its functions under this section. Special advisory and technical experts and consultants appointed pursuant to this subsection shall, while performing their functions under this section, be entitled to receive compensation at rates fixed by the Secretary, but not exceeding the daily pay rate, for a person employed as a GS–18 under section 5332 of title 45, United States Code, including traveltime, and while serving away from their homes or regular places of business they may be allowed travel expenses, including per diem in lieu of subsistence, as authorized by section 5703 of such title 5 for persons in the Government service employed intermittently.

Technical assistance.

5 USC 5332 note.

80 Stat. 499; 83 Stat. 190. Report to Congress.

(g) The Board shall, at the end of each fiscal year, report its activities during the preceding fiscal year to the Congress. Such report shall include an assessment of the extent of compliance with the Acts cited in subsection (b) of this section, along with a description and analysis of investigations made and actions taken by the Board, and the reports and recommendations described in clauses (5) and (6) of subsection (b) of this section. The Board shall prepare two final reports of its activities under subsection (c). One such report shall be on its activities in the field of transportation barriers to handicapped individuals, and the other such report shall be on its activities in the field of the housing needs of handicapped individuals. The Board shall, prior to January 1, 1975, submit each such report, together with its recommendations, to the President and the Congress. The Board shall also prepare for such submission an interim report of its activities in each such field within 18 months after the date of enactment of this Act.

Report to the President and Congress.

Appropriation.

(h) There are authorized to be appropriated for the purpose of carrying out the duties and functions of the Board under this section $1,000,000 each for the fiscal years ending June 30, 1974, and June 30, 1975.

EMPLOYMENT UNDER FEDERAL CONTRACTS

Sec. 503. (a) Any contract in excess of $2,500 entered into by any Federal department or agency for the procurement of personal property and nonpersonal services (including construction) for the United States shall contain a provision requiring that, in employing persons to carry out such contract the party contracting with the United States shall take affirmative action to employ and advance in employment qualified handicapped individuals as defined in section 7(6). The provisions of this section shall apply to any subcontract in excess of $2,500 entered into by a prime contractor in carrying out any contract for the procurement of personal property and nonpersonal services (including construction) for the United States. The President shall implement the provisions of this section by promulgating regulations within ninety days after the date of enactment of this section.

Ante, p. 361.

(b) If any handicapped individual believes any contractor has failed or refuses to comply with the provisions of his contract with the United States, relating to employment of handicapped individuals,

87 STAT. 3

such individual may file a complaint with the Department of Labor. The Department shall promptly investigate such complaint and shall take such action thereon as the facts and circumstances warrant, consistent with the terms of such contract and the laws and regulations applicable thereto.

(c) The requirements of this section may be waived, in whole or in part, by the President with respect to a particular contract or sub-contract, in accordance with guidelines set forth in regulations which he shall prescribe, when he determines that special circumstances in the national interest so require and states in writing his reasons for such determination. **Waiver authority.**

## NONDISCRIMINATION UNDER FEDERAL GRANTS

SEC. 504. No otherwise qualified handicapped individual in the United States, as defined in section 7(6), shall, solely by reason of his handicap, be excluded from the participation in, be denied the benefits of, or be subjected to discrimination under any program or activity receiving Federal financial assistance. *Ante,* p. 36

Approved September 26, 1973.

---

LEGISLATIVE HISTORY:

HOUSE REPORTS: No. 93-244 (Comm. on Education and Labor) and
                No. 93-500 (Comm. of Conference).
SENATE REPORTS: No. 93-318 accompanying S. 1875 (Comm. on Labor
                and Public Welfare) and No. 93-391 (Comm. of
                Conference).
CONGRESSIONAL RECORD, Vol. 119 (1973):
    June 5, considered and passed House.
    July 18, considered and passed Senate, amended, in lieu
        of S. 1875.
    Sept. 13, Senate agreed to conference report.
    Sept. 18, House agreed to conference report.
WEEKLY COMPILATION OF PRESIDENTIAL DOCUMENTS, Vol. 9, No. 39:
    Sept. 26, Presidential statement.

# Appendix D

CHECKLIST FOR COMPLIANCE AGENCY
SYNOPSIS OF OBLIGATIONS OF
CONTRACTORS UNDER SECTION 503
OF REHABILITATION ACT OF 1973 AND
SECTION 402 OF VIETNAM VETERANS
READJUSTMENT ASSISTANCE ACT

## CHECK LIST FOR COMPLIANCE AGENCY

1.  ------------------------------------------------------------
    (Name of contractor)

    ------------------------------------------------------------
    (Name of contractor's contact official)

    ------------------------------------------------------------
    (Address)

    ------------------------------------------------------------
    (Telephone)

2.  Does the contractor having a contract of $50,000 or more and 50 or more employees have a written Affirmative Action Program for the handicapped/veterans? YES —— NO ——

3.  Does contractor have "Equal Opportunity is the Law" notices posted in conspicuous places? YES —— NO ——

4.  Does contractor post notices indicating where and when job applicants and Employees may inspect the Affirmative Action Program? YES —— NO ——

5.  Were 503 and 402 Regulations distributed to contractor? YES —— NO ——

6.  Does contractor list suitable job openings (Salaries up to $25,000.00) with the State Employment Service? YES —— NO ——

(Compliance Officer)

------------------------------------------------------------
(Agency)

------------------------------------------------------------
(Address)

------------------------------------------------------------
(Date)

------------------------------------------------------------

## SYNOPSIS OF OBLIGATIONS OF CONTRACTORS
## UNDER SECTION 503 *

Under the affirmative action obligations imposed by Section 503 of the Rehabilitation Act of 1973, as amended, you are required to take affirmative action to employ, and advance in employment, qualified handicapped individuals, if you have contracts for $2,500 or more.

In addition, you are required to develop and maintain a written affirmative action program setting forth your policies, practices, and procedures as regards employment of the handicapped if you have contracts of $50,000 or more and have 50 or more employees. When entering initial contracts, you are allowed a period of 120 days from the commencement of the contract to develop this program (CFR 60-741.5).

Specific requirements to be included in your affirmative action program are outlined in detail in part 60-741.6 of the regulations. However, to summarize, with respect to basic requirements relating to employment and advancement of handicapped workers, all physical and mental job requirements must be job related. Any information obtained from preemployment inquiries about their physical or mental condition and from medical examinations may be used only for the purpose of proper job placement and in accordance with job related qualification requirements. In the event that questions should arise, you are responsible for showing that the physical and mental job qualification requirements are job related.

As part of your affirmative action program you are to review your personnel policies and procedures to make sure that they do not discriminate, or have the effect of discriminating, against the handicapped.

In order to balance your need to know who is entitled to affirmative action under Section 503 with the individual worker's right of privacy, the affirmative action obligations apply only to those with clearly visible handicaps or known handicaps, and to those who voluntarily come forward and identify themselves as handicapped, or by any other means. For such individuals,

---

* Compliance officers may provide the contractor with copies of the synopses which explain, in brief, the affirmative action obligations imposed by Sections 503 and 402.

you are required to make a reasonable accommodation to their handicaps. In addition, you must post notices to all applicants and employees who might benefit under the affirmative action program, inviting them to identify themselves. This invitation is to state that the information is voluntarily provided, and will be kept confidential.

# SYNOPSIS OF OBLIGATIONS OF CONTRACTORS UNDER SECTION 402

Under the affirmative action obligations imposed by Section 402 of the Vietnam Era Veterans' Readjustment Assistance Act of 1974, you are required to take affirmative action to employ, and advance in employment, qualified disabled veterans and veterans of the Vietnam era, if you have a contract of $10,000 or more. You are required to list job openings and file reports with the Local State Employment Office as stated in Part 60-250.4(b)(d) of the 402 Regulations.

If you have a contract of $50,000 or more and have 50 or more employees, you are required to develop and maintain a written affirmative action program setting forth your policies, practices and procedures as regards employment of disabled veterans and veterans of the Vietnam era. When entering initial contracts, you are allowed a period of 120 days from the commencement of the contract to develop this program (60-250.5(a)).

Specific requirements to be included in your affirmative action program are outlined in detail in Part 60-250.6 of the 402 Regulations. However, to summarize, with respect to basic requirements relating to employment and advancement of disabled veterans and veterans of the Vietnam era, all physical and mental job requirements must be job related. Any information obtained from pre-employment inquiries about their military records, physical or mental condition and from medical examination may be used only for the purpose of proper job placement and in accordance with job related qualification requirements. In the event that questions should arise, you are responsible for showing that the requirement, question, or medical information is job related.

As part of your affirmative action program, you are to review your personnel policies and procedures to make sure that they do not discriminate, or have the effect of discriminating, against disabled veterans or veterans of the Vietnam era.

In order to balance your need to know who is entitled to affirmative action under Section 402 with the individual worker's right of privacy, the affirmative action obligations apply only to those with clearly visible disabilities, and to those who voluntarily come forward and identify themselves as disabled veterans or veterans of the Vietnam era. You are required to make a reasonable accommodation to those veterans with disabilities. In addition, you must post notices to all applicants and employees who might benefit under the affirmative action program, inviting them to identify themselves. This invitation is to state that the information is voluntarily provided, and will be kept confidential.

Finally, you are required to list all suitable employment openings which exist at the time of the contract and those which occur during the performance of the contract including those not generated by this contract, with the appropriate local office of the State employment service and to file at least quarterly with this same employment office, reports of your veteran hiring activities. (See Part 60-250.4(d)).

*Appendix E*

SUMMARY OF STATE LAWS PERTAINING TO
DISCRIMINATION AGAINST THE
HANDICAPPED

Summary of provisions under State laws pertaining to discrimination in employment because of physical handicap

*ALABAMA*—No law

*ALASKA*—Same law and provisions as those regarding discrimination due to age

*ARIZONA*—No law

*ARKANSAS*—No law

*CALIFORNIA*—

LAW APPLIES TO—Employers; employment agencies; labor organizations; state and local governments.

EXCLUSIONS AND EXEMPTIONS—Employers of fewer than 5; domestic service; family employment; non-profit social clubs, fraternal, educational or religious associations or corporations.

PROHIBITED PRACTICES—*Employer*: To refuse to hire or employ, to discharge, dismiss, reduce, suspend, or demote; *Labor unions*: To restrict from membership; *Person*: To discriminate in the selection of an individual for training or apprenticeship program; *Employer, employment agency*: To print, circulate a statement, inquiry, or advertisement directly expressing a limitation, specification, or discrimination; using discriminatory applications for employment, or making pre-employment inquiries which are discriminatory; *Employer, Employment Agency, Labor Union*: To discriminate against a person who has opposed unfair practices, filed a complaint, or testified; and, for any person to aid or abet the accomplishment of acts prohibited by this law.

PENALTIES—Up to $500 fine, up to 30 days in jail, or both.

ENFORCEMENT AGENCY—State Fair Employment Practices Commission

*COLORADO*—No law

*CONNECTICUT*—Same law and provisions as those regarding discrimination due to age.

*DELAWARE*—No law

*DISTRICT OF COLUMBIA*—Same law and provisions as those regarding discrimination due to age

*FLORIDA*—

LAW APPLIES TO—State employers or employers supported by public funds

EXCLUSIONS AND EXEMPTIONS—None

PROHIBITED PRACTICES—To refuse employment or discriminate

PENALTY—Misdemeanor of 2nd degree

ENFORCEMENT AGENCY: Commission on Human Relations

*GEORGIA*—No law

*HAWAII*—Same law and provisions as those regarding discrimination due to age

*IDAHO*—No law

*ILLINOIS*—

LAW APPLIES TO—Employers; governmental units in State; labor organizations.

EXCLUSIONS AND EXEMPTIONS—Religious corporations, associations, educational institutions, or societies; employers of fewer than 15 persons.

PROHIBITED PRACTICES—*Employer*: To refuse to hire, to segregate the individual, to discriminate against individual in hiring, tenure; *Employment Agency*: To fail to properly classify, refer for employment, accept applications; to otherwise discriminate; To take a job order that is discriminatory; *Labor Organizations*: To limit, segregate or classify; to in any way affect adversely wages, hours, or conditions of employment; *Employer and labor organization*: To discharge, expel, or otherwise discriminate for opposing unlawful employment practices; or filing a charge, testifying, participation or assistance in proceedings under the law.

PENALTIES—Contempt citation

212 *Antidiscrimination Legislation*

ENFORCEMENT AGENCY—Illinois Fair Employment Practices Commission

COMMENT—Illinois also passed the Equal Opportunities for Handicapped Act which required an affirmative action program for the hiring, placement, and advancement of handicapped individuals of all state departments, agencies, boards, and commissions; the watchdog agency is the Interagency Committee on Handicapped Employees.

*INDIANA*—No law

*IOWA*—Same law and provisions as those regarding discrimination due to age

*KANSAS*—

LAW APPLIES TO—Employers, labor organizations, non-sectarian corporations, organizations engaged in social work, the state and political subdivisions thereof, employment agencies.

EXCLUSIONS AND EXEMPTIONS—Employers of fewer than 4 persons; nonprofit fraternal or social associations or corporations; family employment.

PROHIBITED PRACTICES—*Employer*: To refuse to hire; to discharge; discriminate regarding terms or conditions of employment; to limit, segregate, separate, or classify; make preemployment inquiry which expresses a limitation, specification or discrimination; *Employment Agency*: To refuse to list and properly classify, to refuse to refer for employment, to discriminate, to comply with employer's requests which express a limitation; *Labor organization*: To exclude or expel from membership; to discriminate against members or employers; *All three*: To discriminate in apprenticeship or training programs; may not participate in printing or advertisement which expresses a limitation, specification, or discrimination.

PENALTIES—Fine up to $500, one year in jail, or both

ENFORCEMENT AGENCY—Kansas Commission on Civil Rights

*KENTUCKY*—No law

*LOUISIANA*—No law

*MAINE*—Same law and provisions as those regarding discrimination due to age

---

*MARYLAND*—Same law and provisions as those regarding discrimination due to age

---

*MASSACHUSETTS*—Same law and provisions as those regarding discrimination due to age

---

*MICHIGAN*—No law

---

*MINNESOTA*—

LAW APPLIES TO—Employers, labor organizations, employment agencies

EXEMPTIONS AND EXCLUSIONS—family employment; domestic service; religious or fraternal corporations, associations, or societies with respect to religious qualifications which are bona fide occupational qualifications.

PROHIBITED PRACTICES—*Employer*: To refuse to hire, to maintain system of employment which unreasonably excludes individual from employment; to discharge or otherwise discriminate; *Employment Agency*: To refuse or fail to accept, register, or classify or refer individual for employment; *Labor organization*: To deny full and equal membership rights, to expel from membership, to discriminate, to fail to classify individual properly or refer for employment, or otherwise discriminate; *All three*: to encourage the accomplishment of anything forbidden by this Act; to require pre-employment information expressing limitations, etc.; to participate in the printing or advertising of information expressing a limitation, segregation, or discrimination; to discriminate against a person who has opposed unfair practices, filed a complaint, or testified.

PENALTIES—Pay damages to aggrieved party of not less than $25 nor more than $500 and/or order hiring, reinstatement, or upgrading of aggrieved party.

ENFORCEMENT AGENCY—Department of Human Rights

---

*MISSISSIPPI*—

LAW APPLIES TO—State services, political subdivisions of the state, or any other employer supported in whole or in part by public funds

PROHIBITED PRACTICES—Discrimination

PENALTIES—None

ENFORCEMENT AGENCY—None

---

*MISSOURI*—No law

---

*MONTANA*—Same law and provisions as those regarding discrimination due to age

---

*NEBRASKA*—

LAW APPLIES TO—Employers, labor organizations, employment agencies.

EXCLUSIONS AND EXEMPTIONS—Religious organizations and corporations; family employment; Employer of fewer than 15 persons; domestic service; private club; Indian Tribe.

PROHIBITED PRACTICES—*Employer*: To fail or refuse to hire; to discharge, discriminate with respect to compensation, terms or conditions or privileges of employment; to limit, segregate, or classify employees; *Employment Agency*: To fail or refuse to refer for employment; to discriminate, or to classify individuals; *Labor Organizations*: To exclude or expel from membership, to discriminate, to limit, segregate, or classify membership; to refuse to refer for employment; to cause or attempt to cause an employer to discriminate; *Employer, Labor Organization, Joint Labor-Management Committee*: Control apprenticeship and training programs; *Employer, Labor Organization, and Employment Agency*: To print or advertise information expressing a limitation, segregation, or discrimination; to discriminate against a person who has opposed unfair practices, filed a complaint, or testified.

PENALTIES—Fine of not more than $100 or imprisonment of not more than 30 days or both.

ENFORCEMENT AGENCY—Equal Opportunity Commission

---

*NEVADA*—Same law and provisions as those regarding discrimination due to age

---

*NEW HAMPSHIRE*—Same law and provisions as those regarding discrimination due to age.

*NEW JERSEY*—Same law and provisions as those regarding discrimination due to age.

*NEW MEXICO*—Same law and provisions as those regarding discrimination due to age.

*NEW YORK*—Same law and provisions as those regarding discrimination due to age with the addition of one extra prohibited practice: *Employers, Employment Agencies, Labor Organizations, Joint Labor-Management Committees*: To discriminate in admission to apprenticeship or training programs.

*NORTH CAROLINA*—

LAW APPLIES TO—State Governmental Bodies, Employers

PROHIBITED PRACTICES—No discrimination in public and private employment

PENALTY—None

ENFORCEMENT AGENCY—None

*NORTH DAKOTA*—No law

*OHIO*—No law

*OKLAHOMA*—No law

*OREGON*—Same law and provisions as those pertaining to discrimination due to age with the addition of two sections:

*Employer*: must re-employ individual who has sustained compensable injury at employment which is available and suitable; it is prohibited to refuse to hire, promote, to bar, discharge, reduce in compensation, suspend, demote, discriminate in work activities because of physical handicap.

*PENNSYLVANIA*—Same law and provisions as those regarding discrimination due to age.

*PUERTO RICO*—No law

## RHODE ISLAND—

LAW APPLIES TO—Employers, Employment Agencies, Labor Organizations, the State and all its political subdivisions

EXCLUSIONS AND EXEMPTIONS—Employers of less than 4 persons; religious corporations, associations, educational institutions, or societies; family employment; domestic service.

PROHIBITED PRACTICES—*Employer*: To refuse to hire; discharge; discriminate with respect to hiring, compensation terms, conditions or privileges of employment; may not use any referring source known to discriminate; may not encourage or compel violation of this Act or obstruct any person from complying with the Act; prior to employment, may not elicit any information, make and keep record of such information, or use an application that asks for information which implies discrimination. *Employment Agency*: To fail or refuse to classify properly; to fail or refuse to refer for employment; discriminate; may not comply with employer's discriminatory request; may not encourage or compel violation of the Act. *Employer and Employment Agency*: May not establish or announce a policy of denying or limiting employment opportunities; may not print or publish notice or advertisement which indicates a preference, limitation, specification or discrimination. *Labor Organization*: To deny full and equal membership rights; expel from membership; fail to refer for employment or classify properly; otherwise discriminate; *All three*: To discriminate against an individual who has opposed unfair practices, filed a complaint, or testified. *Licensing agency*: No discrimination.

PENALTY—None (Order to cease)

ENFORCEMENT AGENCY—Commission for Human Rights

---

## SOUTH CAROLINA—No law

---

## SOUTH DAKOTA—No law

---

## TENNESSEE—

LAW APPLIES TO—Employers, State agencies and subdivisions

EXEMPTIONS AND EXCLUSIONS—None

PROHIBITED PRACTICES—Discrimination

PENALTY—punishable as provided by general misdemeanor laws

ENFORCEMENT AGENCY—Human Development Commission

---

*TEXAS—*

LAW APPLIES TO—State, employers

EXEMPTIONS AND EXCLUSIONS—None

PROHIBITED PRACTICES—Discrimination

PENALTY—None

ENFORCEMENT AGENCY—None

---

*UTAH—*No law

---

*VERMONT—*

LAW APPLIES TO—Employers, Employment agencies, Labor organizations

EXCLUSIONS AND EXEMPTIONS—None

PROHIBITED PRACTICES—To discriminate against any physically handicapped person with respect to employment or labor membership.

PENALTY—Civil action for damages or equitable relief

ENFORCEMENT AGENCY—None

---

*VIRGINIA—*

LAW APPLIES TO—Employers

EXCLUSIONS AND EXEMPTIONS—Employers covered by the Federal Rehabilitation Act of 1973

PROHIBITED PRACTICES—To discriminate in employment or promotional practices

PENALTY—Grievant can file complaint with any circuit court in county or city where alleged discrimination occurs and receive an injunction against such discrimination

ENFORCEMENT AGENCY—None

*WASHINGTON*—Same law and provisions as those regarding discrimination due to age.

———————

*WEST VIRGINIA*—Same law and provisions as those applying to discrimination due to age also apply to blindness (no other physical handicap included in the law).

———————

*WISCONSIN*—Same law and provisions as those applying to discrimination due to age.

———————

*WYOMING*—No law

———————

# Appendix F

## SECTIONS 402 AND 404 OF THE VIETNAM ERA VETERANS' READJUSTMENT ASSISTANCE ACT

Public Law 93-508
93rd Congress, H. R. 12628
December 3, 1974

# An Act

To amend title 38, United States Code, to increase vocational rehabilitation subsistence allowances, educational and training assistance allowances, and special allowances paid to eligible veterans and persons under chapters 31, 34, and 35 of such title; to improve and expand the special programs for educationally disadvantaged veterans and servicemen under chapter 34 of such title; to improve and expand the veteran-student services program; to establish an education loan program for veterans and persons eligible for benefits under chapter 34 or 35 of such title; to make other improvements in the educational assistance program and in the administration of educational benefits; to promote the employment of veterans and the wives and widows of certain veterans by improving and expanding the provisions governing the operation of the Veterans Employment Service, by increasing the employment of veterans by Federal contractors and subcontractors, and by providing for an action plan for the employment of disabled and Vietnam era veterans within the Federal Government; to codify and expand veterans reemployment rights; and for other purposes.

*Be it enacted by the Senate and House of Representatives of the United States of America in Congress assembled,* That this Act may be cited as the "Vietnam Era Veterans' Readjustment Assistance Act of 1974". Vietnam Era Veterans' Readjustment Assistance Act of 1974.

SEC. 402. Chapter 42 of title 38, United States Code, is amended as follows:

(1) by inserting in the first sentence of section 2012(a) "in the amount of $10,000 or more" after "contract" where it first appears, by striking out ", in employing persons to carry out such contract," in such sentence, and by striking out "give special emphasis to the employment of" and inserting in lieu thereof "take affirmative action to employ and advance in employment" in such sentence; Employment under Federal contracts. 38 USC 2012.

(2) by striking out in the third sentence of section 2012(a) "The" and inserting in lieu thereof "In addition to requiring affirmative action to employ such veterans under such contracts and subcontracts and in order to promote the implementation of such requirement, the"; and

(3) by striking out in the first sentence of section 2012(b) "giving special emphasis in employment to" and inserting in lieu thereof "the employment of".

38 USC 2011. SEC. 404. (a) Part III of title 38, United States Code, is amended by adding at the end thereof a new chapter as follows:

## "Chapter 43—Veterans' Reemployment Rights

"Sec.
"2021. Right to reemployment of inducted persons; benefits protected.
"2022. Enforcement procedures.
"2023. Reemployment by the United States, territory, possession, or the District of Columbia.
"2024. Rights of persons who enlist or are called to active duty; Reserves.
"2025. Assistance in obtaining reemployment.
"2026. Prior rights for reemployment.

## "§ 2021. Right to reemployment of inducted persons; benefits protected

"(a) In the case of any person who is inducted into the Armed Forces of the United States under the Military Selective Service Act (or under any prior or subsequent corresponding law) for training and service and who leaves a position (other than a temporary position) in the employ of any employer in order to perform such training and service, and (1) receives a certificate described in section 9(a) of the Military Selective Service Act (relating to the satisfactory completion of military service), and (2) makes application for reemployment within ninety days after such person is relieved from such training and service or from hospitalization continuing after discharge for a period of not more than one year— 50 USC app. 451. 50 USC app. 459.

88 STAT. 1595

"(A) if such position was in the employ of the United States Government, its territories, or possessions, or political subdivisions thereof, or the District of Columbia, such person shall—

"(i) if still qualified to perform the duties of such position, be restored to such position or to a position of like seniority, status, and pay; or

"(ii) if not qualified to perform the duties of such position, by reason of disability sustained during such service, but qualified to perform the duties of any other position in the employ of the employer, be offered employment and, if such person so requests, be employed in such other position the duties of which such person is qualified to perform as will provide such person like seniority, status, and pay, or the nearest approximation thereof consistent with the circumstances in such person's case;

"(B) if such position was in the employ of a State, or political subdivision thereof, or a private employer, such person shall—

"(i) if still qualified to perform the duties of such position, be restored by such employer or his successor in interest to such position or to a position of like seniority, status, and pay; or

"(ii) if not qualified to perform the duties of such position, by reason of disability sustained during such service, but qualified to perform the duties of any other position in the employ of such employer or his successor in interest, be offered employment and, if such person so requests, be employed by such employer or his successor in interest in such other position the duties of which such person is qualified to perform as will provide such person like seniority, status, and pay, or the nearest approximation thereof consistent with the circumstances in such person's case,

unless the employer's circumstances have so changed as to make it impossible or unreasonable to do so. Nothing in this chapter shall excuse noncompliance with any statute or ordinance of a State or political subdivision thereof establishing greater or additional rights or protections than the rights and protections established pursuant to this chapter.

"(b) (1) Any person who is restored to or employed in a position in accordance with the provisions of clause (A) or (B) of subsection (a) of this section shall be considered as having been on furlough or leave of absence during such person's period of training and service in the Armed Forces, shall be so restored or reemployed without loss of seniority, shall be entitled to participate in insurance or other benefits offered by the employer pursuant to established rules and practices relating to employees on furlough or leave of absence in effect with the employer at the time such person was inducted into such forces, and shall not be discharged from such position without cause within one year after such restoration or reemployment.

"(2) It is hereby declared to be the sense of the Congress that any person who is restored to or employed in a position in accordance with the provisions of clause (A) or (B) of subsection (a) of this section should be so restored or reemployed in such manner as to give such person such status in his employment as he would have enjoyed if such person had continued in such employment continuously from the time of such person's entering the Armed Forces until the time of such person's restoration to such employment, or reemployment.

U.S. Government employment.

State or private employment.

Noncompliance of employer.

Status rights.

88 STAT. 1596

Reserve component members.

"(3) Any person who holds a position described in clause (A) or (B) of subsection (a) of this section shall not be denied retention in employment or any promotion or other incident or advantage of employment because of any obligation as a member of a Reserve component of the Armed Forces.

State employee.

"(c) The rights granted by subsections (a) and (b) of this section to persons who left the employ of a State or political subdivision thereof and were inducted into the Armed Forces shall not diminish any rights such persons may have pursuant to any statute or ordinance of such State or political subdivision establishing greater or additional rights or protections.

## "§ 2022. Enforcement procedures

Ante, p. 1594.
Post, p. 1598.

"If any employer, who is a private employer or a State or political subdivision thereof, fails or refuses to comply with the provisions of section 2021 (a), (b) (1), or (b) (3), or section 2024, the district court of the United States for any district in which such private employer maintains a place of business, or in which such State or political subdivision thereof exercises authority or carries out its functions, shall have the power, upon the filing of a motion, petition, or other appropriate pleading by the person entitled to the benefits of such provisions, specifically to require such employer to comply with such provisions and to compensate such person for any loss of wages or benefits suffered by reason of such employer's unlawful action. Any such compensation shall be in addition to and shall not be deemed to diminish any of the benefits provided for in such provisions. The court shall order speedy hearing in any such case and shall advance it on the calendar. Upon application to the United States attorney or comparable official for any district in which such private employer maintains a place of business, or in which such State or political subdivision thereof exercises authority or carries out its functions, by any person claiming to be entitled to the benefits provided for in such provisions, such United States attorney or official, if reasonably satisfied that the person so applying is entitled to such benefits, shall appear and act as attorney for such person in the amicable adjustment of the claim or in the filing of any motion, petition, or other appropriate pleading and the prosecution thereof specifically to require such employer to comply with such provisions. No fees or court costs shall be taxed against any person who may apply for such benefits. In any such action only the employer shall be deemed a necessary party respondent. No State statute of limitations shall apply to any proceedings under this chapter.

Hearing.

## "§ 2023. Reemployment by the United States, territory, possession, or the District of Columbia

Ante, p. 1594.

"(a) Any person who is entitled to be restored to or employed in a position in accordance with the provisions of clause (A) of section 2021(a) and who was employed, immediately before entering the Armed Forces, by any agency in the executive branch of the Government or by any territory or possession, or political subdivision thereof, or by the District of Columbia, shall be so restored or reemployed by such agency or the successor to its functions, or by such territory, possession, political subdivision, or the District of Columbia. In any case in which, upon appeal of any person who was employed, immediately before entering the Armed Forces, by any agency in the executive branch of the Government or by the District of Columbia, the United States Civil Service Commission finds that—

"(1) such agency is no longer in existence and its functions have not been transferred to any other agency; or

"(2) for any reason it is not feasible for such person to be restored to employment by such agency or by the District of Columbia.

the Commission shall determine whether or not there is a position in any other agency in the executive branch of the Government or in the government of the District of Columbia for which such person is qualified and which is either vacant or held by a person having a temporary appointment thereto. In any case in which the Commission determines that there is such a position, such person shall be offered employment and, if such person so requests, be employed in such position by the agency in which such position exists or by the government of the District of Columbia, as the case may be. The Commission is authorized and directed to issue regulations giving full force and effect to the provisions of this section insofar as they relate to persons entitled to be restored to or employed in positions in the executive branch of the Government or in the government of the District of Columbia, including persons entitled to be reemployed under the last sentence of subsection (b) of this section. The agencies in the executive branch of the Government and the government of the District of Columbia shall comply with such rules, regulations, and orders issued by the Commission pursuant to this subsection. The Commission is authorized and directed whenever it finds, upon appeal of the person concerned, that any agency in the executive branch of the Government or the government of the District of Columbia has failed or refuses to comply with the provisions of this section, to issue an order specifically requiring such agency or the government of the District of Columbia to comply with such provisions and to compensate such person for any loss of salary or wages suffered by reason of failure to comply with such provisions, less any amounts received by such person through other employment, unemployment compensation, or readjustment allowances. Any such compensation ordered to be paid by the Commission shall be in addition to and shall not be deemed to diminish any of the benefits provided for in such provisions, and shall be paid by the head of the agency concerned or by the government of the District of Columbia out of appropriations currently available for salary and expenses of such agency or government, and such appropriations shall be available for such purpose. As used in this chapter, the term 'agency in the executive branch of the Government' means any department, independent establishment, agency, or corporation in the executive branch of the United States Government (including the United States Postal Service and the Postal Rate Commission).

"(b) Any person who is entitled to be restored to or employed in a position in accordance with the provisions of clause (A) of section 2021(a), and who was employed, immediately before entering the Armed Forces, in the legislative branch of the Government, shall be so restored or employed by the officer who appointed such person to the position which such person held immediately before entering the Armed Forces. In any case in which it is not possible for any such person to be restored to or employed in a position in the legislative branch of the Government and such person is otherwise eligible to acquire a status for transfer to a position in the competitive service in accordance with section 3304(c) of title 5, the United States Civil Service Commission shall, upon appeal of such person, determine

*Regulations.*

*Compliance order; compensation for loss of wages.*

*"Agency" in the executive branch of the Government."*

*Restoration to legislative position.*
*Ante, p. 1594.*

*Transfer to executive position.*

whether or not there is a position in the executive branch of the Government for which such person is qualified and which is either vacant or held by a person having a temporary appointment thereto. In any case in which the Commission determines that there is such a position, such person shall be offered employment and, if such person so requests, be employed in such position by the agency in which such position exists.

Restoration to judicial position. Ante, p. 1594.

"(c) Any person who is entitled to be restored to or employed in a position in accordance with the provisions of clause (A) of section 2021(a) and who was employed, immediately before entering the Armed Forces, in the judicial branch of the Government, shall be so restored or reemployed by the officer who appointed such person to the position which such person held immediately before entering the Armed Forces.

## "§ 2024. Rights of persons who enlist or are called to active duty; Reserves

"(a) Any person who, after entering the employment on the basis of which such person claims restoration or reemployment, enlists in the Armed Forces of the United States (other than in a Reserve component) shall be entitled upon release from service under honorable conditions to all of the reemployment rights and other benefits provided for by this section in the case of persons inducted under the provisions of the Military Selective Service Act (or prior or subsequent legislation providing for the involuntary induction of persons into the Armed Forces), if the total of such person's service performed between June 24, 1948, and August 1, 1961, did not exceed four years, and the total of any service, additional or otherwise, performed by such person after August 1, 1961, does not exceed five years, and if the service in excess of four years after August 1, 1961, is at the request and for the convenience of the Federal Government (plus in each case any period of additional service imposed pursuant to law).

50 USC app. 451.

"(b)(1) Any person who, after entering the employment on the basis of which such person claims restoration or reemployment, enters upon active duty (other than for the purpose of determining physical fitness and other than for training), whether or not voluntarily, in the Armed Forces of the United States or the Public Health Service in response to an order or call to active duty shall, upon such person's relief from active duty under honorable conditions, be entitled to all of the reemployment rights and benefits provided for by this chapter in the case of persons inducted under the provisions of the Military Selective Service Act (or prior or subsequent legislation providing for the involuntary induction of persons into the Armed Forces), if the total of such active duty performed between June 24, 1948, and August 1, 1961, did not exceed four years, and the total of any such active duty, additional or otherwise, performed after August 1, 1961, does not exceed four years (plus in each case any additional period in which such person was unable to obtain orders relieving such person from active duty).

"(2) Any member of a Reserve component of the Armed Forces of the United States who voluntarily or involuntarily enters upon active duty (other than for the purpose of determining physical fitness and other than for training) or whose active duty is voluntarily or involuntarily extended during a period when the President is authorized to order units of the Ready Reserve or members of a Reserve component to active duty shall have the service limitation governing eligibility for

December 3, 1974        - 21 -        Pub. Law 93-508

reemployment rights under subsection (b) (1) of this section extended by such member's period of such active duty, but not to exceed that period of active duty to which the President is authorized to order units of the Ready Reserve or members of a Reserve component. With respect to a member who voluntarily enters upon active duty or whose active duty is voluntarily extended, the provisions of this subsection shall apply only when such additional active duty is at the request and for the convenience of the Federal Government.

Additional active duty.

"(c) Any member of a Reserve component of the Armed Forces of the United States who is ordered to an initial period of active duty for training of not less than three consecutive months shall, upon application for reemployment within thirty-one days after (1) such member's release from such active duty for training after satisfactory service, or (2) such member's discharge from hospitalization incident to such active duty for training, or one year after such member's scheduled release from such training, whichever is earlier, be entitled to all reemployment rights and benefits provided by this chapter for persons inducted under the provisions of the Military Selective Service Act (or prior or subsequent legislation providing for the involuntary induction of persons into the Armed Forces), except that (A) any person restored to or employed in a position in accordance with the provisions of this subsection shall not be discharged from such position without cause within six months after that restoration, and (B) no reemployment rights granted by this subsection shall entitle any person to retention, preference, or displacement rights over any veteran with a superior claim under those provisions of title 5 relating to veterans and other preference eligibles.

Duty for less than three months.

50 USC app. 451.
Six-month discharge period.

5 USC 101 et seq.

"(d) Any employee not covered by subsection (c) of this section who holds a position described in clause (A) or (B) of section 2021(a) shall upon request be granted a leave of absence by such person's employer for the period required to perform active duty for training or inactive duty training in the Armed Forces of the United States. Upon such employee's release from a period of such active duty for training or inactive duty training, or upon such employee's discharge from hospitalization incident to that training, such employee shall be permitted to return to such employee's position with such seniority, status, pay, and vacation as such employee would have had if such employee had not been absent for such purposes. Such employee shall report for work at the beginning of the next regularly scheduled working period after expiration of the last calendar day necessary to travel from the place of training to the place of employment following such employee's release, or within a reasonable time thereafter if delayed return is due to factors beyond the employee's control. Failure to report for work at such next regularly scheduled working period shall make the employee subject to the conduct rules of the employer pertaining to explanations and discipline with respect to absence from scheduled work. If such an employee is hospitalized incident to active duty for training or inactive duty training, such employee shall be required to report for work at the beginning of the next regularly scheduled work period after expiration of the time necessary to travel from the place of discharge from hospitalization to the place of employment, or within a reasonable time thereafter if delayed return is due to factors beyond the employee's control, or within one year after such employee's release from active duty for training or inactive duty training, whichever is earlier. If an employee

Leave of absence for active or inactive duty training.
Ante, p. 1594.

covered by this subsection is not qualified to perform the duties of such employee's position by reason of disability sustained during active duty for training or inactive duty training, but is qualified to perform the duties of any other position in the employ of the employer or his successor in interest, such employee shall be offered employment and, if such person so requests, be employed by that employer or his successor in interest in such other position the duties of which such employee is qualified to perform as will provide such employee like seniority, status, and pay, or the nearest approximation thereof consistent with the circumstances in such employee's case.

*Induction period considered as leave of absence.*
*Ante, p. 1594.*

"(e) Any employee not covered by subsection (c) of this section who holds a position described in clause (A) or (B) of section 2021(a) shall be considered as having been on leave of absence during the period required to report for the purpose of being inducted into, entering, or determining, by a preinduction or other examination, physical fitness to enter the Armed Forces. Upon such employee's rejection, upon completion of such employee's preinduction or other examination, or upon such employee's discharge from hospitalization incident to such rejection or examination, such employee shall be permitted to return to such employee's position in accordance with the provisions of subsection (d) of this section.

*Active and inactive duty training.*

"(f) For the purposes of subsections (c) and (d) of this section, full-time training or other full-time duty performed by a member of the National Guard under section 316, 503, 504, or 505 of title 32, is considered active duty for training; and for the purpose of subsection (d) of this section, inactive duty training performed by that member under section 502 of title 32 or section 206, 301, 309, 402, or 1002 of title 37, is considered inactive duty training.

## "§ 2025. Assistance in obtaining reemployment

"The Secretary of Labor, through the Office of Veterans' Reemployment Rights, shall render aid in the replacement in their former positions or reemployment of persons who have satisfactorily completed any period of active duty in the Armed Forces or the Public Health Service. In rendering such aid, the Secretary shall use existing Federal and State agencies engaged in similar or related activities and shall utilize the assistance of volunteers.

## "§ 2026. Prior rights for reemployment

"In any case in which two or more persons who are entitled to be restored to or employed in a position under the provisions of this chapter or of any other law relating to similar reemployment benefits left the same position in order to enter the Armed Forces, the person who left such position first shall have the prior right to be restored thereto or reemployed on the basis thereof, without prejudice to the reemployment rights of the other person or persons to be restored or reemployed.".

(b) The table of chapters at the beginning of title 38, United States Code, and the table of chapters at the beginning of part III of such title are each amended by adding at the end thereof

# Index of Cases

# Index

# Racial Policies of American Industry Series

Order from:  Kraus Reprint Co., Route 100, Millwood, New York 10546

# STUDIES OF NEGRO EMPLOYMENT

Vol. I. *Negro Employment in Basic Industry: A Study of Racial Policies in Six Industries (Automobile, Aerospace, Steel, Rubber Tires, Petroleum, and Chemicals)*, by Herbert R. Northrup, Richard L. Rowan *et al.*                    1970. $15.00

Vol. II. *Negro Employment in Finance: A Study of Racial Policies in Banking and Insurance*, by Armand J. Thieblot, Jr. and Linda Pickthorne Fletcher.                    1970.    *

Vol. III. *Negro Employment in Public Utilities: A Study of Racial Policies in the Electric Power, Gas, and Telephone Industries*, by Bernard E. Anderson.                    1970. $8.50

Vol. IV. *Negro Employment in Southern Industry: A Study of Racial Policies in the Paper, Lumber, Tobacco, Coal Mining, and Textile Industries*, by Herbert R. Northrup, Richard L. Rowan, *et al.*
1971. $13.50

Vol. V. *Negro Employment in Land and Air Transport: A Study of Racial Policies in the Railroad, Airlines, Trucking, and Urban Transit Industries*, by Herbert R. Northrup, Howard W. Risher, Jr., Richard D. Leone, and Philip W. Jeffress.    1971. $13.50

Vol. VI. *Negro Employment in Retail Trade: A Study of Racial Policies in the Department Store, Drugstore, and Supermarket Industries*, by Gordon F. Bloom, F. Marion Fletcher, and Charles R. Perry.
1972. $12.00

Vol. VII. *Negro Employment in the Maritime Industries: A Study of Racial Policies in the Shipbuilding, Longshore, and Offshore Maritime Industries*, by Lester Rubin, William A. Swift, and Herbert R. Northrup.                    1974.    *

Order from the Industrial Research Unit
The Wharton School, University of Pennsylvania
Philadelphia, Pennsylvania 19104

* Order these books from University Microfilms, Inc., Attn: Books Editorial Department, 300 North Zeeb Road, Ann Arbor, Michigan 48106.